Bigfoot Exposed

D1557316

Bigfoot Exposed

An Anthropologist Examines America's Enduring Legend

DAVID J. DAEGLING

A Division of
ROWMAN & LITTLEFIELD PUBLISHERS, INC.
Walnut Creek • Lanham • New York • Toronto • Oxford

EASTERN SHORE PUBLIC LIBRARY
Accomac, Virginia 23301

AltaMira Press
A division of Rowman & Littlefield Publishers, Inc.
1630 North Main Street, #367
Walnut Creek, California 94596
www.altamirapress.com

Rowman & Littlefield Publishers, Inc.
A wholly owned subsidiary of The Rowman & Littlefield Publishing Group, Inc.
4501 Forbes Boulevard, Suite 200
Lanham, Maryland 20706

PO Box 317
Oxford
OX2 9RU, UK

Copyright © 2004 by AltaMira Press

All rights reserved. No part of this publication may be reproduced, stored in a retrieval system, or transmitted in any form or by any means, electronic, mechanical, photocopying, recording, or otherwise, without the prior permission of the publisher.

British Library Cataloguing in Publication Information Available

Library of Congress Cataloging-in-Publication Data

Daegling, David J., 1960–
Bigfoot exposed : an anthropologist examines America's enduring legend / David J. Daegling.
p. cm.
Includes bibliographical references and index.
ISBN 0-7591-0538-3 (hardcover : alk. paper) – ISBN 0-7591-0539-1 (pbk. : alk. paper)
1. Sasquatch–United States. I. Title.
QL89.2.S2D34 2004
001.944–dc22

2004011392

Printed in the United States of America

∞™ The paper used in this publication meets the minimum requirements of American National Standard for Information Sciences—Permanence of Paper for Printed Library Materials, ANSI/NISO Z39.48-1992.

Contents

Preface vii
1 Encounters with Monsters 1
2 The Natural History of Bigfoot 9
3 The Social History of Bigfoot 25
4 Bigfoot Scrutinized: Why the Greatest Hits Are All Misses 61
5 The Patterson Film 105
6 Further Musings on Footprints 157
7 Three Red Herrings 189
8 A Science of Sasquatch? 203
9 The Eyewitness Problem 221
10 The Bardin Booger 237
11 The Phenomenon 247
References 261
Index 269
About the Author 276

Preface

One could argue that Bigfoot happened to me—as it seems to happen to most people—accidentally. Growing up in northern California in the 1960s meant that I could count on coming across hairy-monster stories in the papers occasionally. The details were consistent enough among the reports to make a child wonder whether there was something to them. I was drawn to the beast and became a collector of monstrous tales, becoming practiced at recounting the more dramatic narratives on campouts and sleepovers as a youth. Years later, having moved away from Bigfoot country, I could still summon the stories from memory if a late night poker game was short of conversation or if, on various paleontological excavations, we ran out of gossip while rummaging through the earth for fossil primates.

Graduate study in anthropology became increasingly attractive after brief career experiments as a disk jockey, swimming pool supply clerk, and outdoor lighting installer ended, to the benefit of all concerned. Studying functional anatomy on Long Island marked my descent into full-blown scientific geekdom: I found my life's passion trying to figure out how to describe the internal forces that deform animal bones. Bigfoot was not on my radar as far as research was concerned. But I did spring the odd tale to colleagues over a beer now and then, and this practice would bring the monster back into my life.

Early in 1993, Jon Marks, the book review editor of the *American Journal of Physical Anthropology* and a colleague at Yale, asked me to review Grover

Krantz's *Big Footprints* for the journal. The director of the Peabody Museum of Natural History at Yale University learned of the review and, needing to fill up the schedule for the 1996 fall public lecture series, saved himself airfare and hotel expenses by collaring me to fill one of the slots by talking about Bigfoot. The preparation for that talk, in retrospect, launched this book. I learned that since I had left northern California in the early 1970s, Bigfoot had been very busy, not just among the coastal redwoods but all over the country. The Bigfoot hunters were saying the same thing they had been saying when I was a kid: nobody will look at the evidence, and the scientific community owes us at least that courtesy. It was a fair plea because there were items of evidence that still seemed to defy every explanation except the one involving an undiscovered animal. So I decided to have a closer look. What I found is detailed in the pages that follow.

Why the lure of Bigfoot is irresistible to some while others are immune to it is a fascinating question. I do not know for certain why I ever cared about the monster; perhaps a psychoanalyst would decide that it began at four years old, when I was terrorized by the abominable snow monster (the infamous "bumble") of the Christmas television special *Rudolph the Red-Nosed Reindeer.* Whatever the reason, I do empathize with those who hunt for Bigfoot. The elusive nature of the quarry makes this a quest of intrigue and adventure; it is not difficult to understand how this search becomes obsession. Monster hunts do not yield tangible fruits in the form of actual monsters, but for me, this foray into the realm of Bigfoot has been a detour worth taking.

A NOTE ON SOURCES

The Associated Press issued a release in November of 1992 under the headline *Trap Designed to Catch Bigfoot Has Outlasted Its Creators.* Who built the cage that sits, unoccupied, in the Oregon forest is something of a mystery, since the organization that designed and installed it is long defunct. The story appropriately summarizes a problem one encounters in researching Bigfoot—specifically, the issue of discovering facts with no apparent source and arguments whose authorship is uncertain. These days, Bigfoot lives on the Internet; cyberspace provides the ideal forum for information exchange in a field where traditional scholarly channels have little to offer the enthusiastic monster hunter.

The Internet is something of an anomaly as a scholarly resource. Data can disappear in an instant. Web pages can be left unattended like ghost ships adrift; broken links often mean dead ends. This book contains many web citations for the simple reason that much Bigfoot research has never seen the printed page. Unless indicated otherwise, all web citations are accessible as active links as of January 2004. I make note of the websites that are no longer accessible as of this writing, and where these are cited, I have printed copies of the website content as it existed when it was online. As is the case with traditional book research, I am operating under the assumption that the web-based material is factual in the eyes of its author(s). I have avoided citing anonymous sources except for certain newspaper reports where no byline is provided. Material listed in the bibliography has appeared in print in some form or another; for exclusively web-based sources, the full citations are given in the notes. The reader may notice duplicate entries for some book titles in the bibliography; the reason for this is that my copies of some of these works are later printings that appeared some years after the original first editions were released. The page numbers provided are correct only for the particular edition cited, even though the content in question will also be found in the original publication.

Much of the information gathered for this book was obtained through correspondence or conversations I have had with investigators and interested parties over the years. Within the notes, entries of "personal correspondence" indicate written or printed material in the form of letters, annotations, or word processing files. Correspondence by electronic mail is always designated as such. Entries of "personal communication" refer to actual conversations I have had with the named individual, either in person or by telephone.

ACKNOWLEDGMENTS

Collecting information on Bigfoot is not a tidy scholarly endeavor. Letters, conversations, public statements, and private musings end up being as important as the published word. Misinformation is not the exception in this field; it is the rule. The rumors that circulate, pro and con, are often spurious. Even so, these are the leads that must be followed. I could not have accumulated the information required for detailed critique were it not for the people named below. The fact that so many loose ends persist is in spite of their efforts.

Michael Dennett paved the way for this book. His refutation of "irrefutable" Sasquatch evidence is a model of skeptical inquiry. My hope is that this book lives up to that standard. Certainly without his help and insight, this book would have never been started. Mike corrected some errors of fact and provided helpful editorial comments on the manuscript. Several pictures appear here with his permission. Ben Radford, managing editor of the *Skeptical Inquirer*, has been equally generous with his time and information. Sasquatch believers may be a lonely lot, but Ben is an ideal colleague and collaborator in the even smaller universe of Bigfoot skeptics.

A cynical observer might suppose that those favorably disposed to the reality of Bigfoot might be unwilling to share information with a skeptical investigator. With few exceptions, I did not find this to be the case. Those who seek Bigfoot will no doubt reject this book's conclusion, but it is testament to their character that much of the information that is damaging to their cause was freely given. There are two photographs, central to the arguments presented here, that I was unable to obtain permission to reprint. The artistic reconstruction of these images was provided by Zina Deretsky.

In 1996, Peter Byrne was kind enough to host two strangers (my wife and I) in Hood River, Oregon, give us a tour of The Bigfoot Research Project facilities, and suggest prime camping locations for encountering Bigfoot (we did not see it that night, but we could imagine it happening). Since that time, I have enjoyed our many discussions on the enduring mystery, even in a public forum where we have argued for very different conclusions.

All Bigfoot investigators owe a debt to Daniel Perez for his tireless collection and criticism of Bigfoot evidence. Daniel was still willing to treat me as a serious investigator when, upon arriving at his home, I promptly locked my keys in the car (with the engine running, no less). Our discussions that evening turned out to be a critical five hours of research in preparing this book. Daniel has also been exceedingly generous in sharing information for over ten years. His *Bigfoot Times* was the source of much of the information reported here and is available for subscription at 10926 Milano Avenue, Norwalk, CA 90650-1638 or Perez@worldnet.att.net.

During the time I was researching this book, the Bigfoot community lost two of its most articulate and passionate investigators, and I lost two friends. Barbara Wasson was always delightful company and impressed upon me that the issue confronting us was very much one of psychology as much as of zoology. René Dahinden provided me with a wealth of information from his decades of searching, and he did so with the understanding that my motivation was to tear it down. His investigation of the Patterson film (and Daniel

Perez's subsequent work) made it possible to do the critical analysis described in these pages.

For favors large and small, perhaps forgotten by the givers but remembered with gratitude by myself, I also thank Mike Warren, John Krigbaum, Eric Sargis, Rebecca Fisher, Pierre Lemelin, Tod Deery, Linda Foster, Lyle Laverty, Lena Crain, Larry Lund, Ray Crowe, Jay Tischendorf, and Bobbie Short. My colleagues Daniel Schmitt, Amos Deinard, Andrew Rapoff, Tony Falsetti, and Scott McGraw provided guidance in the articulation of some of the arguments presented in the book. Above all, I want to thank my wife, Marnie Wiss, who not only embraced my distraction with Bigfoot but endured the crankiness (in all senses of the term) that accompanied the writing of the book. Much of the decipherable prose herein is due to her editorial hand. Russ Bernard critically examined earlier drafts and provided substantive input for the argument set forth in chapter 9. Jeff McKee and Ken Feder also offered valuable criticism of the manuscript. At AltaMira Press, Mitch Allen provided indispensable guidance for the organization of the book, and Kristina van Niekirk did masterful work in keeping this organization intact through the various transformations from manuscript to book.

1

Encounters with Monsters

I almost saw a Bigfoot that night. If my brother's curiosity hadn't overcome his fear, I might have had a great monster story.

The three of us—myself, my brother, and my high school buddy Jim—wearily unloaded our packs by a lake in the High Sierra, finishing our third days' hike into the wilderness. The afternoon heat, the thin air, and our growing blisters convinced us to stop early. We set up camp in thick forest that ran right up to the lake margin to stay out of the direct sun. Of course, the mosquitoes liked hanging out in this cool shade as well, and we were soon motivated to get our tents up and ourselves inside them to stop the bloodletting. The rest of the day passed slowly; I lay on my back contemplating the scores of thirsty beasts perched on the tent mesh. Every half hour or so, one of the more resourceful of the lot found its way past this blessed partition, through some poorly sewn seam, and my repose was instantly transformed into a flailing of hands and a hail of cursing until the intruder was well squashed. Such was my entertainment that afternoon.

With the setting of the sun, the winds began to stir around the mountains and a welcome chill descended, convincing the mosquitoes to call off their vigil. We emerged and set about fixing dinner in the growing darkness. There would be a moon that night, but it was two days past full so we would not have the benefit of its illumination until well past dishwashing time. We finished eating our reconstituted freeze-dried offerings, and without talking about it, each of us wandered about collecting firewood. We had to hang the food as well, as these national park bears were famous for their resourceful means of liberating food from backpacks. Finally, our chores done, we settled down to the fire. Beyond its light, the blackness had taken hold of the forest, and that was my brother's cue to begin another campfire story.

My brother, Eric, eight years my senior, had grown up when stories of Bigfoot had begun to come out of the woods of northern California. Bigfoot is the generic term for North America's version of the yeti or abominable snowman of Himalayan fame; it is also commonly called the Sasquatch, which is a name derived from the folklore of the Coast Salish, a Native American group from what is now Washington State and British Columbia.[1] When my brother told stories of such hairy monsters, I could never tell whether he put much stock in them but, at the very least, he appreciated their entertainment value. He and I had been on many backpack trips together, and the legendary Sasquatch always became a focal point of conversation on these trips. This night would be no exception.

I didn't quite know what to make of all these Bigfoot stories either, but I knew I was much more comfortable being a true believer while at home in the suburbs of the Bay Area. Darkness in a backyard is one thing; when you are days—not hours—away from civilization, the blackness of the forest wasn't just scary, it felt ominous. While my brother reeled off the stories in a matter-of-fact fashion, I kept reminding myself that such a thing couldn't be real. Even so, I couldn't stop from turning around every few minutes and scanning the edge of the woods. Was I really expecting to see something?

This was Jim's first backpack trip, and he wasn't accustomed to the pleasures of freeze-dried cuisine, plodding through melting snowfields, or bathing in mountain streams. He also wasn't crazy about having conversations around the fire concerning 7-foot hairy monsters. But the last thing either of us would dream of doing would be to lose face with our fearless leader by asking him to change the subject. So we listened and laughed, albeit nervously.

Eric had just finished the evening's stories and was getting up to throw some more wood on the fire. Pointing across the lake, Jim asked, "What would you do if you saw Bigfoot coming out of those mountains right now?" He and I took turns seriously discussing the proper course of action, concluding that running away in a blind panic was perhaps not the sanest option but would probably be what we would do if that happened. Eric was amused.

The levity of the moment was shattered by a plaintive wail, followed by a bellow of incredible volume. The sound was not coming from Jim's hypothetical Sasquatch across the lake, however. This was something at the edge of our camp, out of view, but very, very close. To be making a noise this loud, it also had to be big. The wailing and the bellowing didn't stop. What the hell was it? A bear? No, bears growled, and this was no growl. A bobcat? I'd heard one a long time ago, and that was plenty frightening, but this sound was different. A marmot? Sure, if they have a 280-pound variety in these parts, that might explain everything. The worst part of it wasn't the sound itself, what was scaring me to death was not knowing what was making it. I was more frightened than I had ever been. The subject of my brother's campfire stories was about to make an appearance.

Jim was up immediately, heading toward his backpack while stating in a surprisingly matter-of-fact tone, "I am getting the hell out of here!" He began collecting his stuff and throwing it haphazardly into his pack. We had both obviously settled on what the source of this noise was. I, meanwhile, sat paralyzed by the fire. This could not really be happening, I thought. I waited for the noise to stop or for the noisemaker to appear but was too shocked to do anything. I kept running through my inventory of known animal sounds and was drawing a blank. More bellowing.

My brother, meanwhile, was also somewhat distressed, but whether because of age, wilderness experience, or simple curiosity, he was going to get to the bottom of this. He walked over to his pack, got his flashlight, and moved, with appropriate caution, toward the source of the noise. Still parked stupidly by the fire, I figured I owed it to my brother to at least see what would transpire.

As the beam of the flashlight shone into the darkness beyond camp, our Bigfoot became fully illuminated, still wailing. It had fur all over its body, four skinny legs with cloven hooves, and a magnificent set of antlers. I looked at this handsome buck and wondered how it could make such a horrific racket and why on earth it chose this place and time to start trumpeting. Even though this little mystery had been solved and we now knew that a monster attack was not forthcoming, it still took a long time for me to settle down.

The fear of that experience was all about the unknown. What would have happened if my brother hadn't gotten his flashlight? I would have lost a night's sleep and would have forever wondered what had wandered into the edge of our camp. The simple truth was that a buck made that noise. The cause of the event was the same, regardless of how any one of us may have interpreted it.

People have been telling similar stories for years but with decidedly more dramatic outcomes. The literature on Bigfoot is replete with tales of encounters with animals considerably less mundane than noisy deer. Some people see Sasquatches, others smell them, still others hear their cries. Trackways that defy zoological explanation are found in the wilderness. Pictures have been taken. Films made.

Is Bigfoot real? The answer is yes, if we define reality as a matter of human experience. Bigfoot has become entrenched in American popular culture and it is as viable an icon as Michael Jordan. Usually, however, what we're asking with that question is whether at the bottom of all the human experiences and the cultural manifestations there is something biological going on. Is there a species of ape living in the woods of North America?

There are two mysteries involved here. First, if there is a large hominoid living in the North American wilderness, why don't we know about it with the same certainty that we know about bears or moose? Second, if there isn't such a beast, what are people seeing and who or what is making the tracks?

Many journalists, psychologists, folklorists, scientists, and a dedicated number of nonprofessionals have attempted to answer these questions. Still, more than forty-five years after Bigfoot hit the newswires as a result of strange happenings in northern California, we have neither an animal nor a satisfying explanation as to why folks see giant hairy men that don't exist. The problem, however, isn't necessarily the animal's elusiveness or eyewitnesses' taste for moonshine. Rather, the reason for the mystery's persistence may have more to do with how people deal with the unknown and how powerful belief is in governing our perception of what is real.

That night in the mountains I slept soundly, although I'd been scared silly just hours before. But my experience provides some insight into how monster stories are born and why legends take on a life of their own. If my brother hadn't gotten his flashlight or perhaps if the buck had simply left after a few calls, we would not have discovered what made the noise. I certainly would have never guessed correctly who the noisemaker was. (I'd never heard deer make noise before, so I assumed they never did.) My experience would have been very different: I wouldn't have slept, I would have insisted on a moratorium on campfire conversations involving Bigfoot, and I would have had the perfect monster story. I very well may have decided in the end that I had encountered Bigfoot. I would have been wrong, but neither you nor anyone else would be in a position to prove it.

If Bigfoot was only ever seen and heard but left no other traces, then we could argue the beast away by reasoning that without corroborating evidence, it was simply a modern-day manifestation of dragons, leprechauns, or trolls. But what sets Bigfoot apart from standard-issue monsters is that it leaves all sorts of corroborating evidence in the form of footprints, hair, nests, and habitat disturbance. There is no shortage of this evidence. You can easily find hundreds of people who will swear to you that they've seen one, the documented footprints number in the thousands, and there has been enough Bigfoot hair collected to weave a few area rugs. Several motion pictures starring Sasquatch exist, and it is featured in a hefty collection of still photographs.

So the question isn't whether there is any evidence; the real question—the important question—is whether any of this evidence is any good. Those researchers, both amateur and professional, who argue that Bigfoot is a real species of undiscovered animal (I'll call these people *advocates* from now on) are quite aware of what evidence is out there. None of these advocates—not a single one—believes that all the evidence is legitimate. Many of them are perfectly happy dismissing most of it, as long as some small portion passes muster. For their belief in the reality of the Sasquatch to be valid, they don't need the bulk or even the majority of the evidence to be legitimate. John Green, a journalist who has investigated the phenomenon of Bigfoot from the outset, once uttered what would become the mantra for those who seek the legendary Sasquatch: "If you establish at any point that even one report is accurate, then you have an animal. And, if you have an animal, then you have literally thousands of animals."[2]

Green is right on the mark. It is irrelevant how much chicanery and deception has occurred in the search for Bigfoot because the true testimony of a single eyewitness, the legitimacy of a single footprint, or the authenticity of any piece of grainy film would prove the reality of the creature. And Green's biology is as sound as his logic. Bigfoot cannot be a singular thing if we are to consider it in the zoological sense; if this is an earth creature, then we must have populations of these hairy giants roaming the wilderness of North America. There can't be just one.[3]

Despite the hope that Green's optimism brings to the Bigfoot enterprise, there is a rub: establishing truth, legitimacy, or authenticity is not a straightforward endeavor. This is the essence of the mystery of Bigfoot. There is not a single piece of Bigfoot evidence that is unequivocal. Despite the weekly proclamations on cable television, there is no smoking gun that establishes that the Sasquatch is out there. It's all over the place, in every corner of the lower forty-eight states, it's 8 feet tall and smells like a bad clam on a hot August day, and we still can't drag one of them out of the woods. Something is going on that requires explanation.

This book delves into the contradictions and the enigmas that make Bigfoot a problem seemingly without resolution. There is, I believe, a satisfactory explanation to the phenomenon that is neither simple nor necessarily intuitive. To arrive at this explanation, we have to delve into the mystery in considerable detail from a variety of angles. The legend I focus on here is the North American one: Bigfoot allegedly has relatives elsewhere around the globe, but my interest in this book is the question of an ape-like creature in the United States and Canada.

The first problem that must be addressed is whether the very idea of an animal matching the description of Bigfoot is plausible, given what we know about the natural history of other animals; this is the focus of chapter 2. The third chapter summarizes the major events that have defined Bigfoot as an object of inquiry; this part of the book also looks at those who have hunted Bigfoot and those fewer individuals who have chronicled the history of the animal and produced a Sasquatch literature. Chapter 4 begins the analysis of the phenomenon by discussing how we might go about studying something as ephemeral as Bigfoot in a scientific manner. Does the evidence permit scientific examination? If we try to look at the evidence through an objective lens, what emerges at the end of the analysis? When the best-known evidence for Bigfoot is scrutinized, we begin to get a clearer picture of what underlies the phenomenon.

Chapter 5 is devoted entirely to the centerpiece of Bigfoot evidence, the 1967 film of a Sasquatch taken by Roger Patterson. The authenticity of the film is defended more stridently by the advocates than any other single piece of evidence. John Green put it bluntly: "I have heard of no one, in any field, who obtained a copy of the film for thorough study and then publicly taken and defended the position that there is anything the matter with it."[4] Most scientists who have devoted time and resources to such an examination concur with Green; a few do not. These arguments deserve scrutiny since some of them baldly state that the film has to be genuine.

The real problem Bigfoot presents is that, as the anthropologist Marjorie Halpin observed, it is "a being of the mind that leaves footprints in the earth."[5] Without the footprints, we could write the whole thing off. Chapter 6 deals with the thorny issue of giant footprints where there are not supposed to be any giants to make them. In this chapter, the question of making, faking, and interpreting footprints gets full attention. While chapter 6 presents a serious dilemma for the skeptically inclined, the advocates' dilemma is presented in chapter 7. There is no body. This issue has been dealt with, dismissed, and explained away in a series of arguments over the years, and the question addressed in this chapter is whether we should be satisfied with these explanations.

The easiest way for academic institutions to ignore the problem of Sasquatch is to dismiss the enterprise as pseudoscientific. Chapter 8 addresses the fairness of such a charge. The question is not only whether the search for a mysterious animal is intrinsically unscientific, but also whether the facts and arguments of that search to date belong beneath the tent of scientific inquiry. If the quest for Bigfoot can be a scientific endeavor, then it should be, in some measure, soluble.

A last problem to be confronted, in chapter 9, is the persistent eyewitness accounts that exist independent of footprints, films, and hair samples. Is it possible to explain what people are experiencing other than by invoking an unknown animal? The eyewitness is the final piece of the puzzle. If we can explain what might be happening here, Bigfoot's true nature should begin to emerge.

Chapter 10 involves one final digression. I explore a Bigfoot legend that lives on in the most unlikely of places—the forests and swamps of north-central Florida. It is an instructive exercise for learning how legends are born, what keeps them going, and most importantly, why such things matter to people who are faced with problems far greater than the question of feral apes roaming the woods. In chapter 11, my purpose is to take the totality of what Bigfoot is—the history, the footprints, the endless encounters, and the lure of the creature—and offer an explanation of what is behind it all.

NOTES

1. Suttles (1980:245).
2. Green made the comment in June 1979; quoted in Wylie (1980:144).
3. The reader will recognize that the name of the creature is capitalized throughout this work. I do this out of precedent, since it is customary to see "Bigfoot" rather than

"bigfoot" in supportive books on the subject. There is a certain irony in this tradition, in that authors advocating the animal's existence bestow legendary status on it by insisting on capitalization (singular mythological creatures are considered proper nouns, whereas in zoology, one writes of "deer" rather than "Deer"). There seems to be no consensus on the correct plural form, with Bigfoot, Bigfoots, and Bigfeet in usage. I use Bigfoot as both the singular and plural form.

4. Green (1978:113).

5. Halpin (1980:24).

2

The Natural History of Bigfoot

The story has been told not once, but hundreds of times. It is often seen at night, its eyes glowing in the shine of headlights. It is covered with hair. Its massive frame is anywhere from 7 to 12 feet tall. Its facial features are reminiscent of apes, yet also vaguely human. Its odor is so foul that people have been known to pass out from the stench. It walks on two legs with a speed and fluidity of motion not seen in humans. It does not run from people like most wild animals; it simply walks away, unconcerned. If someone forgets such an encounter, it is only because the incident was so traumatic that it is suppressed from consciousness.

Monsters can only move from the realm of legend into the scope of scientific inquiry if they can somehow achieve flesh-and-blood status. Most supporters of Bigfoot's reality appreciate this, thus they will argue that Bigfoot is simply another member of the earth's biosphere, albeit one that the scientific establishment has failed to recognize. Bigfoot must fit within the paradigm of evolutionary biology if it has any hope of achieving scientific legitimacy. It has to conform to principles of ecology, evolution, and ultimately common sense if it is to be taken seriously as a zoological phenomenon. If Bigfoot is to demand our attention, it must first be plausible.

When credentialed scientists have spoken out in favor of there being an undiscovered primate behind the phenomenon, a cornerstone of the argument has been that, from the perspective of natural history, the existence of

Sasquatch-creatures cannot be ruled out a priori. If, however, the existence of such animals is biologically impossible, then whatever tales come back from the woods with frightened hikers need not be taken at face value. If the beast can't exist, then we know very well who has been making giant footprints on the fringes of civilization—some people with a little too much time on their hands.

The argument from natural history—that a creature of Bigfoot's description is biologically, ecologically, and evolutionarily plausible—has several components to it. The first has been termed the "continuity test."[1] This simply states that if Bigfoot is a real animal, it is a product of evolution and therefore has an evolutionary history that can be discerned. If there are fossils of Bigfoot, then the idea of animals surviving today cannot be summarily dismissed. A second imperative of a natural history argument is that, given that Bigfoot is subjected to the same evolutionary forces as all other crawling beasts, it must conform to ecological principles. These principles are not at all difficult to articulate. As John Green so aptly noted, if Bigfoot is a real animal, there cannot be just one.

We can reasonably dismiss the possibility that a single or even the same handful of monsters have been frightening people from Oregon to Florida for the last century or more. We are allowed to do so by adhering to some known facts of natural history: individual mammals do not extend their home ranges across entire continents, and life expectancy for mammals in the wild does not extend for 100 years. If the monster stories are real, then procreation is an activity the monsters must be engaging in. These giants must be capable of sufficient reproduction to maintain their numbers and they have to live someplace where they can find enough to eat, where their numbers won't be devastated by predation or disease, and—because these must be mammals—they can manage to stay warm. Some aspect of Bigfoot behavior and ecology also needs to answer the most obvious question: how it is that a giant primate—perhaps the largest that ever lived—remains hidden from view, especially given that it inhabits the forests that people visit routinely?

Constructing a hypothetical natural history for Bigfoot is a worthwhile exercise, if only because it forces the advocate to constrain the argument. For example, the more sober advocates maintain that Bigfoot must be a primate of some sort, owing to its ape-like description.[2] This admission immediately imposes limitations on what constitutes permissible inferences. If Bigfoot is a primate, we can rule out parthenogenesis (reproduction without fertilization) as the means of perpetuation of the species, we need not bother with the speculation that the animal subsists on wood, and we are well advised to ignore the possibility that Bigfoot is constructed of titanium.[3] We can also articulate certain expectations as to what we should observe in Bigfoot populations, based on our observations of other primate and mammal populations (see fig. 2.1).

This brings us to the thorny aspect of the natural history argument—that of consistency. Individual variation is something that biologists expect to see in animal populations, living and extinct. In fact, it would be naive to argue that Bigfoot sightings, footprints, and fossils (if there are any) must be perfectly monotonous to be credible. Variation is the rule in nature, not the exception. Indeed, evolution is impossible without it. But we are entitled to expect a certain level of consistency in what Bigfoot has to offer in terms of material evidence and even eyewitness accounts. For any living species of animal, there are

FIGURE 2.1
Bigfoot bust sculpted by veteran Sasquatch hunter Paul Freeman. Freeman claimed to have seen Bigfoot on several occasions, beginning in 1982. Photo by Michael Dennett, used with permission.

limits to variation: no animal is infinitely variable in size, proportion, anatomy, or behavior. I would not believe an account of deer attacking and devouring a mountain lion any more than you would find credible a report of an orangutan sporting fish scales. If Bigfoot represents a real animal, then we should expect to see variation in appearance and behavior, but within the limits that we observe for other primate species.

To entertain the idea that Bigfoot represents a zoological species, then, we need to demonstrate four things: (1) Bigfoot has an evolutionary history that can reasonably place the animal in contemporary North America; (2) the habitats of North America can sustain a population of these primates; (3) the totality of evidence—from prehistory, historical accounts, and contemporary anecdotes—is consistent with the biology of a large-bodied primate; and (4) there is a sensible explanation as to why a Sasquatch has never been collected. If we can support these contentions, then perhaps the taboo of talking about Bigfoot in scientific circles needs to be lifted.

THE FOSSIL RECORD

The Americas do have an impressive fossil record as far as primates go, but the kinds of animals and the times that they lived do not lend much support to the idea of Bigfoot. In fact, North America was home to the oldest and most primitive primates, a motley collection of small squirrel-like forms, the plesiadapiforms, but by 50 million years ago they were already on the way out (some paleontologists contend that this group is sufficiently weird that they should not be called primates). A second wave of primates occupied the North American continent until about 32 million years ago, with one species persisting until perhaps 10 million years later.[4] There is nothing more recent in the North American record, and, in any case, the forms that were here do not match the size or description of Bigfoot at all. South America boasts an evolutionary radiation of monkeys—with an incomplete but informative fossil record—that runs to the present day. Deriving something like Bigfoot from these primates is not a position many advocates endorse, because there is no evidence for the evolution of giant primates, much less humongous apes, anywhere in the Western hemisphere.[5] Thus, most advocates choose an extra-continental origin for the creature.

Despite these problems, Bigfoot is by no means impossible from the perspective of primate evolution. The fossil record of primates, if it teaches us anything, reveals that this group of animals is incredibly diverse and capable of radiating into a number of ecological niches. Primate diversity today—impressive in its own right—pales in comparison to what we see in the past. A good-sized lemur today is scarcely larger than a well-fed housecat, but in historical times there were lemurs approaching the size of cattle foraging in the forests of Madagascar.

Bigfoot, however, is obviously no giant lemur. Among other traits, it walks on two legs, which makes it a close relative of humans on the basis of parsimony alone. At the very least, it is some kind of ape, convergent with us by virtue of locomotion but not, apparently, in terms of its brains, since tools and fire do not appear to be part of its behavioral repertoire. Since there are several primate fossils so small that the details of their anatomy cannot be discerned without a microscope, we can surmise that something the size of Bigfoot ought to be leaving a tangible fossil record. Ideally, we should have a continuous record of fossilized Sasquatch remains right up to modern times, preferably in the locales where the beast currently terrorizes unsuspecting outdoor types.

But the fossil record is seldom so accommodating. Most primate paleontologists will tell you that the fossil record of recognizably modern gorillas and chimpanzees is virtually nil, and the remainder would concede that any fossils representing their ancestors are controversial. Chimpanzees and gorillas are real animals that had real ancestors, but it is not the fossil record that allows us to draw that conclusion. The truth of the matter is that the fossil record is spotty. But if we rightly place the burden of proof where it belongs, then it seems reasonable to ask that, since the advocates cannot produce a single living Bigfoot, they at least come up with a fossil or two.

The fossil record might be the one thing Bigfoot has going for it, up to a point. From the late Miocene up through the Pleistocene (from perhaps 8 million years ago to about 150,000 years ago), South Asia was home to a primate genus named *Gigantopithecus* ("giant ape"), appropriately named because it was obviously the largest primate that had ever lived by the time it allegedly went extinct. As extinct primates go, this was a late survivor, as it is likely that the animal encountered evolving human lineages during the latter part of its existence.[6] Both species of *Gigantopithecus*, *G. giganteus*, and *G. blacki*, are known exclusively from jaws and teeth. No other part of the skeleton is known. The inventory of *G. blacki* specimens numbers over 1,000.[7]

What can we tell from jaws and teeth about an animal's overall biology? While we can't get a very reliable estimate of overall body size from teeth alone, the fact that *Gigantopithecus* teeth generally dwarf those of other great apes makes it a safe assumption that the animal was massive by any primate standard. Studies of the teeth also tell us something about the primate's ecology as well as its evolutionary relationships. The consensus is that *Gigantopithecus* is closely related to present-day orangutans[8]; in fact, it is very difficult to distinguish large fossil orangutan teeth from the smaller representatives of *Gigantopithecus* in fossil assemblages. Two studies of the chewing surfaces of *G. blacki* teeth establish that this ape was a fairly eclectic feeder, an omnivore not unlike present-day chimpanzees.[9]

Does *Gigantopithecus* fit the bill as Bigfoot's ancestor? It would appear to be big enough, and its generalized diet seems to match the cumulative data from Bigfoot eyewitnesses. It is impossible to say, based on the fossils, that *Gigantopithecus* was not bipedal. The fit was good enough for Bigfoot's most outspoken advocate in academia, Dr. Grover Krantz. Krantz, who passed away in 2002, was professor of anthropology at Washington State University. Unapologetic in his support of Bigfoot as a valid species, Krantz served as editor on two volumes dedicated to the question of Bigfoot, argued for the reality of the creature in another book, and penned several journal articles on the subject. In one of these, he argued that Bigfoot was the contemporary representative of *Gigantopithecus blacki.*[10] His argument rested on the speculation that the two halves of the lower jaw (the mandible) were spread far apart in the back where the bone articulates with the base of the skull. These widely separated halves of the mandible indicated a bipedal posture for this primate, according to Krantz, because in an upright form the jaw had to be separated in the back to permit the head to rest comfortably on a vertical neck. The veracity of the argument is moot, since it relies on Krantz's assessment of the jaw's architecture. The critical parts of the jaw's anatomy were not, in fact, preserved on the fossils, and Krantz did not offer supporting anatomical evidence that his jaw reconstruction could be predictably linked to locomotion. The combination of bipedalism and size permitted the connection between the Sasquatch and the fossils that Krantz desired. Yet the inference was a stretch: paleontologists usually won't commit to a label of bipedality for a species unless some representative fossils from the pelvis or lower limb are preserved. Inferring bipedality from parts of the skull is something of a gamble.

Krantz also wanted to lend legitimacy to the Sasquatch enterprise by giving the animal a scientific name. It is a rule in the biological sciences that you have to designate a particular individual, or part thereof, as a *type specimen* to use as an example of the species being named. The problem in this case, however, is that there were no contemporary remains to be so designated. But Bigfoot left signs of its existence in the form of footprints, and so understanding the need for a type specimen Krantz offered up a specific set of Sasquatch footprints as the material evidence for the living form. Procedurally, this was perfectly legitimate, as there is precedent for naming species on the basis of trace fossils (e.g., fossil droppings or trackways) in the paleontological literature. The fact that Krantz used traces to define a living species was unusual, but not, scientifically speaking, illegal. Bigfoot was named *Gigantopithecus.*

Krantz, in effect, was formalizing the argument from natural history by establishing a connection between the fossil record and Bigfoot, but the argument suffers from a gaping void that I have noted already: there is no fossil record of Bigfoot in North America. Not one fossil from any time or place on the continent can be attributed to *Gigantopithecus* or any other ape. It did live in China, but we have no evidence that it ever found its way here. Whether this is a trivial point or not will be explored more fully later. For the time being, we can say the fossil evidence provides a circumstantial case for Bigfoot, but what do we make of these circumstances? The Pleistocene fossil record for mammals in North America is a good one (the Pleistocene epoch included the ice age glaciations in North America and ran from about 1.8 million years ago to 11,000 years ago): we have excellent documentation of a host of extinct forms as well as some which survive to the present day. But we have never pulled a Bigfoot out of the La Brea tar pits in Los Angeles, a site famous for the hundreds of mammalian fossils recovered there. Some Bigfoot experts speculate that Sasquatch was a latecomer to the continent, crossing over the Bering land bridge (a terrestrial corridor joining what is Russia and Alaska today) more or less contemporaneously with the ancestors of Native Americans. Skeletal remains of Native Americans are very spotty the further back one goes, but their numbers do increase as we converge on the present. With Bigfoot, the record does not get better or worse through time because there is no record at all.

The status of Bigfoot as *Gigantopithecus* is not universally embraced by those sympathetic to modern-day hairy giants. Bigfoot, in its incarnations in the Americas and the Old World, is seen as a beacon of hope for those who wish to have relict Neanderthal populations eking out an existence in the shrinking wilderness.[11] By contrast, it has been suggested that Bigfoot fits best as a scaled-up robust australopithecine,[12] a heavy-jawed bipedal cousin of ours that lived in Africa until perhaps 1 million years ago. Ray Crowe, publisher of a Sasquatch newsletter called *The Track Record* and director of the International Bigfoot Society,[13] has argued for classification of Bigfoot as *Homo erectus*.[14] The issue cannot be resolved without a type specimen. Krantz's tactic of using a footprint is no help since we do not have fossilized tracks of most early hominid species (hominids are a taxonomic group that I define as including the common ancestor of great apes, humans, and all their descendants). In any case, the question of taxonomy is not essential to the argument of whether hairy giants are possible. In the end, it is a distraction because it asks: "What is it?" before establishing whether there is an "it" to begin with.

BIGFOOT HABITAT AND ECOLOGY

Bigfoot advocates will tell you that most Sasquatches reside in the forests of the Pacific Northwest. Proceeding from this premise, the argument from natural history also requires the demonstration that a population of Bigfoot can survive in this preferred habitat of wet, coniferous montane forest. Multiple arguments can be articulated pro and con with respect to this matter, provided we entertain certain assumptions. For example, one can argue that Bigfoot's existence is implausible on the principle of congruence based on its alleged habitat. By Krantz's taxonomy, Bigfoot is a great ape; all great apes occupy tropical habitats today (and it is the rare primate species—ourselves and a few monkeys—that lives beyond subtropical regions). A great ape living in a seasonal temperate climate is at best unexpected; after all, as the great apes' closest living relative, we did not venture far out of the warm climes until we had fire and shelter firmly established in our behavioral repertoire. A gorilla would starve among the conifers of the Cascades if the snows of winter didn't freeze it first; surely Bigfoot, with its greater caloric requirements, would do the same. *Gigantopithecus*, by all indications a tropically adapted form, would have had to survive the long trek over the Bering land bridge over countless generations. Under this line of reasoning, Bigfoot is implausible.

But we can also turn the argument right around and make a credible counterpoint. Bigfoot's size is hardly a liability, rather it is an asset and a predictable one at that. Just as the Polar and Kodiak bears of subarctic regions are much larger than their ursid cousins of lower latitudes, so is Bigfoot much larger than its tropical brethren. Bigfoot is adhering to a well-known principle of biology known as Bergmann's rule[15]: simply stated, animals tend to get bigger the further one moves from the equator. The idea is that getting bigger keeps you warmer because your body's surface area-to-volume ratio decreases as you get larger. This means Bigfoot doesn't have to worry about freezing to death during the long Northwest winters. But doesn't a big animal have to eat more? Indeed it does, although there is a nifty tradeoff with getting bigger and staying warmer: metabolically you can get away with eating relatively less (i.e., per unit body weight) than smaller animals and you can afford to eat bulkier, nutrient-poor food that smaller animals can't process. Under this scenario, Bigfoot's size and presumed omnivorous habits are the perfect adaptation to its forest home.

How does one resolve these contradictory arguments? What premises of the arguments are valid? The crucial point is that the arguments are unfettered by data on the object of study. Speculation has free reign when the ecology of Bigfoot is contemplated. One only has to choose the appropriate eyewitness account to bolster a particular claim. And there are plenty to choose from.

Questions of ecology are an essential consideration in terms of a species' natural history. Bigfoot books often devote page after page to speculations about their subject's preferred foods, migration patterns, and sleeping arrangements. But in trying to establish the basic question of Bigfoot's existence, we put the cart before the horse when we use musings about behavioral ecology to argue in favor of or against the animal's existence. Feral apes shouldn't do well in forests where the winters are long. On the other hand, we know that great big animals can live in temperate forests and do quite well. Moose and grizzly bears are very large and quite real. That is perhaps sufficient on its own to argue that Bigfoot isn't impossible, but by itself it is a weak argument for the beast's reality.

HOW DOES BIGFOOT REMAIN HIDDEN?

The remaining aspect of Bigfoot's natural history that is profitably considered with respect to the issue of plausibility is whether there are credible behavioral or ecological explanations as to how Bigfoot, far and away the tallest beast in the forest, can remain cryptic after decades of pursuit? It is the sharpest question in the skeptic's arsenal and the one question the advocates cannot dodge.

From a perspective of natural history, there are four main lines of argument as to why Bigfoot remains undiscovered (we will revisit this issue in some detail in chapter 7). The first is that ***Bigfoot lives in a remote habitat that is generally inaccessible to people.*** Peter Byrne, a retired big-game hunter who has pursued Bigfoot intermittently for over forty years, is fond of noting that in the Pacific Northwest, there are several accounts of planes that have gone missing in the region since World War II, and the whereabouts of the wreckages are still unknown.[16] John Green once described Bigfoot habitat as "mile after mile of mountain covered with heavy forest growth that completely cuts off any view of the ground."[17] The mountains of the Coast Range and Cascades boast dense forests that do not lend themselves to unobstructed, well-illuminated vistas, to be sure. It would seem to follow, however, that if Bigfoot habitat is so well removed from human eyes, it might hide not only Bigfoot but also perhaps dozens of other unknown creatures as well. Yet no one has suggested such a thing, and while there are vast areas of the continent that remain unsettled, there are actually few places in the lower forty-eight states that have not seen human visitors. The remoteness argument is on some level repudiated by the high incidence of Bigfoot encounters: if humans cannot access Bigfoot habitat, then reports of Bigfoot should be virtually nonexistent. The absurdity of the position was not lost on Grover Krantz, who was once amused by a Bigfoot film in which a region of the forest identified as "unexplored" boasted the greatest frequency of discovered tracks.[18]

A second argument for Bigfoot's cryptic nature is that ***Bigfoot is rare and therefore encounters are rare.*** This argument is unsustainable for essentially the same reason. Sasquatch encounters continue unabated and were so frequent as far back as 1980 that John Green opined that since Bigfoot "are reported over such a wide area . . . that even if there are very few of them in one place they must still number many thousands."[19] People see Bigfoot all the time; the argument that the animals are rare is seldom entertained among advocates because it requires them to concede that the vast majority of encounters must be bogus.

The third argument is compelling but at present unverifiable: ***Bigfoot has enhanced sensory capabilities that permit it to escape detection.*** The hypothesis of excellent sensory modalities was the position taken up by the Bigfoot Research Project (TBRP, directed by Peter Byrne in the early 1990s).[20] The reasoning here is simple: Bigfoot can see, smell, or hear people coming before people can do likewise. The implication is that encounters happen only because Bigfoot permits it. I was inclined to regard this as a thinly veiled paranormal explanation, thinking that the fact that people must be "allowed" to see Bigfoot has supernatural, if not mythological, overtones. One of my colleagues, however, prevailed on me to reconsider. David Watts, a primatologist at Yale University, is a world-renowned expert on African ape behavior. His experience with what were often futile attempts to track chimpanzees in the wild convinced him that his objects of study always knew where he was long before he knew where they were. He was convinced that the chimpanzees were better equipped to collect sensory cues than he was—be it the result of their familiarity with the forest or better neurophysiological capabilities. He eventually found the chimps not because he became a flawless tracker but rather because the chimps eventually got used to his presence and stopped bothering to run away. Does this explain Bigfoot's elusive nature? If Bigfoot is just another primate, shouldn't we expect that eventually they would become accustomed to having curious humans around?

The final argument confronts the bothersome fact that no specimen of Bigfoot has been successfully collected. John Green reasons that this is accounted for by the fact that ***Bigfoot is extremely hard to kill.***[21] The explanation is supported by eyewitness anecdotes: there are several accounts of Bigfoot being shot, yet a body has never been secured after the fact, usually because the bullet did not slay the beast and it simply ran away. Bigfoot has been hit by both cars and trucks,[22] but even these high-speed collisions have not yielded a dead Sasquatch. Given Bigfoot's large size, the argument is not completely without foundation. Even if you have a big gun, you have to know what you are doing to kill a grizzly bear, and the animal is not likely to grant you a second chance should you miss the mark. Given a choice, no wild animal is going to elect to die at a hunter's feet. The explanation that Bigfoot does not die easily at the hands of people can perhaps suffice for any particular case. But it is prudent to ask how it is that Bigfoot always survives these violent encounters.

ALTERNATIVE EXPLANATIONS

Expressing some thoughtful skepticism toward the argument from natural history does not easily settle the mystery of Bigfoot. If there is no animal behind it all, then the skeptical view needs to offer an alternative explanation. We have to explain why people see Bigfoot when there is no such animal.

Generally, these alternative explanations take two forms. The first confronts the possibility that Bigfoot is not an animal but does not then subscribe to the notion that people see something that isn't there. This view comes from Bigfoot's paranormal camp, an interesting group that has Bigfoot teleporting in and out of flying saucers, morphing into different entities, and dematerializing at will. It's a completely effective rejoinder to skeptical complaints that we can't bag a specimen, so long as you accept the premise that alien visitations, shape-shifting, and violation of thermodynamic principles are credible processes operating in the world today. The seasoned Bigfoot hunters, by and large, take a dim view of this set of explanations, recognizing that explaining one unknown through a host of others amounts to a pseudoscientific shell game. Public statements connecting Bigfoot with UFOs is considered bad form among certain self-appointed Bigfoot experts.[23] Throughout its history, Bigfoot has been plagued by paranormal undercurrents. But more on that later.

The second alternative to the natural history argument is favored by the scientific community and was articulated most precisely in 1980 by Kenneth Wylie in his book *Bigfoot: A Personal Inquiry into a Phenomenon.* The argument is simple: Bigfoot is a contemporary mythological figure that is perpetuated through hoaxes. Yet Wylie appreciated that this succinct assessment of the phenomenon belies the complexity of the issue. Not all Bigfoot encounters are fabrications or practical jokes. Some people perceive Bigfoot and cannot be convinced otherwise, and these people are telling the truth. In some sense, the easiest way around the problem is to accept that they did, in fact, see a Sasquatch. A compelling case can be made, however, that what is really happening is people are seeing something that is not Bigfoot at all, but when they interpret the experience, Bigfoot is imprinted on their consciousness. How can this be?

Contemporary Western culture is not enamored with myths. We're enlightened through science and technology, after all, and thus we have dispensed with superstition and the silliness of monsters. People used to believe in dragons, but we like to think we are more rational now. We think we have moved beyond the need for monsters and demons, so we have no use for myths.

It is useful to ask why we ever needed myths in the first place. Certainly, myths were attempts to understand the universe when there were not better means available. Every culture has an origin myth. The question of origins comes naturally when we contemplate the human condition. Where do I come from? Why am I here? Is my life experience meaningful? If these questions are no longer relevant to the contemporary person, then we can truly say that myth has no place anymore in the human psyche.

I submit (and this is neither a novel nor radical insight) that myth remains a powerful and essential force in human society. Myths still tell us why things are the way they are when the newspapers and the scientists don't provide us with all the answers. As the literary critic Roland Barthes remarked, "Myth is a value, truth is no guarantee for it; nothing prevents it from being a perpetual alibi."[24] In other words, myth is all about meaning, and the reality of the elements within the narrative has no bearing on utility. Anyone doubting the popularity of myth today need only spend an evening watching professional wrestling. Bogus is not necessarily meaningless.

What does the idea of the essential nature of myth contribute to the enigma of Bigfoot? Put bluntly, when Bigfoot appears this means something well beyond a mere sighting of a large bipedal ape. Bigfoot is not just seen, or smelled, or heard, it is experienced; people do not merely gaze at it and get on with their lives. The eyewitnesses often regard encounters as life-changing. People don't construct websites devoted to the bear they saw last summer, but they do for Bigfoot.

These observations hardly settle the issue, however. We may still need myths, and Bigfoot may fit the bill, but that does not exactly mean that Bigfoot is not out there. In his book *Where Bigfoot Walks: Crossing the Dark Divide*, naturalist-writer Robert Pyle makes the point that Bigfoot is a mythological figure regardless of its material existence. Bears and wolves figure prominently in native mythologies, but we don't then stupidly conclude that the animals don't exist.

We will return to the idea of Bigfoot as myth in the last chapter, but at this point we are getting ahead of ourselves. Myth alone is an incomplete explanation. Fictional monsters can't leave footprints and they shouldn't photograph well either.[25] There is a mountain of evidence to confront first before relegating Bigfoot to the world of vampires and werewolves.

On balance, the argument from natural history compels us to pursue the matter of Bigfoot more deeply. There are real problems posed. We should have remains in North America, yet we have none. Inferring the ecology of giant bipedal apes is little more than a futile thought experiment devoid of objectivity, but we cannot say with certainty that a giant primate could not survive in North America. Perhaps this is an animal that has a gift of sensory acuity that allows it to live unmolested in our midst. It seems strong enough to withstand our violence. On the other hand, there seem to be so many of them that some accident must befall their kind occasionally to facilitate discovery.

From the perspective of natural history, the arguments pro and con are something of a wash: the existence of Bigfoot is not impossible but perhaps merely implausible. Given this inconclusive verdict, it is apparent that the question of Bigfoot hinges on the details. Bigfoot may or may not have a natural history in the sense of evolutionary biology, but it most certainly has the appearance of one with respect to those who have pursued it. In this apparent history there has been an accumulation of evidence over the years that brings new generations of seekers to investigate the mystery. It is a curious history as stories of discovery go, because after four decades of pursuit, the hunters of Bigfoot appear to be no closer to their quarry.

NOTES

1. Glickman (1998:2).

2. The insistence on primate status for Bigfoot is not universal, although nonprimate hypotheses are a minority view. The possibility that Bigfoot is a surviving giant ground sloth was broached by an audience member at the Sasquatch Symposium in Harrison Hot Springs, British Columbia, on May 28, 1994.

3. Grover Krantz was treated to just such a speculation (1992:41). It was offered as a means to explain the great depth of tracks for which Bigfoot is famous. Parenthetically, this provides an excellent explanation of why shooting Bigfoot generally has little effect on the creature's well-being.

4. Conroy (1990:127, 138).

5. There have been claims—ultimately unsubstantiated—of apes in South America; see Keith (1929).

6. Ciochon, Olsen, and James (1990).

7. Woo (1962).

8. Fleagle (1999:476–480).

9. Daegling and Grine (1994); Ciochon, Piperno, and Thompson (1990).

10. Krantz (1986).

11. See Porshnev (1974) and Shackley (1983) for full development of the hypothesis.

12. Strasenburgh (1984).

13. See http://www.internationalBigfootsociety.com/index.php.

14. Crowe (2002), Early man as a model for Bigfoot. This was written for Craig Heinselman's CRYPTO pdf newsletter *Hominology Special Number II.* Accessible at http://www.strangeark.com/crypto/Homin2.pdf.

15. Conroy (1990:32).

16. Byrne (1976:91–92). The now defunct website of the Bigfoot Research Project, an organization that Byrne headed, put this number at seventy-two since World War II.

17. Green (1971:70).

18. Krantz (1992:17).

19. Green (1980:64).

20. The project posted the hypothesis of excellent sensory capabilities on its website under its Frequently Asked Questions. These have been reposted on other Bigfoot Internet sites since the project's closing.

21. Green (1971:77).

22. See Green (1978) for a sampling of such accounts.

23. Both John Green (in the *Sasquatch Odyssey* video production, 1999, Big Hairy Deal Productions) and Loren Coleman (2003:172), despite serving as past purveyors of Sasquatch-UFO lore, have repudiated such a linkage on the grounds that such explanations do not advance the scientific case for Bigfoot.

24. Barthes (1978:123).

25. Of course, a paranormal perspective would hold that photography of ghosts or spiritual energy fields is theoretically possible.

3

The Social History of Bigfoot

Bigfoot's natural history remains an open question. As yet there is no definitive evidence that a large bipedal ape inhabits the North American forests, the product—like ourselves—of a long and relentless process of evolution. Even so, the history of zoology reminds us that there may exist animals that we do not yet know about: the saola, a primitive ungulate, was discovered in Viet Nam in 1992, and the turn of the twentieth century began with the discovery of a 500-pound relative of the giraffe, the okapi.[1]

It is undeniable that Bigfoot is part of human experience, whether it is animal or myth. It has a social history. What I mean by this is very simple: people have heard stories of Bigfoot, people have encounters with Bigfoot, people see Bigfoot tracks, and people deem Bigfoot to be worthy of conversation. Human interest is thus central to Bigfoot's social history.

There are good reasons for making the distinction between natural and social history. If natural history can be thought of as a compendium of evidence and observation, social history is about how people discover, distribute, and interpret that evidence. With respect to the basic question of zoological existence, the argument from natural history comes up a little short. If we can examine the social history—the stories, their interpretation, the people who make the plaster casts of footprints—and we can conclude that there need not be a strange animal behind these items, then the phenomenon of Bigfoot is one step closer to resolution. Essentially, the remainder of this book deals with this social history, because it is in this context where we are forced to evaluate the best evidence for Bigfoot. We cannot consult the fossil record because it is empty, and even though one can find the occasional Bigfoot museum, there are no monstrous remains to be studied—only footprints and stories about who might have made them. From the perspective of biology, the evidence is ambiguous rather than objective. Still, we can entertain the idea that the stories people are telling point to something that we cannot explain except by reference to an undiscovered species. In this chapter, I will outline the highlights of Bigfoot's history, with a view toward treating the evidence at face value. I reserve the more critical examination of this history for later chapters.

A QUESTION OF ORIGINS

The first step in trying to see whether natural and social histories are congruent is to try to establish the origins of the phenomenon. Determining where and how a tradition starts is critical when one's aim is to distinguish truth from legend. For example, if the contemporary obsession with alien visitations could be traced to a single event in UFO lore, it might be possible to dissect that event, find out who saw what and when, compare the narratives of those involved, and arrive at some synthesis in which the facts get sorted out. If the inspiration for the story was actually a crashed weather balloon, we would be likely to put less stock in subsequent tales of flying saucers and their curious occupants. On the other hand, if a flying saucer from the event was on display at the Smithsonian, we would be apt to pay closer attention to complaints of nocturnal abductions and uninvited probing. Neither conclusion (misidentified instrument versus otherworldly aircraft) to the historical event actually proves or disproves the reality of alien abduction, but each serves to inform us about how confident we ought to be that something strange is going on.

Bigfoot is not the only monster tradition that has wide popular appeal. The same cable television channels that broadcast Bigfoot specials also feature programming on the possibility of plesiosaurs lurking under the surface of Loch Ness. In this case, the identification of the phenomenon's origin is fairly damning to the advocate position. Ronald Binns, in his 1984 book *The Loch Ness Mystery Solved*, establishes that this particular monster tradition simply did not exist prior to 1933. From this fact, Binns is able to articulate a strong case that the monster is the product of human invention and imagination.

Hypothetically speaking, if the Bigfoot phenomenon could be traced to a single contemporary source, it would be prudent to dismiss the possibility that it has anything to do with actual animals because Bigfoot would have no natural history to speak of. For the point of argument, let us say that no Bigfoot stories existed prior to 1958 (the reason behind my choice of this particular year will become apparent shortly). That is, before this date, no one had ever reported seeing a Bigfoot, no previous oral tradition of hairy apes in the forest existed, and no one had ever found gigantic humanlike tracks that they couldn't explain. Let us also impose a condition that corresponds to the current state of affairs: there is no body or unequivocal specimen of any kind.

From the standpoint of evolutionary biology, we could ascribe the instantaneous appearance of Bigfoot to two possibilities. First, as luck would have it, nobody had run into one of these 7-foot, 800-pound monsters until 1958. Perhaps the retreating populations had run out of hiding places then, or people who had encounters just didn't recognize a Sasquatch or its traces for what they were. The second possibility is that Bigfoot is something other than an animal; more specifically, Bigfoot is an invention of the human mind, possessing only a social history with no corresponding natural history. A misidentified bear might be the inspiration for the invention, or a strange sound in the night might be sufficient to flesh out a whole monster. It is even possible that the alleged event was a fabrication of someone desperate for attention or a sophomoric prank.

We thus have to weigh two alternatives: Bigfoot is spontaneously discovered or Bigfoot is invented out of whole cloth for any number of reasons. Neither alternative is impossible. Embracing the first possibility requires us to buy into the idea that a population of giants could reasonably remain undetected for recorded history. Accepting the second explanation depends on how we view the human animal. Do people make perceptual mistakes? Do people lie? Is there any such thing as a practical joker? The answer is clearly yes to all of these. We are compelled to acknowledge that the idea of invention is a perfectly valid explanation.

This concession does not settle the issue, however. Before settling on fabrication as the source of Bigfoot, we first have to decide whether or not our first explanation has any teeth to it. What if nobody lived in the forests of western North America before 1958? If the first reports emanated from a region that was truly unknown and unexplored, we might give some cautious credence to them. If Bigfoot was sighted rummaging through a dumpster behind a shopping mall in Yakima, however, it is unlikely that many of us would take that initial report at face value. What brings us to make those initial judgments is a matter of familiarity of experience. By definition, an unexplored stretch of wilderness is unknown. Nobody knows exactly what is in there, so if reports of a strange animal start emerging from these woods, we might not deem it impossible just so long as the animal described is, by some standard, plausible (tales of eight-legged linoleum rhinos with paisley eyes would not, presumably, prompt sponsorship of an expedition from the National Geographic Society). On the other hand, an initial account of a hairy monster appearing in an urban setting, where people are familiar with the environs, would soon be relegated to the status of legend. In this case, there is no reasonable expectation on biological or rational grounds that we could have missed such a thing. We would, properly, conclude that the most likely explanation was one of misperception, imagination, or fabrication.

Finding the first account or source for Bigfoot turns out to be a monumentally difficult task. What we now call Bigfoot stories existed well before the monster got its name. A number of scholars have attempted to trace the legend or the animal to its historical origin, but tales of hairy giants living on the fringes of human habitation have been around forever.[2] It is also important to note that stories of Bigfoot-like creatures (bipedal, hairy, and not human) are by no means restricted to the forests of western North America. As Ivan Sanderson amply documented in his 1961 book *Abominable Snowmen: Legend Come to Life*, you can find eyewitnesses for these beasts on every continent (except Antarctica, which appears to be a monster-free zone).

Thus, a skeptic's dream scenario in which there is a single point of origin for Bigfoot—preferably an account in which there are fantastic mythological elements to cast suspicion on its reality—is simply wishful thinking. If we allow that the North American Bigfoot is an undiscovered primate and we base this conclusion, in part, on eyewitness testimony, we must acknowledge that eyewitnesses are attesting to similar beings throughout the globe. If we assert that it is merely a legend, then we are forced to concede it is a universal one with the expected cultural variations. In either case, the phenomenon is likely as old as humanity itself.

There is a widespread but mistaken impression that Bigfoot as a phenomenon started *de novo* with the discovery of gigantic, strangely proportioned footprints by a road construction crew in a remote region of northern California in 1958. Rather, what happened was that a wire service picked up the local story and it ran all over the country and in many places abroad. What made the dispatch so dramatic was a photograph of the tracks' discoverer, Gerald Crew, holding a cast of one of the prints. The size of the cast was breathtaking; it would have been laughable were the picture not accompanied by a sober report of scores of tracks peppering the freshly graded road in this largely uninhabited stretch of coastal California. Bigfoot was now big-time news, but neither the story nor the tracks were unprecedented.

The significance of the event was only that a local legend went global. The cast of the giant foot merely foisted an alleged beast onto public consciousness well beyond the local taverns. There had been previous tales of such beasts from the Pacific Northwest—some historical, a few contemporary—but here was an image that sold the idea to a larger audience. This was Bigfoot's coming-out party, and the publicity surrounding the find foreshadowed the media circus that has surrounded the phenomenon ever since. The details of these tracks' appearance deserve careful scrutiny, and I will return to these later in the chapter.

The instant appeal of Bigfoot had precedent from the other side of the world. The footprint of an alleged yeti, photographed by Eric Shipton late in 1951 on a high Himalayan mountain pass,[3] had made the rounds of the world's newspapers soon after. This image popularized the notion of the "abominable snowman" for the masses, but just as the northern California find had an existing legend as a foundation, the Shipton photograph documented only the latest set of tracks discovered. The yeti tradition was strengthened by sightings of beasts and trackways dating from at least 1887.[4]

The Himalayan compendia of evidence only bolstered the case for Bigfoot. Tom Slick, the wealthy Texas oilman who had bankrolled three expeditions in search of bipedal hairy apes in Asia during the late 1950s, funded a similar expedition to find Bigfoot in the Bluff Creek area of the Trinity Alps beginning in 1959,[5] in the same general area where the famed tracks were spotted the year before. Slick's expeditions never discovered anything conclusive on either continent, although in each case some suggestive finds were made.[6] The mere fact that someone was paying to send people into the field looking for these things, however, lent the phenomenon an air of credibility.

Advocates and skeptics alike consider the 1958 incidents (Bigfoot made several visits to the road-building operation) to be watershed events in Bigfoot's social history. The phenomenon was instantly and irretrievably out in the open once the story hit the newswire. This was much more than a monster story. The 1958 events are regarded as the beginning of the contemporary era of Bigfoot[7] for a number of reasons. First, the image of the cast—an undeniably physical manifestation of the event—was a symbol that this mystery could be solved by conventional scientific means: Bigfoot could, perhaps, really be studied in the same way that one could study bears or dinosaurs. Hallucination was out as a complete explanation. Second, the footprints themselves became a standard for later comparisons—if they were legitimate, then anything found subsequently could be evaluated against them in an objective manner. The third reason 1958 marked a sea-change in Bigfoot's social history is probably appreciated more by the skeptics than the advocates: the giant ape seemed to get a lot busier in the aftermath of the events. The data have snowballed ever since.

HISTORICAL ACCOUNTS BEFORE 1958

Bigfoot stories existed before Jerry Crew immortalized the monster, but the monster didn't yet have its popular name. Some of these stories produced local excitement in the form of newspaper reports but did not stay in public consciousness for long. Since 1958, a few of these encounters have been immortalized through countless retellings in the advocate literature. These are stories rich in detail but—because of their age—deficient in documentation. They deserve our attention not only because they establish the social history prior to Bigfoot's public debut in 1958, but also because they also provide a sense of what Bigfoot was before it became "Bigfoot." They do not lack for drama.

A trapper, who gave his name as Bauman, told a young Teddy Roosevelt—the future president—of a frightening encounter near one of the forks of the Salmon River in the Bitterroot Mountains.[8] The exact date of this run-in is not known, but various estimates put the time between the early and mid-1800s.[9] In any case, it is clear that the event itself and Bauman's relating it to Roosevelt were separated for several decades.[10]

An unknown beast was raiding Bauman's camp while he and his partner (who curiously is never named) were out checking and setting traps during the day. They surmised from the tracks left in camp that this raider was of the two-footed variety. Bauman awakened one night to a rather rank odor and, opening his eyes, saw the silhouette of a giant form at the front of their lean-to. Taking offense at the intrusion, Bauman fired his rifle at point-blank range—and missed. The intruder was momentarily scared off but returned to ransack the camp the next day. The two trappers were unnerved as they suspected that they were being watched and, on their last day, followed by something just beyond the forest fringe. After having spent the previous day together for protection, on this day they decided to expedite their departure and split up: Bauman would collect the remaining traps and his partner would strike camp. Bauman would not see his partner alive again. The condition of the camp when Bauman returned told the story. Apparently, the beast snuck up on the man in camp, buried his fangs in his throat, and then mutilated the body "in uncouth, ferocious glee."[11] Bauman was not anxious for a repeat encounter, so he left the camp and the surrounding area quickly. Ivan Sanderson picked up the story in his 1961 book, and it is a rare Bigfoot book that does not include Roosevelt's account.

1924 was something of a bad year for human-Bigfoot interaction. Two of the most famous Bigfoot encounters took place in the Pacific Northwest then. Which account is more fantastic all depends on your point of view. In the first, Albert Ostman was prospecting alone near Toba Inlet, British Columbia,[12] when he noticed that his camp was being disturbed by some animal while he slept at night. What was unusual about these disturbances was that the intruder was somewhat tidier in rummaging through his gear than the average bear. Then, one night the visitor decided to make off with some of Ostman's stuff—including Ostman himself, who was trapped in his sleeping bag. He was carried to a box canyon where he was held captive by a nuclear family of Bigfoot: Pop had carried him there, the mother Bigfoot "did not seem too pleased with what the old man dragged home,"[13] and a curious son and shy daughter rounded out the domestic unit. Ostman offered detailed descriptions of anatomy and behavior, and some language ability on the part of the Sasquatch family was apparent. After nearly a week in captivity, Ostman's food supplies dwindled, so one morning he hatched a plan of escape. Over breakfast, Ostman hoodwinked the old man into thinking his chewing tobacco was food and got the unwitting Bigfoot to eat a whole box of chaw. The Sasquatch got quite sick and Ostman escaped. Ostman signed a sworn affidavit attesting to the truth of his story in 1957.[14]

After that event, Ostman decided that prospecting was not for him. Meanwhile, Bigfoot was trying to persuade other miners to come to the same conclusion in the Cascade Range further inland. Not far from Mount St. Helens is

Ape Canyon, so named because one day in 1924 a miner named Fred Beck shot a Bigfoot there. By Beck's account, the wounded beast tumbled off a cliff into the canyon below. Apparently, the body found its way into a torrential stream and was never found. Like Bauman's and Ostman's stories, Beck's is such a popular anecdote that its inclusion in post-1958 Bigfoot books seems obligatory. Beck was one among a group of miners who had encountered bipedal furry beasts of alarming stature while out in the bush working the mine.

Before Beck had his violent encounter, one of his partners had shot another ape-like form in the head when he saw it peering out from behind a tree. Apparently unfazed by the insult, the creature fled without difficulty. In retrospect, the shootings were a poor decision. After nightfall, the miners found themselves trapped in their windowless cabin under attack by at least two of the offended apes, who hurled rocks and perhaps boulders at the cabin walls, pounded on the roof and door, and knocked out a length of wood from the cabin wall long enough to insert a hairy arm inside. That is all the miners saw of the creatures that night. By daybreak the attack had stopped, but the men had had enough and elected to abandon the mine. The newspapers in the region got hold of the story as the miners emerged from their encounter, thus the incident enjoyed some documentation. That is, at least the account of the incident was documented. Giant footprints found around the cabin seemed to corroborate that something unusual had happened.[15]

Not all pre-1958 encounters with Bigfoot were punctuated with violence or abduction. One William Roe was able to observe an adult female Sasquatch at very close range in 1955. His account rivaled Ostman's in the level of detail, although Roe's encounter lasted minutes rather than days. At first Roe watched the Bigfoot unobserved, which seems to have allowed for an extended encounter. But the Sasquatch eventually got wind of him and beat a deliberate retreat. Roe would later recall that at one point he had his rifle leveled at the creature but could not shoot because, "I felt now that it was a human being and I knew I would never forgive myself if I killed it."[16] Roe swore to the truth of his story in an affidavit signed in 1957.[17] That Ostman had signed his just six days before was no coincidence, but I will address that issue in the next chapter.

The Fred Beck story reminds us that the 1958 footprints were not the first trackways to be reported. But even the footprints observed in 1924 were not the first: mysterious prints troubled the continent's explorers over a century earlier. An accomplished geographer named David Thompson found a set of tracks that he deemed extraordinary in the snow near Jasper, Alberta, in January 1811. Thompson was one of the first westerners to explore this region. Puzzled by the size and form of the tracks, Thompson expressed reluctance to find the trackmaker. The proportions of the tracks seem to fit the bill as far as Sasquatch was concerned, but Thompson may not have been familiar with the legend and did not offer an opinion as to the precise identity of the tracks' owner. His companions insisted they did not belong to a bear.[18]

The capture of a Bigfoot would quickly settle the question of its reality, of course, and there is an intriguing late nineteenth-century account that suggests to some advocates that this may have, in fact, happened. British Columbia's *Daily Colonist* ran a story on July 4, 1884, reporting capture of a hairy beast by a railroad crew near the town of Yale.[19] Described as a gorilla, the animal was christened "Jacko" for no apparent reason; it weighed 127 pounds and stood less than 5 feet tall. The animal's mode of progression is never stated, but the size and description of the animal is enough of a fit with a small Sasquatch that, for some researchers, it is a foregone conclusion that Bigfoot had been captured. What eventually became of Jacko and his remains is unknown, but he was apparently not in Yale for very long.

These stories by no means provide an exhaustive account of all sightings and encounters with Bigfoot before 1958 but are included here as they occupy a prominent place in the Bigfoot literature. One problem that emerged in Bigfoot research after 1958, with Bigfoot's growing media popularity, was the rise of hoaxing, fabrication, and innocent misinterpretation—any seasoned advocate will concede the point.[20] There has been, consequently, the tendency to assign more weight to any encounter that was documented before Bigfoot became a cultural phenomenon. The question of whether this assumption is justified needs to be explored at some length if the social history is to give us insight into natural history: old accounts and new accounts should have a lot in common if an animal is at the source. For the moment, we will put off the question and continue fleshing out Bigfoot's storied past.

BIGFOOT DEBUTS AND THE EMERGENCE OF THE BIGFOOT HUNTER

As noted above, the modern era of Bigfoot was ushered in with the picture of a bemused Jerry Crew holding the cast of a monstrous footprint. Crew may have immortalized Bigfoot when he cast one of the prints infesting his workplace in 1958, but fame, apparently, was not his motivation. Instead, it seems that he had been somewhat annoyed that his tale of finding giant footprints was not being taken seriously.[21] So he went to the town of Anderson to call on his friend Bob Titmus, a taxidermist and picked up some plaster to cast what he and everyone else on site was seeing. Titmus would become an important figure around the Bluff Creek area because not only was he particularly adept at finding Bigfoot tracks, he also quickly got in the habit of casting them before wind and rain had a chance to erode the details. He was an anomaly among the elite Bigfoot hunters in that he had actually had his own encounters with the beast, first having seen it on the beach from his vantage point on the deck of a ship in 1942.[22]

The location of the Crew footprints would turn out to be the epicenter of Bigfoot activity in the decade that followed. Predictably enough, the Tom Slick expedition was based in the area. Years later, the Patterson film would be made just a few miles away along the banks of Bluff Creek, and the three sets of Sasquatch tracks that Bigfoot researchers marveled at in the summer of 1967 were found a few miles upslope on Blue Creek and Onion Mountains.[23] In all, Green has filed over seventy reports from the immediate vicinity.[24]

The fact that Crew poured plaster into one of the tracks turned Bigfoot into a problematic monster for the scientific community. John Green and Bob Titmus were impressed enough with Bigfoot's sign that they couldn't imagine how anybody could fake such tracks. What Jerry Crew actually thought was going on is not terribly clear. In the *Humboldt Times* account of the affair, he sides with Titmus on his assessment that the tracks were genuine, but because he declined to speculate on what made them, it is not certain what he meant by this. Later accounts of the event state that initially he had figured the tracks were a prank,[25] and he seemed most interested in demonstrating that the tracks were there rather than worrying about whom they belonged to.

What facts do we have about the Crew tracks? The tracks appeared multiple times and in each case a great number were found. Their discovery each morning by the road crew indicated they were made at night. They wandered along the road, around the logging and road-building equipment, and up and down the steep slopes adjacent to the emerging road. The tracks measured about 16 inches in length and 7 inches in width—far outside the adult human range in size and quite unusual in proportion. Stride length was reported to range from 4 to 10 feet and the depth of the tracks ranged from 1 to 3 inches in soil where a big man's boot print barely indented the ground. In addition, the thing that made the tracks was apparently able to make its way with ease over hillside terrain that was reported to be beyond a human's ability to negotiate. Nobody managed to see the track maker. If someone was playing a joke, they were going to a great deal of trouble for no tangible reason. By one account, the nighttime visitor also was fond of tossing about full 50-gallon oil drums on a lark and chucking sizable culverts into ravines as a protest against human intrusion. The contractor of the expedition, described by advocate Ivan Sanderson as "hard-boiled and pragmatic,"[26] was a man named Ray Wallace. He was reportedly furious at the effect the events were having on his subcontracting operation. Men were quitting and progress was slow.

These footprints lent credence to the oral history of encounters with hairy giants that residents of the Pacific Northwest, white settlers and Native Americans alike, had been articulating for decades. The time was right for a full-scale field investigation. It took the form of The Pacific Northwest Expedition and it was one of the few Bigfoot searches that enjoyed full and adequate funding. The benefactor was Tom Slick, the Texas millionaire who had already funded three expeditions in the Himalayas in search of the yeti.[27] All were busts. The expedition in northern California was organized in November 1959 and whimpered to a halt some three years later. This effort is famous merely by virtue of the bizarre congregation of personalities involved, for it failed in its goal of securing a Bigfoot or of establishing its existence.

Yet the Pacific Northwest Expedition is an essential component of Bigfoot's social history because the clash of egos that blew apart any hope of a functional operation served to define how each of the major Bigfoot hunters would pursue their quarry in the decades that followed. No two followed similar paths, probably because they developed an antipathy for one another personally and methodologically. These individuals were instrumental in disseminating the legend and pushing for Bigfoot's scientific legitimacy. It is worth the digression here to meet these players because they will be in control of Bigfoot's history from this point forward.

Slick recruited Peter Byrne to head up the expedition. Byrne was a natural choice, having been the point man in Slick's Himalayan ventures. He is one of the rare people who qualify as a "professional" in this field in that for long stretches he has made his living off of Bigfoot. In person, Peter is soft spoken, even tempered, and, for someone who has devoted years of his life to the discovery of a giant unknown primate, seems surprisingly dispassionate about the subject. Irish by birth, he is articulate, engaging, and strikes one as the type who could sell ice to the Inuit given an hour to make his pitch. Before his various full-time stints looking for Sasquatch, Byrne was a big-game hunter and guide in India and Nepal. He was Slick's choice to get the job done—partly because of his outdoor experience, but also out of familiarity and friendship. That Byrne, however, was regarded as an interloper with no North American experience among his expedition fellows is indisputable. Upon his arrival in 1960, when the expedition had been running for some time, Peter disbanded what was left of the original group and opted for a fresh start, keeping Titmus on for a short time.[28]

So deep was the resentment that those who later wrote about the expedition could not even bear to use Peter's name in written accounts; Byrne's sin was that he had not paid his dues by exhaustively chasing down leads in North America prior to the expedition. In later years, Byrne would use his experiences on the Slick expeditions to convince other benefactors to launch two large-scale Bigfoot research efforts in Oregon: the Bigfoot Information Center in The Dalles during the 1970s and the Hood River–based Bigfoot Research Project in the 1990s. These projects were both focused on achieving a scientific resolution of the Bigfoot phenomenon, though there was little interest evident on Byrne's part in arriving at a negative conclusion. Much of the effort in both projects was devoted to raising public awareness of Bigfoot, but Byrne's critics argued that the main point was raising public awareness of Byrne himself. Both goals were realized: Byrne helped bring Bigfoot into public consciousness and in so doing raised his own profile as well. His appearance in feature films and TV documentaries about the Sasquatch is practically a given, which is a testament to his charm and eloquence.

Byrne's projects were unique in that they were well funded and remained operational for a number of years. Byrne claims that, at one point, the support enabled him and his staff to pursue their work uninterrupted for nine years.[29] What became of the research projects? Neither made visible progress in realizing its goal, and the prospects for financial survival of these endeavors consequently dimmed over time and both ceased. The Bigfoot Information Center's demise in 1979 was quiet and uneventful. Author Ken Wylie discovered it by trying to call Byrne and finding the phone line disconnected.[30] It was not surprising. The center itself was little more than a trailer with various items of Bigfoot paraphernalia that could be viewed for the modest sum of 75 cents.[31]

What was particularly bizarre about the center was its location in The Dalles on the Columbia River. Among the varied landscapes of Oregon, it is hard to conceive of a less practical location from which to launch a search for Sasquatch. Unlike the thickly forested and moist environs of the Coast Range or the western slopes of the Cascades, The Dalles abuts the high desert of eastern Oregon. The landscape is not exactly devoid of trees, but it is largely open grassland and scrub. Still, one fruit of Byrne's early work in Oregon was his 1975 book *The Search for Bigfoot: Monster, Myth or Man*, which was, for the most part, a collection of anecdotes of recent and historical encounters. As a persuasive scientific argument, the book falls well short of the mark, but it did keep the public—and his potential backers—interested, at least for a time.

The Bigfoot Research Project was based in what are the ostensibly more Bigfoot-friendly environs of Hood River, some 20 miles west of The Dalles. The town sits next to the Columbia River, but the forested slopes of the Cascades rise from the gorge, making this a more palatable base for Bigfoot-hunting operations. This project, adopting the TBRP acronym for its correspondence and press releases, had real teeth to it in terms of actual research. Remote sensors were set up in the woods in the vicinity of selected "Category A" sightings ("A" events were judged highly credible through an assortment of objective and subjective measures). An 800-number hotline was set up for reporting sightings, and a database was developed to decipher any "geotime" patterns (correlating times and locations of encounters) to Bigfoot sightings. Apparently well heeled this time around, Byrne even had a helicopter at the ready just in case they needed to get into the field and dart a specimen at a moment's notice. TBRP was not restricted to collecting contemporary data. In 1993, Byrne contacted a certified forensic investigator, Jeff Glickman, to analyze the 1967 Patterson film full time.[32] The impact of TBRP was large in comparison to the defunct Information Center; the media were interested and the Internet was buzzing about it. The press was as favorable as one could hope for when Bigfoot was the headline.

Byrne was working on a draft of a major report on the circumstances and analysis of the Patterson film in 1998 when TBRP suddenly and inexplicably closed its doors. A terse press release announced that Byrne had left TBRP and that the organization was defunct. In a bizarre twist, the formation of the

North American Science Institute (NASI) was announced at that same instant, with Glickman at the helm. The organization had the same purpose and used the same facilities as TBRP and apparently experienced no serious interruption of funding. It was not clear whether the backers were the same, but the only tangible changes that could be discerned were the name change and the fact that Byrne was out and Glickman now ran the show.

Byrne no longer actively pursues Bigfoot; his present passion is conservation and he currently oversees a national game reserve in Nepal that he helped create years ago. He remains, however, a staunch Bigfoot advocate and is among the more persuasive of that disparate group when the cameras are rolling. In being an effective fundraiser and persuasive spokesman, he lent an air of professionalism to the pursuit of Bigfoot that other searchers regarded as irrelevant to the endeavor.

In terms of demeanor and outlook, Byrne's counterbalance on the Pacific Northwest Expedition was René Dahinden. Unpolished and impatient, Dahinden disliked Byrne constitutionally. The feeling was mutual.[33] The two shared a dedication to the search, and there the similarities ended. Dahinden thought Byrne was in it for the wrong reasons, explaining it to me this way: "With Byrne, the search for Bigfoot is pie; if he actually found one, it would be pie a la mode."[34] Byrne loved the search and the notoriety that surrounded it, and Dahinden suspected that the quarry itself was practically irrelevant to him. Whether this is the case is arguable; Byrne presents an air of sincerity and he qualifies as a true believer in that he's perfectly satisfied that Bigfoot exists as a flesh-and-blood creature.

René Dahinden found his purpose in life at the age of twenty-three when he heard tales of Bigfoot while working on a farm in Alberta in 1953.[35] Soon after, he moved to British Columbia to begin his quest for the Sasquatch. The search continued, more or less unabated, from then until his death in 2001. Despite nearly five decades in pursuit, Dahinden never once spotted his quarry. He heard enough accounts, saw enough footprints, and spent enough time pondering one short, jerky film to keep himself involved in tracking Bigfoot his entire adult life. He created his own job recovering and reselling spent shot at the Vancouver Gun Club in Richmond, British Columbia, so that he could work when he wanted and, when the mood struck, could take off "to the bush" in his truck with its makeshift camper to see what might be going on beyond the reach of civilization. His commitment to the search was total and unapologetic, though this resolve cost him a marriage and more than a few friends along the way.[36]

Dahinden was born in Switzerland and spent enough of his childhood there that he retained a thick and distinctive accent throughout his life. He was eminently quotable, save for the fact that every other utterance was peppered with a string of profanity. "*Something* is making those goddamn footprints,"[37] was his terse justification for the search. The statement epitomizes Dahinden's approach: what really mattered to him was resolving the mystery. Self-described as a true believer when he first embarked on the search, Dahinden gradually grew more and more skeptical of the creature's existence as he grew older and definitive proof of the Sasquatch never materialized.[38] He never gave up completely because there was just enough evidence that he felt hadn't been adequately explained to leave the door open. But he got to the point where he lost patience with "evidence" that he felt was nothing of the sort: "The last thing I want is to hear another guy tell me he saw a hairy monster."[39]

Dahinden had no formal scientific training, but the years of looking for Bigfoot and coming up against dead end after dead end turned him into a fairly rigid empiricist. In the peculiar universe of Bigfoot research, however, what counts as empirical evidence is tricky. He seemed to recognize before anyone else—and long before any of the professional scientists involved—that most of what was being collected as evidence was "garbage."[40] In his later years, Dahinden's first impulse on hearing or seeing new evidence was to determine first and foremost whether a human agent was at work. In other words, the first order of business was to rule out a hoax. If he could not be convinced that such shenanigans were impossible, he remained skeptical.

Dahinden's fame in the community of Bigfoot aficionados was established well before he published *Sasquatch: The Search for North America's Incredible Creature* with Don Hunter in 1973. This book detailed Bigfoot activity through the 1960s, a period that is arguably the most important as far as evidence is concerned. Dahinden's exploits were also detailed in many of John Green's publications, and his central role in the pursuit of Bigfoot was firmly established by 1975. Dahinden was involved in the follow-up of nearly every major find in the field of Bigfoot research. Although he only coauthored the one book, Dahinden garnered perhaps more press than anyone else involved in the field. Part of the reason for this was his early involvement in Bigfoot research in North America, but no less important was his ability to provide good copy. Dahinden established the irascible reputation of the Bigfoot advocate without help from any of his colleagues. He was not averse to calling his rivals "morons."[41] Some of his choicest criticisms were reserved for the "Ph.D. and university types,"[42] Dahinden's code word for the handful of degreed scientists involved in the field who felt it unnecessary to consult with him about his extensive experience with Bigfoot evidence. The unfortunate fallout from this was that his reputation for intolerance alienated many potential researchers. In truth, Dahinden despised neither skepticism nor science; what he detested more than anything else was arrogance. His apparently unhelpful attitude, however, would be vindicated in time when the arrogance displayed by the Ph.D. types would lead them to make colossal blunders in interpretation.

Dahinden was a collector of Bigfoot evidence but did not routinely share the information he had. Barbara Wasson, a tracker and a Bigfoot advocate, was among Dahinden's small circle of close friends and, in an interview with me in 1999 shortly before her death, she expressed frustration that he was never forthcoming about what he actually knew about certain pieces of evidence. She explained that Dahinden preferred to size up people who would seek him out for information and would slowly troll out small bits of what he knew to see what they would do with it. If the reporter or investigator handled the information responsibly (in his view), then he might dole out more. But Wasson believed Dahinden never shared everything he knew.

Dahinden did not restrict his research to Bigfoot evidence per se. He was not shy about investigating the finders or disseminators of that evidence as well. On this front he was not at all apologetic: having endured so many liars and con artists over the years, he considered it an essential part of his pursuit. The central focus of his research was the famous Patterson film of Bigfoot shot in 1967, and he spent at least as much time investigating the filmmakers—Roger Patterson and his partner on the shoot, Bob Gimlin—as he did scrutinizing the movie itself. He was deeply suspicious of anyone involved with the mystery of Bigfoot, not on principle, but because he knew that the thirst for fame and money was equal to the purer motivation of simple curiosity. On some level, he distrusted everyone: scientists, reporters, the amateur seekers tromping through the woods on weekends, as well as the handful of fellow "professional" Bigfoot hunters. He did not particularly like the people who were involved in the search, but the search was his life, so these were the people with whom he was compelled to interact.

The Pacific Northwest Expedition illustrates this dilemma. At certain points, Bob Titmus was appointed project leader. His unorthodox approaches for finding Sasquatch struck Dahinden as absurd, particularly the technique of baiting trees with used sanitary napkins.[43] When Titmus decided an impressive pile of droppings represented a Sasquatch evacuation, Dahinden opined correctly that "horse shit" was the most appropriate term to describe both the scat and its original interpretation.[44] His sour relations with Dahinden notwithstanding, Titmus would become a leading figure in Bigfoot research by virtue of his ability to find trackways, particularly in the Bluff Creek area.

Another participant in the expedition was a hunter by the name of Ivan Marx. Marx had apparently been retained by Slick as a tracker on Titmus's recommendation based on his good work using hounds.[45] While all he seemed to accomplish on the Slick expedition was to drive Dahinden home to British Columbia (by psychological rather than vehicular means), Marx ended up being by far the most successful of the expedition participants after the fact, as he would be involved in over half a dozen encounters with Bigfoot in succeeding years. Despite these successes, Marx did not enjoy much acclaim among his peers. But that is a story for another chapter.

John Green was another expedition member. Of those involved who later wrote about the experience, Green seems the least embittered. He saw retrospectively that the expedition was doomed: "the average Sasquatch hunter is so pig-headed that two of them together are pretty sure to have a falling out before long."[46]

Green is the original collector and the writer among the big-time Bigfoot hunters. He has amassed thousands of reports of footprints and sightings over four decades and has published over half a dozen monographs and books on the subject. He is well suited to the task of assimilating the mountains of data on the Sasquatch: a newspaperman by trade, he was trained at the School of Journalism at Columbia University. Green has been as intimately involved in Bigfoot as anyone over the years, following closely every major find in the search and faithfully documenting Sasquatch activity from every corner of North America. If there is a definitive work in the Bigfoot field in terms of documentation, it would have to be his 1978 book *Sasquatch: The Apes among Us*. Here are nearly 500 pages of data, if one uses a liberal definition of the term, that describe not just one monolithic beast from the rainforests of the Pacific but a menagerie of animals scattered all over the continent that are involved in all manner of activities in all variety of habitat. In reporting most of what he has heard indiscriminantly, Green doesn't necessarily buy all the stories he has collected, but he doesn't dismiss many of them either. He simply reports them for public consumption.

The stock Bigfoot stories are carefully and thoroughly described in Green's writings, but the weird stuff is folded into the mix as well in *The Apes among Us*. He mentions connections to UFOs but withholds endorsement of these stories only by remarking that using one mysterious phenomenon to explain another is unhelpful.[47] Green also introduces some of Bigfoot's midwestern cousins: "fluorescent Freddie" hails from French Lick, Indiana, sports green fur on his 10-foot frame, and isn't hard to spot at night since his eyes glow red. Uniontown, Pennsylvania, was nearly the scene of a Sasquatch homicide in 1974 when a woman decided to take the law into her own hands and discharge her shotgun into a 7-footer approaching her porch in a threatening manner. No charges were filed, however, as the intruder vaporized in a flash of light on being shot. Some of Green's reports strain credibility in terms of the paranormal attributes of the creatures, while others appear implausible on geographic grounds. Bigfoot on Staten Island? Two sightings occurred within a month of each other. Green considers the nearby swamp and garbage dump to be important components to the story. There is a Bigfoot tradition in Palmdale, California, a community at the foot of the San Gabriel Mountains on the edge of the Mojave Desert. It would be one of the last places on earth one would envision as giant primate habitat, but activity has been frequent enough to prompt the locals to form the CBFO (California Bigfoot Organization) to keep tabs on their giant interloper.

Green has not devoted his energies to field research in the manner of Byrne or Dahinden, but our inventory of Bigfoot evidence would be impoverished were it not for his penchant for cataloging reports. The amount of material is impressive, but what exactly is being documented is something of an enigma. The disparities among reports—three-, four-, and five-toed tracks, hair of every conceivable tint and shade, eyes of various colors—are no particular impediment to the solution to the mystery for Green. It was he, you recall, who made the pertinent observation that, of all the reports, only one need be true to establish the reality of the heretofore unknown creature. John Green is certain that this minimal requirement is already satisfied: somewhere among the noise of these reports are a few kernels of truth. While Green acknowledges "there is a question whether Sasquatches exist at all,"[48] his operational assumption is that the animal is really out there, given his penchant for making rather definitive statements about Sasquatch ecology: "it has learned to swim, to see in the dark, and to survive in a wide variety of climates."[49]

Kenneth Wylie draws a telling portrait of Green as a true believer[50]: the tainted evidence is not troubling, the absence of specimens is hardly unexpected, and some thoughtful sorting through the multitude of encounters leads to a clear and conclusive picture of the beast itself. From diet (omnivorous), activity patterns (nocturnal), and demeanor (shy and retiring) to taxonomy (a persistent *Gigantopithecus*), the biology of the Sasquatch is already largely worked out if you look at the data carefully enough and can separate the wheat from the chaff. Green tires quickly of the skepticism that constantly greets his efforts, yet he rarely feels compelled to answer his critics.

An important difference between Green on the one hand, and Byrne and Dahinden on the other, is that Green has always advocated getting the scientific community involved in the mystery. His frustration with the scientific establishment for ignoring or laughing off the enterprise is palpable in his writings, but he has supported and cooperated with those scientists who have entered the Bigfoot fray. Dahinden despised the dogmatic and condescending attitude of scientists; Byrne seemed to see no need to get credentialed academics involved until the search proved successful, although he was not averse to consulting with scientists for a specific purpose. Green, on the other hand, sees the uninterested posture of mainstream science as a travesty,[51] one so important that he is willing to put aside past slights to cajole academics to get involved and stay involved.[52]

Tom Slick died in a plane crash in 1962,[53] and all the expedition material that had been archived in his care was apparently lost or thrown out. Few think that this evidence is a critical loss. Many of Slick's crew would remain active in the search, and, with the exception of Ivan Marx, all would spend much energy examining and evaluating the crown gem of Bigfoot evidence. It is a 16mm movie of a Sasquatch walking along a creekbed, not far from where Bigfoot had disrupted Ray Wallace's road-building operation less than a decade before.

BIGFOOT IS FILMED

On Friday, October 20, 1967, at about 1:30 in the afternoon, Roger Patterson and Bob Gimlin were on horseback traveling along the Bluff Creek drainage.[54] They were there to film a documentary about Bigfoot. It was a good place to look by all accounts, as the previous summer René Dahinden and John Green had verified that no less than three sets of distinct Sasquatch tracks had been found nearby in conjunction with another road-building operation.[55] Patterson and Gimlin had arrived the week before, camping not far from the base of operations of the Slick Expedition. They were hoping to find footprints, but they got much more. As they rounded a bend in the creek, they came on a squatting Bigfoot that quickly stood up and began walking away from them. In the meantime, Patterson's horse startled, reared, and fell. Patterson grabbed his rented movie camera from the saddlebag and began running toward the retreating Bigfoot, filming as he ran. He managed to steady his hand for some of the film, but the Bigfoot's course of travel forced him to change his position to track it. After a minute, the filming was over. By that night, the roll of film had been shipped, via air courier, to Yakima, Washington, for processing,[56] and the two men were telling their story to the Eureka *Times-Standard*, which ran it on the front page the next day. The two men got word out to Green and Dahinden of their remarkable luck, and by Sunday afternoon Patterson, Dahinden, and Green were watching the film in Yakima at the home of Patterson's brother-in-law.

John Green recalls the sense of optimism the film engendered, remarking: "We had the film, we thought it was all over."[57] Dahinden was intrigued but perhaps somewhat less sanguine about the value of the film at first. Eventually, though, he would hold up the film as being the pivotal evidence for Bigfoot. Bob Titmus got to the filmsite on October 29 and had the presence of mind to cast ten consecutive tracks from the event. The film was shown to a group of anthropologists and zoologists at the University of British Columbia on October 26.[58] Their initial reaction was tepid, and the film's status has not risen in academic circles through the years. For the Bigfoot community, however, the Patterson film was and is the beacon of hope, more than thirty-five years after the fact. The simple truth is that no one has yet proven the film to be a hoax.

The film is intriguing. There are but a few moments where Patterson's hand steadies enough for us to see the subject in motion. The subject is female, judging by her prominent breasts, and her heavyset proportions appear to be due to a well-muscled frame. Hers is a fluid walk that does not resemble a human gait in several details. In the most famous frame of the film, the subject turns head and shoulder toward the camera to dart a quick glance at her pursuer. She moves quickly and deliberately, but beyond this it is difficult in any single viewing of the film to draw any definite conclusions. With the subject occupying such a small portion of each frame and the unsteadiness of the camera itself, the film is, if anything, ambiguous.

Even so, the film stands as the centerpiece of Bigfoot evidence. The few academics who endorse Bigfoot have staked their reputations on the film's authenticity. To suggest that the film is a hoax borders on blasphemy in advocate circles. As recently as 1992, John Green complained that "it has never been properly studied by competent persons in North America."[59] In fact, the only institutional support for the film (outside of self-styled Bigfoot research organizations) prior to that time had come from the then Soviet Union, where a group of Russian scientists from the Darwin Museum in Moscow analyzed and endorsed the film in 1984.[60] Since Green's comment, however, the film has been subjected to thorough kinematic, biomechanical, and metric analyses. The majority of these agree that the film shows a real animal on the grounds that a human being in a costume could not duplicate what is on the film, and the technology of 1967 could not have fudged the image to make it so. If that is true, the matter is settled. I will devote a later chapter to this issue.

A CORPSE: IF NOT BIGFOOT, THEN WHAT?

The only thing better than a film would be a body. Advocates have always known that the body of an actual Bigfoot—living or dead—provides the only certain way out of the mystery. For a time, beginning in 1968, they almost had one. The body in question was a stiff, in both the figurative and literal sense, encased in a block of ice.[61] It was first examined by Bigfoot sleuths in, of all places, a cramped trailer in rural Minnesota. The caretaker of the body was a man by the name of Frank Hansen who had been entrusted by an unknown eccentric millionaire living on the West Coast to show the creature at various carnivals and fairs throughout Middle America. The origin of the Iceman, as it came to be known, was a smallish iceberg in the frigid seas off the coast of the Kamchatka peninsula, in the northern reaches of the western Pacific, half a world away. Who exactly found the Iceman is unclear, but somehow the thing made its way to Hong Kong where it was sold to the rich man in the United States, who Hansen hinted was a movie mogul but who apparently wished to eschew publicity of his acquisition.

Ivan Sanderson, who at the time had authored the most comprehensive treatise on Bigfoot and other hairy bipeds, had heard that Hansen had something very interesting in his freezer. He brought with him Bernard Heuvelmans, an established and respected academic who, with the publication of *On the Track of Unknown Animals* in 1958, more or less founded the emerging field of cryptozoology, the science of hidden animals. Both men had an obvious interest in what Hansen had to show them and they would end up spending two days examining the creature though its icy façade. They were very impressed with what they saw. Even though the ice obscured much of the detail, they could still make out the length, coloration, and distribution of hair, details of the extremities, the compelling face (with the eyes missing from their sockets), and the unambiguous genitalia. It wasn't human, but it wasn't an ape either.[62]

Since Hansen had the Iceman on loan, presumably permission to thaw the Iceman out of its tomb was not his to give, and the conclusions that Sanderson and Heuvelmans drew would have had to be made based only on what they could see through the ice. Both investigators, however, had seen enough to go to press with the story. Sanderson publicized the find in both *Genus* and *Argosy*,[63] while Heuvelmans announced the find in dramatic fashion in the *Bulletin of the Royal Institute of Natural Sciences of Belgium* in 1969, going so far as to name the Iceman as a new zoological species: *Homo pongoides*.[64]

Sanderson was so impressed with the icy figure that he pressed John Napier, a world-renowned expert on human and primate anatomy, to use his association with the Smithsonian Institution to get an official government body to investigate the matter further. The subsequent events would figure prominently in Napier's 1972 book, *Bigfoot*. The Smithsonian issued a press release, and Hansen was informed of the National Museum's impending involvement into the affair. This, apparently, was too much for the Iceman's reclusive owner, who instructed Hansen to return the body. A likeness could be used for public display in the future, but Hansen didn't think he would ever get to show the original again. The specimen that Sanderson and Heuvelmans had studied was gone. Whether the original Iceman has ever been seen since is a matter of debate, but that story will be told in the next chapter.

A CRIPPLED SASQUATCH

The next major incident in Bigfoot's social history occurred right on the heels of the Iceman, just two years following the Patterson film. The events were centered in the town of Bossburg in eastern Washington State, just south of the Canadian border. Like the 1958 find of tracks, the significance of the incident is very much a matter of perspective. For some Bigfoot advocates, the professional anthropologists in particular, it provided the compelling evidence that the Sasquatch was a zoological reality.

As winter settled into northern Washington late in 1969, some memorable Bigfoot tracks began to surface with regularity.[65] Apparently falling on lean times, this Sasquatch had taken to feeding out of the locals' garbage as a means of sustaining itself and it was leaving plenty indication of its passage. This particular Bigfoot may have been risking discovery on the edges of town because it was probably unable to make its appointed living owing to a substantial handicap: its right foot was terribly deformed, as indicated by its twisted imprint in the soil and snow. Its left foot was a fine example of a standard-issue Sasquatch track: over 17 inches long and 7 inches wide.[66] Both feet were too big to belong to a person, and even the normal track seemed out of proportion with an adult human foot. A veteran of the Slick expedition, Ivan Marx, happened to be living in town at the time and had gotten word out that something interesting was up. All the big players in the Bigfoot fraternity—Dahinden, Byrne, Titmus, and Patterson—would at some point come to Bossburg to have a look at this amazing find (see fig. 3.1).

It is an arguable point that had the Bossburg Bigfoot simply stayed away from town, academics would have avoided the whole Bigfoot business altogether. The Bossburg tracks, however, turned out to be the decisive item of evidence as far as the interested scientists were concerned. Not that there was anything approaching institutional interest in the footprints; for the most part, academia could not be bothered to even acknowledge the tracks were being found. There were, however, exceptions within the ranks of professional academics. It was this set of crippled prints that convinced Dr. Grover Krantz that a real, but as yet unrecognized, animal was lurking in the North American landscape.[67] John Napier similarly surrendered his skepticism on close examination of the finds: "It is very difficult to conceive of a hoaxer so subtle, so knowledgeable—and so sick—who would deliberately fake a footprint of this nature. I suppose it is possible, but it is so unlikely that I am prepared to discount it."[68] Jeff Meldrum, a member of the Biological Sciences faculty at Idaho State University and Krantz's professional heir-apparent in the field of anthropology, has identified the specific pathology as an example of *metatarsus adductus*.[69]

There were details of anatomical minutiae in the crippled tracks that would seem to require a very high level of expertise: one of the toes was displaced so badly by the twisted deformity that it left scant impression in the ground, and

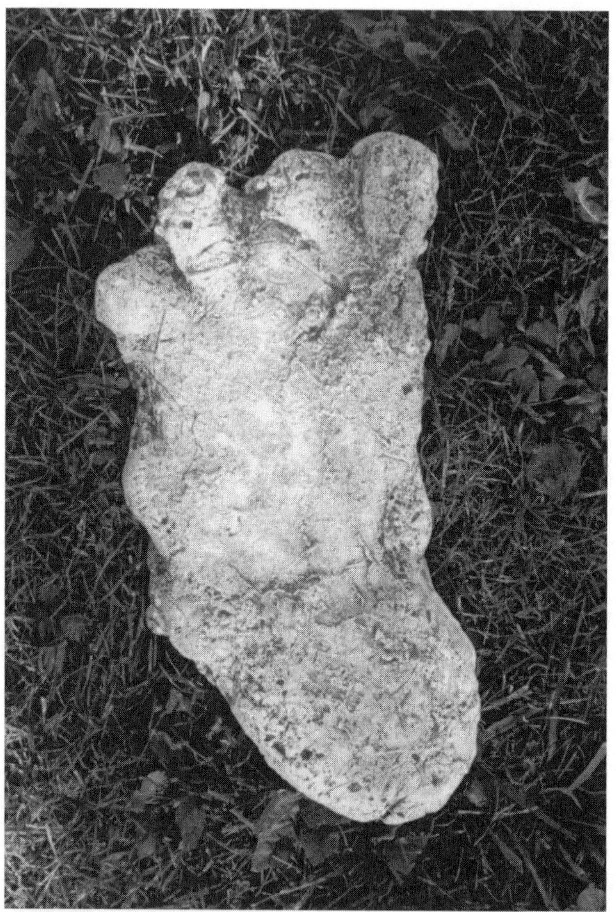

FIGURE 3.1
Cast of deformed footprint found in Bossburg, Washington, over the winter of 1969–1970. The nature of the deformity and the proportions of the footprint have made this one of the most celebrated Bigfoot finds. Many Bigfoot proponents have argued that such tracks would be impossible to fake. Photo by Michael Dennett, used with permission.

on the outside edge of the foot were two bumps that betrayed a fracture, dislocation, or some other correlate of the crippled Bigfoot's anatomy. The deformed print had a story to tell.

Krantz saw the tracks on the ground in Bossburg and put his own knowledge of primate anatomy to work on deciphering just what this story was.[70]

He observed, as no one who saw the prints could not fail to notice, that the tracks were simply too large to belong to a person. But in the crippled tracks he saw something even more unbelievable than the deformity of the track itself. Krantz insisted that when you lined up the bumps and the bends on the track with what would correspond to the underlying foot skeleton, the proportions were all wrong. In other words, this wasn't simply the outline of an enlarged human foot that some prankster had carved out of a spare piece of plywood on a slow evening at home.

Krantz used the details of the deformity in the print to work out how the bones of the foot were laid out. What he concluded was that the calcaneus (the heel bone) was relatively elongated to support a talus (ankle bone) that was set well forward in the Sasquatch foot when compared to the human anatomy. Thus, the tibia (shin bone) articulated with the talus at a position on the foot that was quite different from what one would expect in a giant human being (see fig. 3.2).

But Krantz noted that this was exactly the kind of biomechanical adjustment one would expect in something that was scaled up to the size implied by the prints. Being well versed in the principles of allometry (*allo* = different, *metry* = measurement, the study of size and its consequences in biological systems), Krantz had surmised quite correctly that a foot half again the length of a human's betrayed a creature not 50% heavier but rather much more massive, perhaps four times so.[71] He knew this simply by applying the principle that, as you increase the length of part of an organism, the volume (and by extension, in this example, the weight) increases in proportion to the cube of the added length. The key here, in Krantz's reasoning, was that these giant feet had to be propelling a being that weighed not 300 pounds but probably more like 800 pounds.[72] And a human foot, even proportionately enlarged, he figured, would not have been up to the task. The calf muscles attaching to the calcaneus would have had insufficient leverage to provide the crippled Sasquatch with enough power to move it about economically and quickly. Here the elongated calcaneus, the forward-set ankle made sense: this was an adaptive feature that one would expect to find in a Sasquatch with the mass of this crippled individual, and it made perfect sense in terms of natural selection, biomechanics, and the facts of anatomy.

Krantz asserted that no hoaxer could possibly have worked out these details.[73] This comprised Krantz's argument as to why the Bossburg prints represent Bigfoot's smoking gun. He never doubted Bigfoot's reality again.

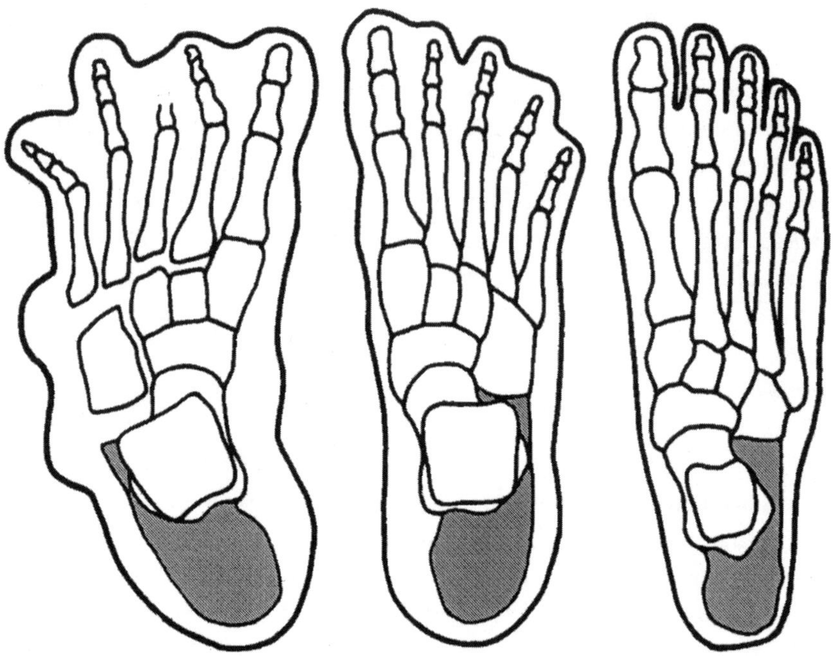

FIGURE 3.2
Grover Krantz's reconstruction of the skeletal anatomy of the Bossburg Sasquatch footprints (left and center). The differences in proportion of the bones of the Sasquatch foot compared to those of a human (right) led Krantz to conclude that a real Bigfoot made the tracks. Specifically, Krantz believed the deformed footprint indicated an elongated calcaneus (heel bone, shaded) that shifted the bone sitting on top of the calcaneus (the talus) to a more forward position in the foot relative to the human condition. The talus forms part of the ankle joint, which, therefore, occupies a somewhat different position in a Sasquatch foot in comparison to human feet. The figure is drawn such that the outline of the foot is viewed from below but the skeleton is viewed from above. Reprinted with permission from Northwest Anthropological Research Notes, Inc., and the *Journal of Northwest Anthropology.*

Another point of interest was that the crippled Sasquatch had not simply left a few prints here and there. René Dahinden, who was on the scene for much of the time when the Sasquatch was active, once counted a trackway that sported a full 1,089 prints. What's more, the tracks appeared to step over a 43-inch, tightly strung barbed wire fence not once but twice during the jaunt.[74] The anthropologists who could be bothered to look at the evidence were not convinced that the series of tracks constituted a hoax.

It would be inaccurate to suggest that between 1969 and 1982 there was a complete hiatus in Bigfoot activity. Tracks were found and Sasquatches were seen during this interval, but the advocates had nothing new of substance to add to their files beyond the odd eyewitness encounter. This was not particularly worrisome because the Patterson film and the Bossburg tracks continued to enjoy support among the Bigfoot community and Grover Krantz and John Napier were lending the hunt an air of legitimacy.

BIGFOOT MEETS PAUL FREEMAN

Bigfoot would intrigue investigators again in 1982 near Walla Walla, Washington, a town more famous for the smell of onions than the stench of Bigfoot prior to that time. East of town lie the Blue Mountains, which thanks to the effort of a single tireless pursuer, would become a hotbed of Bigfoot activity. The protaganist in this subplot, Paul Freeman, is something of an unlikely hero. A large man, Freeman was a meat cutter by trade who, in 1982, traded in his cleaver to start a new career with the U.S. Forest Service.[75] He would become the most successful Bigfoot hunter of all time, tracking the beast over a span of more than ten years despite being hobbled with foot problems brought on by his affliction with diabetes. Freeman's initial assignment was to patrol a watershed area in which public access was restricted.

No sooner had he been on the job than Freeman realized that Bigfoot was no myth—unless, of course, myths could be 8 feet tall, covered with hair, walk on two legs, and leave footprints to boot. The prints at the scene defied description of any known creature, but having seen the trackmaker himself, Freeman knew full well who made them. The preservation of the tracks was exceptional: some displayed dermal ridges ("fingerprints," though in this case on the feet) and successive prints of the right and left feet betrayed an unsettling feature for would-be skeptics—the position of the toes and indeed the form of the tracks themselves differed from print to print. It was an abbreviated trackway by Bossburg standards, consisting of a finite set of prints in a restricted area, but after Freeman dutifully informed his superiors, they were sufficiently intrigued that they dispatched one of their staff wildlife biologists and contacted the Border Patrol, who sent in their expert tracker in the area. Grover Krantz would examine casts of the prints and argue strongly for their authenticity[76] (it is unclear whether he examined this particular set of tracks in the ground, and if he did, when), even though the Forest Service's conclusions were not favorable to Freeman's account or Krantz's conclusion. Then again, the government agency never publicly released any official report.[77]

Freeman's encounters with Sasquatch were only beginning, though his tenure with the Forest Service ended up being rather brief. Whether Freeman's repeated Bigfoot finds while on the job had anything to do with his abbreviated career as a ranger is not clear.[78] In his freelance roamings since leaving the

FIGURE 3.3
Paul Freeman was the world's most successful Bigfoot hunter from 1982 until retiring from the hunt late in the 1990s. He found scores of footprints and several hair samples in addition to photographing and filming Sasquatch in the Blue Mountains near Walla Walla, Washington. Many veteran Bigfoot hunters thought Freeman was too successful to be believed, but his evidence continues to enjoy endorsement from professional scientists and forensic examiners. Photo by Michael Dennett, used with permission.

federal payroll, Freeman was inordinately successful in amassing Bigfoot evidence. He found innumerable tracks in the Blue Mountains outside of Walla Walla (including handprints and knee impressions) and was lucky enough to get some still photos of Bigfoot, record its screams, collect its dung and hair, and even produce some video footage.[79] Jeff Meldrum, already familiar with the evidence amassed by Freeman over the years, was led by Freeman himself to a newly discovered trackway in 1996.[80] The prints, in Meldrum's eyes, betrayed a dynamic foot that made perfect biological sense for a bipedal creature adapted to a rugged existence in the mountainous terrain.[81] The several dozen tracks that Meldrum was able to analyze convinced him that something living had made them[82]—and it is clear that a human agent was not at the top of his list of suspects.

Paul Freeman was not held in high regard by many of the nonacademic advocates who thought he was simply too successful to be believed. But Freeman enjoyed ringing endorsements from Meldrum and Krantz, whose anatomical expertise certainly exceeded that of Freeman's more vocal critics. Freeman died in April 2003 (see fig. 3.3).

A RECLINING SASQUATCH LEAVES ITS MARK

Bigfoot's latest splash as of this writing lies somewhere between the Minnesota Iceman and the Patterson film in terms of its nature and impact. On September 22, 2000, an expedition sponsored by the Bigfoot Field Researchers Organization (BFRO, an affiliation of a diverse group of advocates who promote Bigfoot) discovered an imprint in a muddy road turnout, not of footprints, but of a large animal's heel, thigh, buttock, and forearm.[83] The turnout had been baited with fruit in hopes of attracting a Sasquatch. The tactic apparently paid off when just such an animal laid down in the mud to reach for the fruit. The expedition members contemplating the find concluded that the imprint was attributable to no known living animal, but the size and shape of the impressions were entirely consistent with the form of a gigantic primate.

John Green, Grover Krantz, and Jeff Meldrum were summoned to examine the cast that the discoverers had painstakingly made of the muddy imprint. Idaho State University issued a press release a month later in which Meldrum labeled the find as "significant and compelling" new evidence for Bigfoot.[84] John Green was less restrained; he suggested that interpretation of the cast was so unambiguous that collection of a body was no longer needed as proof—the imprint could settle the matter.[85] Dubbed the "Skookum Cast" based on its discovery in the Skookum Meadows area of the Gifford Pinchot National Forest, the find has generated considerable publicity, including a piece in *Science News*.[86] In something of a coup, a long-time Bigfoot skeptic, Dr. Daris Swindler, a professor emeritus from the University of Washington, examined the cast and concluded that it provided strong evidence for the existence of Bigfoot.[87] Swindler had previously maintained that the subject filmed by Patterson was a person in costume.[88]

What is remarkable about Bigfoot's social history is that an astonishingly small number of investigators have been largely responsible for investigating and disseminating the evidence, such as it is. Without Byrne, Dahinden, Green, Titmus, Marx, Freeman, and Krantz, Bigfoot might well have disappeared from the cultural radar decades ago. The phenomenon of Bigfoot is thus necessarily as much about the people who hunt the thing as it is about the creature itself. The dysfunctional Slick Expedition foretold the bitter rivalries and lack of cooperation that have come to define the Bigfoot community; acrimony is the signature of the field. The relations among Bigfoot hunters, layfolk and academic alike, certainly make entertaining reading and are standard filler in the Bigfoot literature. In the context of resolving the mystery, however, the back stabbing and name calling are not terribly relevant. It is tempting, perhaps, to suggest that the bitterness of the field emerges from the frustration of having nothing to study and of expeditions always coming up short. Academics who have been paying attention to events in their own fields of expertise, however, will quickly tell you that tantrums, poor etiquette, and the double-cross are standard fare in so-called legitimate academic pursuits. Behaving badly does not disqualify anybody from being logical and scientific in his or her approach.

What should concern us about the personalities involved in the hunt for Bigfoot is how they deal with standards of proof. It is generally desired that whatever the scientific pursuit, there should be a single standard of proof acceptable to everyone. This consensus has never been achieved in the search for Bigfoot. That a body is needed as proof is always paid lip service, but invariably a lesser standard creeps into the argument. For Grover Krantz, the inferred anatomy of footprints is sufficient; for John Green, the Skookum Cast is ample proof. Bob Titmus saw the animal twice with his own eyes, so he spent his life pursuing something he already believed was there. Jeff Meldrum believes the evidence to date indicates an undiscovered primate,[89] arguing that some tracks would have been impossible to fake.[90] René Dahinden was never satisfied that anyone could debunk the Patterson film, but he died a skeptic.

Dahinden's skepticism served him well because it allowed him to deal with the essential contradiction posed by the phenomenon (10-foot monster that we can't manage to find). Since there is no unequivocal Bigfoot standard with which to assess an encounter, the only recourse is to affirm the reality of it by systematically ruling out all possibility of human agency. If you can establish that an item of Bigfoot evidence is beyond the realm of human invention, fabrication, or imagination, then you have your animal. It is that simple. Skeptics have understood this from the very beginning. Ruling out the human element in Bigfoot encounters might seem a high standard, but then again no body, living or dead, has been found in forty-five years of active searching.

The cases reviewed above are merely a drop in the bucket of Bigfoot evidence. The advocates have nothing to worry about if any fraction of that volume of evidence is legitimate. It is this issue that now demands our attention. Is there anything in this inventory that compels us to recognize the Sasquatch as a species unknown to science?

NOTES

1. Discovery of the saola is detailed on a web page of the World Wildlife Fund (http://www.panda.org/about_wwf/where_we_work/asia_pacific/where/indochina/mosaic_project/area/saola.cfm). The story of the okapi's discovery can be found at the digital library of the American Museum of Natural History (http://diglib1.amnh.org/articles/okapi/okapi.pdf).

2. Cohen (1970) suggests that pinning down the origin of the legend is fruitless. The origins of wildman traditions, including Native American legends, are untraceable. Consequently, Bigfoot researchers have instead attempted to specify Bigfoot's origin in terms of American or European culture's first awareness of the North American variety of wildman. Trotti (1994) and Zuefle (1997) suggest that the white settler tradition was inspired by a beast from Swift's *Gulliver's Travels* that was co-opted by Daniel Boone for content in tall tales. This would place the origin of the settler's Bigfoot in the early 1800s. Peter Byrne's Bigfoot Research Project uncovered a reference from early in 1785 in London's *Daily Universal Register* that matches the description of Bigfoot. This story has Bigfoot being shipped off to France from North America.

3. Sanderson (1961:13) and Napier (1974:45).

4. Sanderson (1961:259).

5. Coleman (1989).

6. Byrne (personal correspondence via e-mail, July 16, 2003) indicates that four sets of footprints were found and a possible bedding site was discovered. No hair or scat attributable to Bigfoot was found.

7. Glickman (1998:2) formally denoted 1958 as the date marking the division of contemporary from historical accounts. Others, including Green (1978), implicitly followed this dichotomy previously.

8. Roosevelt (1893).

9. Sanderson (1961:108) endorses the earlier date; Coleman (2003:180) suggests the latter.

10. Theodore Roosevelt was born in 1858 and graduated from Harvard in 1880. It would seem that he could not have had a conversation with anyone about Bigfoot until at least 1883 when he established two cattle ranches in the Dakota Territory. I am indebted to Russ Bernard about this point.

11. Sanderson (1961:108).

12. Coleman (2003:46).

13. Green (1971:17).

14. Green (1971:14).

15. Green (1978:89–90).

16. Green (1971:12).

17. Green (1971:12).

18. Green (1994:17).

19. Green (1971:22).

20. John Green (1994:3) suggests that the situation worsened even more after the 1967 film of Bigfoot became public knowledge.

21. Coleman (2003:70).

22. Green (1978:303).

23. Green (1971:47).

24. Green (1994:34).

25. Sanderson (1961:126); Coleman (2003:69).

26. Sanderson (1961:131).

27. Coleman (1989).

28. Personal communication with Peter Byrne via e-mail, July 16, 2003.

29. Wylie (1980:176).

30. Wylie (1980:173).

31. Wasson (1979:90).

32. Cook (1998) and the University of Illinois Computer Science Department website: http://cs.uiuc.edu/whatsnew/newsletter/winter97/glickman.html.

33. The bitterness remained years after the expedition. In 1977, Byrne abandoned his usual decorum and called Dahinden "stupid" and "ruthlessly ignorant." Dahinden countered a year later by likening Byrne to a sack of manure (Perez 2000a). This personal animosity did not prevent the two from cooperating in a late 1990s endeavor to analyze the famous 1967 film shot by Roger Patterson.

34. Personal communication, Bigfoot Daze festival, Carson WA, August 24, 1996.

35. Perez (1990:19–21).

36. Wylie (1980:156–162) and several personal communications with the author in August 1996.

37. Hunter and Dahinden (1975:8).

38. Dennett (1988:7).

39. Personal communication via audiotape, February 20, 1996.

40. Dahinden's talk at the Sasquatch Symposium in Harrison Hot Springs, BC, May 6, 1995.

41. Dahinden's talk at the Sasquatch Symposium in Harrison Hot Springs, BC, May 6, 1995, and in several correspondences with the author from 1995 to 1998.

42. Perez (1990:21).

43. Hunter and Dahinden (1975:89).

44. Hunter and Dahinden (1975:89).

45. Green (1978:161).

46. Green (1978:69).

47. Green (1978:205).

48. Green (1978:461).

49. Green (1980:242).

50. Wylie (1980:163–171).

51. Wylie (1980:167).

52. See Pyle (1995:197) and Krantz (1984:129).

53. Coleman (1989).

54. There are innumerable narratives of the chain of events leading up to and following the film, few of which agree precisely in all details. I rely on Green (1978) and Perez (1992) for the principal points of the story.

55. Green (1971:47–50) and Dahinden, personal communication via audiotape, February 20, 1996.

56. Wylie (1980:185). Perez (2003g) notes that there is no documentation that such an exchange occurred, even though Chris Murphy's investigation suggests that the event was plausible in terms of the air facility in question being open at the stated time.

57. Perez (1992:17).

58. Perez (1992:17).

59. Perez (1992:19).

60. Bayanov, Bourtsev, and Dahinden (1984).

61. As with the Patterson film, this famous episode in Bigfoot's history is detailed in a number of published narratives. I rely here on the details provided by Napier (1974:97–113) and Wylie (1980:220–223).

62. Coleman (2003:112–114) reprints the impressions of the two investigators.

63. Sanderson (1969); Coleman (2003:113, 118).

64. Heuvelmans (1969); Napier (1974:98).

65. Here again one can find numerous accounts of these finds and their aftermath in the literature, with the omission of certain details accounting for differences among these retellings. I draw on Hunter and Dahinden (1975:150–173), Green (1978:160–168), and Napier (1974:122) in describing the events.

66. Napier (1974:122).

67. Krantz (1992).

68. Napier (1974:123).

69. Krantz (1999:298–299).

70. Krantz (1977a, 1977b, 1992).

71. Krantz (1984:131).

72. Krantz (1992:63).

73. Krantz (1984:132–133, 1992:63); Dennett (1994:499–500).

74. Krantz (1992:43); Hunter and Dahinden (1975:154–155).

75. Foster (1997).

76. Krantz (1983, 1992).

77. Dennett (2003:1).

78. According to Robert Sullivan (in an *Open Spaces Quarterly* article accessed online at http://www.open-spaces.com/article-v1n3-sullivan.php), Freeman's obsession with Bigfoot figured in his dismissal.

79. Krantz (1992:50–51); Dennett (1989:268, 1994:502).

80. Meldrum described the incident in his talk at the Harrison Hot Springs Sasquatch Symposium in May 1996.

81. Meldrum's presentation of his 1999 abstract featured the 1996 Freeman trackway with other Bigfoot evidence. Perez (1999a) suggested this was the first time the American Association of Physical Anthropologists had taken notice of the Bigfoot phenomenon, and he reprinted the abstract in *Bigfoot Times.*

82. Meldrum's (1997) review of Vance Orchard's book, *Bigfoot of the Blues* (1993, Earthlight Books) was first published in *Cryptozoology.* It is posted on Bobbie Short's Bigfoot Encounters website: http://www.n2.net/prey/Bigfoot/reviews/blues.htm. Meldrum also defended Freeman's finds in several postings of the now defunct *Internet Virtual Bigfoot Conference* in 1997.

83. http://www.bfro.net/NEWS/BODYCAST/index.asp.

84. Glenn Alford (October 23, 2000). Idaho State University researcher coordinates analysis of body imprint that may belong to a Sasquatch. The press release is posted on the BFRO website: http://www.bfro.net/news/bodycast/isu_press_rel_cast.asp.

85. Statement posted online at http://www.bfro.net/NEWS/BODYCAST/green_statement.asp.

86. Kleiner (2000).

87. Swindler endorsed the imprint in the video production *Sasquatch: Legend Meets Science* (2003, Whitewolf Productions).

88. Goodavage (1996b).

89. Taylor (1999); Stefan Lovgren (2003). Forensic expert says Bigfoot is real. *National Geographic News* 10/23/03 (accessed online at http://news.nationalgeographic.com/news/2003/10/1023_031023_bigfoot.html).

90. Perez (2000b:2).

4

Bigfoot Scrutinized: Why the Greatest Hits Are All Misses

A survey of the Bigfoot literature establishes that certain events stand out in the matter of evidence. Despite the thousands of eyewitness sightings and endless trails of gigantic footprints, there is a remarkably limited amount of Bigfoot data that are amenable to scientific scrutiny. The totality of the evidence is used to invoke public interest, because the apparent ubiquity of Bigfoot activity forces us to recognize that something very strange is going on. But the documentation for the vast majority of the evidence is so poor that for analytic purposes it is essentially useless. A few cases are useful because the investigators involved had the foresight to document what was going on in the form of casts, measurements, pictures, and even films. These are the cases that offer the best hope the advocates have for asserting the legitimacy of Bigfoot. Because these events have data that can be scrutinized, criticized, rejected, or authenticated, they are within the scope of scientific inquiry and are potentially valuable for establishing the existence of an unknown animal. The chronology and essential details of these cases were laid out in the last chapter. Here we will delve into the context of these cases and consider what the data emerging from them can actually tell us.

The persistent complaint of the advocates is that Bigfoot evidence gets dismissed before it is even examined: Jeff Meldrum's point is simply that the data exist and deserve scrutiny.[1] It is a fair point echoed across the board by the advocates; the scientific establishment seems to reject Bigfoot reflexively without so much as feigning an interest in examining the evidence.

It is worth a digression on what exactly we mean when we agree to analyze something "scientifically." In one sense, science is little more than a protocol for observation and explanation. What distinguishes a scientific explanation from a nonscientific one is a willingness to test (either by further observation, experimentation, or prediction) whether or not a proposed explanation is reasonable and sufficient to account for an observation, however mundane or bizarre. In this sense, there is nothing mysterious about practicing science; it involves looking at and manipulating the world in a systematic way so that we can make generalizations about how things work. It is the basis for reliable knowledge, as opposed to anecdotal knowledge. The distinction is important.

The anecdote is the single observation or a collection of stories that, after the fact, do not permit confirmation for any number of reasons. An anecdote isn't necessarily false, it is just unverifiable. Seeing a hairy monster while driving alone at night is a tailor-made anecdote; even if you remember the time and the exact spot on the highway and return with your friends to the scene to find giant footprints, the hairy giant part of your story is still anecdote. The footprints are the facts of the matter. These can be treated scientifically for a couple of reasons: first, you can measure and record them, and second, other people can look at the imprints as well.

This last point is essential for distinguishing anecdote from scientific observation: it is the notion of repeatability. A simple tenet of scientific investigation is that, given a specified set of conditions, different observers can witness the same outcomes. In 1989, University of Utah researchers Stanley Pons and Martin Fleischmann announced that they had observed a nuclear fusion reaction at room temperature[2]—a startling development that had profound implications for human civilization. The press jumped on the story, but when researchers at other institutions tried to replicate the results, they came up empty more often than not. Pons and Fleischman seemed sure of the validity of their experiment, but it did not matter. Because their observation of cold fusion could not be consistently repeated, their confidence counted for naught. The event became anecdote.

The cold fusion example illustrates two other markers of scientific inquiry; the notions of independence and parsimony. Replication of an observation also needs to be independent. Hypothetically, Pons and Fleischman could have repeated their experiment 100 times and found that each time the results they got were identical. Still, they would have encountered widespread skepticism. Why? The problem of bias would remain; there could be something the investigators repeatedly overlooked or data that were always discarded based on an inadvisable protocol. The easiest—and most valid—alternative would be to tell scientists elsewhere how the experiment was set up and see if others could come up with the same results. This provides independent replication. There is a subtle distinction that we also must recognize: it is not enough to simply invite someone else into the lab to examine the notebooks or to verify the computer printouts. This is not independence in the spirit of scientific inquiry; rather, this is just getting someone else to testify on behalf of your results. It does not count as verification. This hair splitting is important, as we will see, because the lofty goal of independence is surprisingly elusive when it comes to tracking big hairy monsters.

The concept of parsimony is in no way unique to science, but it is an invaluable tool for avoiding wild-goose chases. The idea behind parsimony is economy of explanation: of competing explanations, choose the one that is simplest with respect to the theoretical gymnastics involved. The example of cold fusion serves us well here once again. The experiments worked in one laboratory in Utah, but not elsewhere. We could entertain the idea that the laws of physics work differently in that part of the world, or that the scientists elsewhere could not replicate the experiments out of incompetence, or that instruments to measure the effects work better at altitude in the dry air of Salt Lake City. We could even get much more creative: perhaps Bigfoot telepathically influenced results from its haunts in the nearby Uinta Mountains! Without parsimony, there is nothing to restrain the explanations, and it is no stretch to suggest that scientific inquiry could not function without this principle. Parsimony demands that we take the simplest explanation: Pons and Fleischman did not measure what they thought they measured. They made a mistake.

The presence of so-called hard evidence does not solve the problem, because it is not the evidence per se, but rather its interpretation, that makes an endeavor scientific. The Piltdown fossils, discovered in Sussex, England, between 1912 and 1915 provided seemingly concrete proof that humans evolved from big-brained, big-muzzled ancestors.[3] This sat very well with the English scientific establishment at the time for two reasons: first, it provided the first fossil human—and a smart one at that—on British soil and second, it fit neatly into the theory that brains were the initial and essential hallmark of humanity. The bones were real, their context was known, so it followed that the theory was correct.

Piltdown is now famous as a hoax, an ape's jaw having been tampered with to fit a set of human cranial fragments. In 1953, flourine dating established beyond doubt that the fossil fragments did not belong together. Who engineered the hoax remains unknown, but the consensus is that it was an inside job—that is, someone who had a stake in promoting the interpretation that was bound to follow. There were, in the years that followed the discoveries, several anthropologists who suggested correctly that the jaw was sufficiently ape-like that it ought to be so classified. The principals associated with the Piltdown finds, however, never seriously entertained the possibility that a hoax was afoot, in part because the fossils made sense in their view of human evolution. Ironically, this is precisely why the deception was able to persist for several decades. Accomplished scientists mistook personal conviction as a guide to truth.

Science always proceeds from theory, whether it is acknowledged or not. I use the term *theory* in the formal scientific sense rather than in the colloquial sense of speculation or conjecture. A scientific theory is composed of a set of general propositions, coherently related to one another, that serves to explain a class of phenomena. Emerging from a theory's principles are the questions that can be posed to see if the logical extensions of the theory hold water. These questions are hypotheses, and hypothesis testing is the essence of scientific inquiry. Observation and experiment are means for evaluating hypotheses; a string of falsified hypotheses is nature's hint to the scientist that something is not quite right in the overarching theory.

No one ever talks about a theory of Bigfoot, but there is one. If, as Krantz, Meldrum, and the naturalistically inclined advocates insist, Bigfoot can be studied as a zoological being, then there must be sound theoretical reasons why we cannot find it. A scientific theory of Bigfoot requires that the population of alleged beasts obeys all known laws of genetics, evolution, ecology, and physics. We can formalize the study of Bigfoot into a series of testable hypotheses. In this book, I am really only proposing one and focusing on that. The hypothesis is simple: Bigfoot is explicable entirely by human agency. Human agency can take many forms: misperception, fabrication (a euphemism for lying in this context), hallucination, memory distortion, and hoaxing are the ones that concern us here. I will return to the larger question of whether the search for Bigfoot qualifies as a scientific enterprise, but now it is time to focus on Bigfoot's more famous exploits with our hypothesis in hand.

The centerpiece of Bigfoot lore, and by far the most investigated and debated item of evidence, is the Patterson film of 1967. This item is so essential to the advocate's evidentiary arsenal that it merits a separate chapter and discussion. The other major pieces of evidence have to do with impressions: of feet, hands, and even buttocks. There's even a pair of mysteries surrounding whole specimens, one alive and kicking long ago, and a frozen corpse more recently.

THE HISTORICAL BIGFOOT: OLDER IS NOT NECESSARILY BETTER

The "historical" cases (that is, in the Bigfoot universe, pre-1958) are often accorded special status among the advocates for the obvious reason that "[p]rinted reports from any time before the Sasquatch publicity started cannot be the result of the publicity."[4] John Green's idea here is simply that an increase in false alarms is the expected fallout from a dramatic—and therefore well-publicized—Bigfoot story. Earlier tales logically can't be classified as copycat imitations of later accounts. The old stories should not be tainted in the same way that evidence can be today when everybody is familiar with the legend of Bigfoot.

Still, antiquity of evidence has nothing to do with its quality. There is something of an unstated assumption that, prior to the beginning of full-scale investigation with the Slick expedition, the reports that existed were untainted. On one level, this is a reasonable supposition: there was not much of a market for faking before 1958 because Bigfoot was not yet on the cultural radar. On the other hand, it is a romantic notion that the stories of the old-timers will ring truer, and it is altogether naive to suppose that in the good old days honest misperception or intentional deception could not creep into Bigfoot lore as it does today.

The discovery of strange tracks in 1811 by the explorer David Thompson has worked its way into multiple books and web pages sympathetic to the advocate's position. The time and setting are ideal; Jasper in the depths of winter is none too tame an area now. Thompson's confessed apprehension about following the tracks adds some drama to the story, but the details of the prints themselves are explicable without invoking Bigfoot's involvement. The overall dimensions betrayed by the tracks are certainly compatible with standard-issue Sasquatch prints, but other details are all wrong. The observation of claws and only four toes is fairly damning, and there is no indication that Thompson thought the trackmaker to be bipedal—a detail shocking enough that one would expect that he would have been eager to report it. John Napier's opinion on the matter was that this is likely the spoor of a very large grizzly bear; he notes that the imprint of four toes is not unusual among bear tracks, and the presence of claw marks describes a carnivore better than it does a primate.[5]

Even further back in time, not just in North America, but all over the world, we can also identify stories and traditions that ostensibly are talking about Bigfoot, if we accept the premise that a real animal has to be behind such accounts. The history seems to get diffuse the further back we go. In many cases, it is really not clear that we are dealing with Sasquatch either as legend or beast. The wild man tradition in medieval Europe is well known, in local traditions as well as in literature (*Beowulf* being the classic example[6]). Sanderson's global survey[7] establishes the near universality of the idea that mysterious man-like, but at the same time un-human, creatures are roaming on the fringes of familiar landscapes.

The animals described in these accounts don't resemble Bigfoot as it is usually conceived other than they are hirsute and bipedal, and the behaviors in these traditions range from the monstrous (dining on people) to the mundane (knocking on doors to beg for food). We could take a Fortean view and just accept that the accounts reflect a genuine part of nature, but if we want to be at least nominally scientific about it, we label these apocryphal and move on.

Otherwise apocryphal stories graduate to anecdotal status simply by making the headlines. The seizure of "Jacko" is historically documented, thanks to the *Daily Colonist*'s 1884 account. The capture of the hairy beast might well be a true story, but it does not follow that we are dealing with a genuine Sasquatch. Jacko's attributes (black hair, long forearm, 127 pounds, under 5 feet tall) could well be describing a wayward chimpanzee or gorilla. What would an African ape be doing in British Columbia? Grover Krantz suggested that Jacko was briefly part of P. T. Barnum's Circus at the time.[8] Krantz reasons that Barnum must have acquired Jacko from Yale and for a time had him star in the "dog-faced boy" show. The implication that Krantz acknowledges is that Jacko was indigenous to Canada and that P. T. Barnum had a Sasquatch on his hands.

Of course, Krantz's scenario could easily be turned around. The few facts we have don't rule out the possibility that Jacko was part of the circus but somehow got separated from his employer—not an unreasonable inference for explaining the sudden appearance of a strange creature alongside a railroad track. In this scenario, Jacko wasn't adopted by the circus, he was a refugee from it. Barnum was assembling menageries some thirty years before Jacko made his appearance,[9] and railroad tours of his circus, with exotic animals in tow, were underway in the 1870s.[10] George Bailey, who would later join forces with Barnum in the circus business, had been using the menagerie as a circus attraction since 1851, and gorillas and chimpanzees were among the featured animals.[11] The Barnum & Bailey merger happened in 1881.[12] These facts enable us to draw the following conclusion: African apes were on the continent as part of touring circus menageries before Jacko was found. The newspaper report, if true, does not compel the conclusion that a Sasquatch was captured.

In researching the case, John Green notes that among his contacts so long removed from the event, he could only find people who knew people at the time the event supposedly happened. Those people who were there remember hearing the story, but no one knew anyone who actually laid eyes on the beast. Newspapers following up the story weren't helpful to Jacko's cause, whatever his primate affinities may have been: the *Mainland Guardian* issued a terse statement on July 9 insisting that no animal had been captured. Three days later, *The Columbian*, which had also run the original story, reported that an apparent showing of the beast had been well attended with the exception that one party, Jacko, was nowhere to be found.[13] Nothing seems to corroborate the original story. Advocates have wrestled with the question of whether Jacko might fit the description of a juvenile Sasquatch rather than a chimpanzee, but the more basic issue is whether Jacko existed at all.

Albert Ostman's tale of nocturnal abduction is remarkable not only in terms of the narrative but also considering Ostman's meticulous attention to detail. While the experience might be expected to leave an indelible impression, it is a testament to Ostman's memory that the events of 1924 were still fairly fresh in his mind when he first wrote them down in 1957, some thirty-three years after his narrow escape. What occasionally escapes notice in the literature is that Albert Ostman only came forth with his story after hearing of William Roe's more mundane encounter, which supposedly happened in 1955. The two stories are granted exceptional weight by Ivan Sanderson in his 1961 book. Roe and Ostman offer details of their Bigfoots' appearances that are surprisingly congruent with one another. If they were making up such fantastic tales out of thin air, it is almost inconceivable that in concocting their respective monster stories they would agree on seemingly minute details of anatomy. Could identical descriptions of the shape of Bigfoot's head be a coincidence of two independent fabrications? Such similar descriptions just might mean they saw the same thing.

Indeed, the similarity of the descriptions is extremely telling. But it is not implausible to suppose that the shared details of the two accounts have more to do with familiarity with monster stories than with actual monster encounters. The accounts are in no way independent, and in this case it is reckless to argue that their similarities are compelling reasons to believe that either or both are true. The best face we can put on the situation is to suppose that when Roe told his story he hadn't heard Ostman's account, and, given the dates involved, that Ostman could not possibly have heard Roe's. Obviously, the real issue here is not when the story happened but rather when it was told. Roe's story got enough publicity that Ostman did get wind of it in 1957 (Ostman admitted as much[14]). It is believed Roe did not know Ostman's story before airing his own account. Only after hearing of Roe's experience did Ostman come clean about his abduction by hairy giants, presumably emboldened by Roe's sighting to relate his own. At this point, the fact that the events occurred thirty-one years apart is obviously irrelevant to the issue of their independence. Ostman may or may not have been held hostage by a group of Sasquatches, but the fact remains that he did not write down his account of the incident until after he read Roe's tale and no one can confirm him talking about it before 1957.[15] There is a very simple explanation why these accounts agree in descriptive details, and it is not necessarily because anybody saw a Sasquatch.

Parenthetically, the Ostman tale is famous for its richness of detail (much "data" on Bigfoot biology comes from this account[16]), convincing the advocates Sanderson and Green that the tale was almost too incredible to be *dis*believed. Of course, the level of detail offered in an account is no reliable guide to the truth or falsity of the proposition, but Ostman may have been too specific for his own good. In Albert Ostman, René Dahinden found a source for information at a time when the physical evidence for Bigfoot was rare indeed. With so few encounters to investigate, Dahinden grilled the abductee on more than one occasion. He was impressed with what he heard in one sense because Ostman never once changed any details of his story. But there was enough detail about places and times that Dahinden could reconstruct some of the distances traveled by the offending Bigfoot during the abduction itself and by Ostman during his escape. Given the timeline consistently adhered to in Ostman's account, Dahinden's final verdict was that the tale was "totally impossible."[17] The advocates are split on the Ostman story. Barbara Wasson, a psychologist by training, found Ostman's story fit better as a projection of his imagination than a recollection of a real event.[18] That explanation is parsimonious in the context of the facts that we do have.

Much is made of the fact that the men signed sworn affidavits as to the veracity of their claims. That they signed these documents is not in doubt; what concerns us is whether this fact has any relevance. Ostman and Roe were hardly sticking their necks out since, on the documents they signed, there is no clear articulation of penalty should their stories be contradicted. It stretches credulity to imagine that the law enforcement establishment had any motivation for pursuing the matter further, even if business was mighty slow in the summer of 1957. Ostman and Roe's sworn statements do not suffice as scientifically legitimate even if they are legally conclusive, unless, of course, we wish to entertain the idea that sworn affidavits are all that are needed to rid the world of perjury.

Ostman's decision to keep mum about his encounter for three decades undoubtedly compromises the credibility of the account. Documentation of Fred Beck's encounter with some rather violent Sasquatches was provided by the local papers in 1924, so we need not doubt that Beck was where he said he was when the alleged attack took place. Beck's account is famous, but in the inventory of encounters the behavior of Bigfoot in this tale is several standard deviations away from the mean. The Ape Canyon story, if it is representative of Sasquatch behavior, suggests that the ape-like creatures are quite willing to engage in rather visible displays of property destruction. The advocate position on this is that the Beck attacks, like the grisly tale told by Bauman from the century before, were precipitated by violence on the part of the human. Perhaps this explains something, but Albert Ostman was certainly minding his own business when he was unceremoniously abducted in his sleeping bag.

Two footnotes to the Beck saga provide us with some information that permits an informed decision on the whole episode. The first is that after telling John Green his account, and after Patterson had summarized the tale in his 1966 book, Beck decided that he needed to flesh out the body of the story a little more and so dictated another account to his son. The result was privately printed in 1967 under the title *I Fought the Ape-Men of Mount Saint Helens.* Some of the details of this late version have not made it into the second-hand accounts featured in Bigfoot books, and it is not hard to figure out why. In the amended version, Beck attests to his clairvoyant abilities and talks of giant Indian spirits who showed him and his partners the way to the mine, by virtue of an apparition in the form of a white arrow that apparently moved on its own. Beck is also quite firm in his pronouncement that the hairy apes were not animals in the conventional sense—he was convinced his attackers were not of this world.

The second item of interest is that when a posse went to investigate the miner's cabin after the incident, they found giant footprints all around the cabin, providing nominal support for the fantastic story.[19] The presence of these tracks would seem to assuage any reservations about Beck's psychic predispositions unduly coloring the facts. This does not exactly resolve the story in favor of its veracity; the locals were suspicious of the tale despite their familiarity with the legend (or perhaps because of it).[20] One L. H. Gregory apparently led an investigation that found tracks from the incident. These bore marks suspiciously reminiscent of human knuckles, and for some reason they seemed to be exclusively from right feet.[21] Appropriately, rumors have persisted ever since that there were people in the vicinity who planted the tracks and threw the rocks, even though the consensus is that Beck and his fellow miners were not in on the joke.[22]

Nothing in the details of the older (pre-1958) stories make them particularly compelling; in fact, their violent content belies Bigfoot's reputation among the more sober advocates as a passive and uninquisitive creature.[23] Bauman's tale provides even more problems for the Bigfoot advocates. On balance, they would be better off dismissing it. As a prelude to his account, Bauman had said he had been warned not to go into the particularly wild area of this mountain pass, because some evil thing had killed and partly consumed a lone hunter not too long before. The narrative has several elements of folklore embedded in it: told not to go where the bad thing is, the men go. Discovering the bad thing, they decide to leave, but not before making a last mistake in judgment. Bauman's partner paid a terrible price, and Bauman learned too late that he should have heeded the warning; his story is unmistakably mythological in structure.

Roosevelt was inclined to think the offender was a known, but unidentified, wild animal, and Peter Byrne notes that the injuries suffered by Bauman's unlucky partner fit the description of a bear attack.[24] Roosevelt prefaced the account by suggesting that Bauman was susceptible to supernatural suggestion: "when overcome by the fate that befell his friend, and when oppressed by the awful dread of the unknown, he grew to attribute, both at the time and still more in remembrance, weird and elfin traits to what was merely some abnormally wicked and cunning wild beast."[25] Roosevelt was decidedly noncommittal in his endorsement of the story and clearly skeptical of Baumann's reliability as an eyewitness.

If, in fact, we are not dealing with an evil spirit and Bauman is not pulling the future president's leg, then we have an account suggesting that Bigfoot has a penchant for killing, and perhaps dining on, territorial interlopers. How is it that the scores of unarmed backpackers since then, trampling through every corner of the American forests, have managed to escape the ire of Sasquatch? Perhaps Bigfoot doesn't attack all the time, but something just sets it off (being shot at, for example). Invoking an analogy to grizzly bears, most of the time Sasquatch won't care about humans hanging around, but once in a blue moon it just gets ticked off and attacks. Even if we accept the analogy, we ought to have campers getting mangled at least occasionally. John Green has always maintained that Bigfoot is a shy, retiring creature. Yet the Beck, Bauman, and Ostman accounts still figure in his historical evidence.

The problem with accepting these accounts is that they paint a behavioral portrait of Bigfoot that suggests not a shy denizen of the forest, but an aggressive and perhaps gregarious animal. Nothing is cryptic about Bigfoot's activities in these stories, even if we accept the premise that it is easy to hide 8-foot tall monsters in coniferous forests.

These historical cases are pure anecdote, with little beyond newspaper stories to prop them up. When Jerry Crew picked up some plaster from his friend Bob Titmus, a scientific study of Sasquatch became at least nominally possible. The physical evidence for which we have anything approaching adequate documentation dates from 1958 to the present day. What's particularly interesting about the chronology of events is that the problems plaguing these contemporary cases—inadequate documentation or bogus events surrounding "legitimate" data—never seem to get resolved. Bigfoot data never really get any better and thus there is no gravity to the claim that we are closing in on the animal. Like the historical cases just examined, the modern Bigfoot data only look better if we ignore all the details of context. Bigfoot data, despite claims to the contrary, cannot be analyzed at face value, when misperception, fabrication, and expectation are part and parcel of the enterprise.

BIGFOOT, MEET RAY WALLACE

As we established in the last chapter, Jerry Crew found tracks while working on Ray Wallace's road-building operation in 1958, and plenty of other folks, John Green included, saw these on site. It did not escape anyone associated with the events that a prank might be behind it all. What convinced people otherwise was not necessarily the dimensions of the tracks but the reported stride length ranging from 4 to 10 feet and the incredible depth of some of the tracks. The tracks seemed to go over some fairly forbidding terrain as well, and it seemed incongruous that some joker would expend such an effort to make harmless fun.

John Green boiled the events down to only two alternatives. Either someone had designed, delivered, and operated some heavy equipment specifically designed to make Bigfoot tracks, or a Sasquatch was suddenly interested in road-building operations in northern California.[26] Green dismissed the first option as patently ridiculous. How did the equipment get into this remote location? Where was it hidden? How did it get up and down hillsides without leaving evidence of its passage? A print-making machine was just too fantastic a notion to be seriously entertained, so Green settled on the second option.

Green's reasoning was not intended to obfuscate matters, but it is a classic rhetorical trick. He props up the real-live Bigfoot hypothesis simply by deeming the alternative to be beyond reason. We can reexamine the case by leaving open the question of a hoax. The living beast alternative, in this account, is not describing a retiring giant that keeps itself immune to discovery by cryptic behavior. The repeated appearance of Bigfoot does not bear the signature of a 7–10-foot beast that is elusive and shy by reputation. Besides inspecting the heavy machinery, Bigfoot was also expending precious calories leaving signs of his superhuman strength. As with the Fred Beck tale of angry apes pelting a cabin with rocks all night long, such details are sure to keep a story's retelling going well beyond the local tavern, but it forces a question. If inspecting tractors and hurling oil drums and culverts is standard behavior for these creatures, why aren't road crews throughout the mountains in the Pacific Northwest posting guards at night to prevent vandalism by Sasquatch? Panic, fear, and an overwhelming desire to seek other employment would be an understandable reaction to having one's livelihood disrupted by a superhuman monster, but that is not why Ray Wallace's hired hands were quitting.[27] In René Dahinden's view, the most puzzling aspect of the Bluff Creek tracks was not the footprints, but the apparent disinterest and ambivalence of the workers who were encountering them.[28]

Sanderson featured Wallace as the embroiled central personality in the unfolding drama, describing him as a serious man bent on getting his road built, which is at odds with other descriptions of his personality. Under suspicion in part because Bigfoot's activities seemed to correlate well with his own proximity to the area, Wallace's rejoinder to the press was "who knows anyone foolish enough to ruin his own business, man?"[29] An investigation conducted by Elizabeth Allen for the *Humboldt Times*, however, suggested that under the terms of the subcontract, Wallace was under no time constraint at all.[30] There is no evidence that Bigfoot's interest in the operation disrupted it, other than Wallace's complaints to that effect. For whatever reason, when Wallace was away on business, Bigfoot lost interest in the road-building operation.

It would turn out, paradoxically, that Wallace was to become something of a Bigfoot expert. He told John Napier that he had over 15,000 feet of film of Bigfoot.[31] He photographed Bigfoot many times.[32] He even captured a Bigfoot in 1959; Tom Slick and Peter Byrne followed up with due diligence but never claimed the specimen.[33] Another Wallace operation had been visited by Bigfoot before Jerry Crew found his big surprise at work.[34] Cryptozoologist Loren Coleman has Wallace on record admitting he faked tracks, but he insisted it was only to throw the hunters off the real trail. In short, when Ray Wallace was around, Bigfoot was active. It is a story we will revisit; only the names will change.

Wallace died in November 2002. His surviving family told the press that Wallace was indeed behind the 1958 tracks[35] and that this episode was only one of his many exploits.[36] They even produced sets of bogus feet for the reporters that matched the tracks found in the Bluff Creek area from 1958 to 1967. Despite Wallace's reputation, these revelations sent shock waves through the Bigfoot community.

The news should not have come as any surprise; *Strange Magazine* editor Mark Chorvinsky had been claiming for years that Wallace's role in Bigfoot's legend had been marginalized by the advocates, who were embarrassed by Wallace's colorful narratives that made Ostman's account seem positively dull. The claim is fully justified: in their recountings of Jerry Crew's discovery, both Grover Krantz and John Green fail to mention Ray Wallace at all.[37] If the omission is merely oversight, it is coincidentally a convenient one for the advocate's cause.

In fact, for years corollary evidence had existed of Wallace's involvement in producing Bigfoot evidence. A Toledo, Washington, neighbor of Ray Wallace—one Rant Mullens—had been making fake feet for hoaxing purposes since 1930.[38] Mullens confessed to loaning some of his handiwork to Ray Wallace and was apparently miffed when Wallace's use of the wooden feet in 1958 generated more publicity than Mullen's own pranks had in the past (see fig. 4.1).[39]

The Wallace family confession sent the advocates into immediate damage control; the newspaper reports were dismissed as a publicity stunt.[40] The im-

FIGURE 4.1
Rant Mullens in 1982 with a set of fake feet he used to fabricate Bigfoot tracks. Mullens fashioned eight sets of bogus feet since 1930 and provided some of these to other hoaxers, including his Toledo, Washington, neighbor, Ray Wallace. Photo by Michael Dennett, used with permission.

pact of the revelation, however, is that Bigfoot's credibility was eroded significantly in the public eye. The advocates can offer a predictable rebuttal: Wallace started faking Bigfoot once he realized how much attention it could garner. Notoriety can be fun, after all, and fun was by many accounts what Wallace was all about. Such a scenario is possible, but it is not very parsimonious. The simplest explanation is the most plausible: (1) Ray Wallace was a joker (true by all accounts, save for Ivan Sanderson's self-serving assessment); (2) there existed a regional monster legend (historically established)[41]; and (3) things could get pretty slow at the end of a long summer far from the city (a reasonable inference). So, how did he do it?

Minimally, faking a long series of prints requires only a pair of templates. Ordinarily, one would think of strapping these on one's real feet and then stomping about the forest, but the foot templates don't have to be worn at all to be impressed—perhaps deeply—into the ground. A hoaxer has to use some ingenuity to hide their own traces, to be sure, but this isn't by any means an insurmountable task. It only requires that they think the problem through. There is a tendency among Bigfoot pundits to assume that any potential hoaxer is, by virtue of their poor character, also laughably inept. It is irrational as inference: a hoaxer's dishonest character has no bearing on that individual's creativity and imagination. Confidence artists prove the point.

I am not suggesting that the Crew tracks were some sort of cheap and transparent hoax. On the contrary, I think it prudent to entertain the possibility that the whole episode is a brilliant and calculated deception. Loren Coleman received correspondence from a southern Oregon hotel operator who overheard her guests—including a member of the Wallace family—talking about the fun had by Ray Wallace and accomplices the previous summer during some down time along the new road. They spoke of weighted-down bogus feet being hauled up and down the rough terrain with cables used conventionally in logging operations.[42] Some of the pranks were accomplished by simply planting the tracks while an accomplice drove a vehicle slowly along the new roads.[43] This method can account for impossibly large strides and puzzlingly deep impressions.

None of this establishes that a hoax was perpetrated, even if common sense compels us to write off the whole affair. In truth, the documentation surrounding the event was too haphazard to establish much beyond anecdotal descriptions of size, depth, and the stride length associated with the tracks.

That some aspects of the affair were embellished is beyond doubt. The perpetrator was supposedly able to negotiate terrain that was simply beyond human effort; how then, did those investigating verify where these tracks were going? Wallace's anger and apprehension over losing his workers is, in retrospect, disingenuous. The operation was in fine shape when Bigfoot came calling and, as a subcontractor, Wallace was not in danger of taking a bath on the deal.

But what about those anecdotal details? John Green remains adamant that Wallace was incapable of a deception on the scale he witnessed, despite the fact that he had never met him.[44] The size of the prints were certainly within the capability of a resourceful conartist. The length of the stride was between 4 and 5 feet, lengthening to 10 when the monster was really stepping out. A 4–5-foot stride is unusual, but, as we will see in discussion of the Patterson film, it is not at all beyond human capability. As for the 10-foot stride, this claim was made by Wallace, who opined that Bigfoot was in pursuit of a deer at the time.[45]

This leaves the question of the alleged great depth of the tracks. The information is hard to evaluate because two items of relevance, the type of soil involved and how much variation there was in the depth of the tracks, are unknown. A little experimentation on your own in a compliant substrate will convince you that altering the depth of footprint impressions is not all that challenging.

Jerry Crew and his peers saw real impressions in the ground in 1958. That is an incontrovertible fact. Extrapolating beyond this fact is a dicey proposition, and it depends on which of an array of subjective impressions you choose to subscribe. Ray Wallace was a joker, to be sure, but he was not incompetent. As we will discover in a later chapter, he was capable of fooling plenty of experts—perhaps all of them. Most importantly, his family has produced the hardware that was used to produce fake trackways.

SASQUATCH ON ICE

What the Minnesota Iceman represents in the annals of Bigfoot very much depends on your prior inclination. Advocates see the episode as tantalizing, the true tale of the one that got away. Skeptics see the frozen corpse as a testament to human gullibility. It is a story without resolution, because whatever there was in the ice was either replaced or at the very least tampered with. As Ray Wallace turned out to be central to the discovery of the 1958 tracks, so, too, does the fate of the Iceman revolve around one individual.

Frank Hansen, you will recall, was the caretaker of what may have been a frozen Bigfoot when cryptozoologist Bernard Heuvelmans declared it a heretofore unknown species. Ivan Sanderson was equally taken with the specimen—he would remark that through cracks in the ice he could smell the decomposition of the corpse—and he cajoled John Napier to launch an official investigation under the auspices of the Smithsonian Institution.[46] Perhaps it is coincidence that when Hansen was informed of the National Museum's impending involvement into the affair, the tale of the Iceman began to change.

Sadly or predictably (depending on your point of view), the "original" Iceman was replaced with a latex likeness before federal officials could see it or any other scientists could substantiate Heuvelmans' incredible zoological claim. Hansen, who apparently took a much-needed vacation about the time the original went underground,[47] verified that a switch had taken place but tap-danced around the question of his own involvement in the decision to remove the true Iceman from circulation. The two cryptozoologists insisted that they would have detected the switch even if Hansen had not been forthcoming: the latex dummy was simply not the thing they had originally examined, even though it—like the original—could only be viewed through a surrounding block of ice.

The Iceman's origin would also come into question following the switch.[48] Originally, Hansen suggested an extrahemispheric origin for the specimen (though, depending on the day, just who found it seemed to change). Heuvelmans made some important observations that suggested to the government that law enforcement might need to bring its resources to bear on the mystery. Heuvelmans reported, and apparently Hansen had not exactly denied the allegation, that the dislocation of one eye from its socket was not a postmortem artifact but was, in fact, a perimortem result of a gunshot wound that had slain the Iceman. Indeed, the beast seemed to have raised one of its arms in self-defense against its assailant, judging by its posture in its frozen state. Hansen would later confess (although I suspect this is not the best verb to use here) that he, in fact, had pulled the trigger when confronting the monster in the woods of Minnesota. Now the likelihood that this was nothing less than Bigfoot on ice became even more real. The line about a discovery in remote Siberian seas, Hansen explained, was just a carnival barker's trick to get the chumps to come inside and see the Iceman.

The fact that Heuvelmans had rashly named the Iceman *Homo pongoides* also introduced some legal gravity to the case: if the beast in the ice was human (as the moniker *Homo* implies), then the problem of the shooting was not whether the appropriate hunting license had been issued but whether this was a case of cold-blooded murder! No less than J. Edgar Hoover was informed of the potential issue, but apparently leftist radicals were more of a threat to national security at the time than a renegade—and very dead—Bigfoot. No agents were dispatched.[49]

Meanwhile, Napier, with some help from other Smithsonian officials, had done some detective work of their own. In 1967, a company on the West Coast had been approached by Hansen and had successfully made an Iceman for him before the attraction ever began making public appearances.[50] It would be wrong to call this a "replica," since those commissioned to make the model never saw an original to copy in the first place.[51] Napier took the parsimonious view that there was just one Iceman, ever. The switch was merely a case of thawing the "original," repositioning the model, and refreezing the "replica" with a new posture and expression. Following Hansen's narrative contortions and his own investigation, Napier became convinced the whole episode was bogus, and he got the Smithsonian to withdraw from the affair as graciously as one could under the circumstances. The assessment was blunt: "The Smithsonian Institution . . . is satisfied that the creature is simply a carnival exhibit made of latex rubber and hair . . . the 'original' model and the present so-called 'substitute' are one and the same."[52]

Hansen's story of the Iceman never achieved a consistency one would demand of a legitimate historical account; he would remind his audience that he was not "under oath," as it were, and that he reserved the right to disavow everything.[53] The details changed as the questions became more pointed and probing. Neither Napier, nor anyone else, ever tracked down the Iceman's wealthy and enigmatic owner, but after several incarnations of the Iceman's origins story, nobody was seriously looking anymore.

Retrospectively, Napier attributed the intrigue created by the Iceman to Hansen's proficiency at manipulating human curiosity. In fact, when he initially looked into the matter, Napier was not favorably disposed. His assessment was that, by Heuvelmans and Sanderson's descriptions, the body proportions were all wrong for a primate and that, on balance, the thing was a zoological improbability.[54]

Hansen hadn't actively sought out the scientific community, but when it came calling he surely understood that an endorsement could really improve traffic through the fairgrounds. Not even a showman of Hansen's ability could have anticipated how the story could have gotten so big so fast. Someone else was going to demand to see the original, and institutional pressure would be applied to inspect the beast thawed and without the veil of ice. It had to be dispatched quickly. This was all the more necessary if there had never been an original to begin with. With the FBI being summoned, one imagines Hansen was seeing the story becoming something of a liability.

The story of the Iceman example is a signature Bigfoot tale: there exists unimpeachable evidence of Bigfoot, there for all to see, but by an unlikely string of bad luck, the evidence disappears just before the cold eye of science is poised to examine it. It is more dramatic than a case of the camera running out of film or the recently slain Bigfoot disappearing when a hunter returns to retrieve the body, but the form of the narrative is the same. It is perfect fodder for conspiracy theories. Loren Coleman describes the original's disappearance as "mysterious," noting the involvement of the U.S. Customs Service and the FBI.[55] For purposes of persuasion, it is better to argue that evidence was lost rather than to concede it never existed in the first place. Similar arguments plague other futile searches, such as those for Noah's Ark.[56]

In the annals of Bigfoot evidence, the Iceman resurfaces from time to time as a teaser—not evidence per se—but the kind of missed opportunity that reassures the advocates that the search will pay off eventually. The whole sorry episode demonstrates that you can fake the ultimate piece of evidence—a body in three dimensions—and still be able to chum the waters of credulity a good long time. The Iceman's tainted history is enough to convince most advocates that it is not worth invoking as evidence. It is a lesson in how easily anyone—including scientific institutions—can be fooled.

THE BOSSBURG INCIDENT

Bossburg, Washington, was home to a crippled Sasquatch in 1969–1970. The tracks left by this Bigfoot were numerous and anatomically perfect in the eyes of at least one professional scientist. Grover Krantz would leave Bossburg with his professional life changed forever, 100% convinced that Bigfoot was real.[57] Jeff Meldrum would use the tracks as a cornerstone of his anatomical model of a Sasquatch foot.[58] John Napier could not imagine the trackways being a human invention.[59] These anthropologists who had bothered to examine the evidence could not dismiss it as bogus.

Peter Byrne and John Green are not so confident about the tracks. This has nothing to do with the anatomy seen in the footprints but rather the strange events that ensued after their discovery. What started out as one of the greatest finds in the search for Bigfoot quickly degenerated into farce. Green (1978) and Hunter and Dahinden (1973) offer honest yet damning accounts of what is known collectively as the "Bossburg Incident," with the central figure in the affair being one Ivan Marx. Marx, you will recall, was a veteran from the Slick expedition some ten years before and he was able to follow the events of Bossburg very closely, since late in 1969 that is where he happened to be living. While Marx did not discover the Bossburg tracks initially, they showed up close to his home, and Dahinden has reminisced that Marx seemed awfully lucky in finding the tracks when he subsequently went out looking for them. Roger St. Hilaire, a zoologist who accompanied Dahinden on some of his forays here, remarked that the tracks were conveniently located close to the roads (betraying very uncryptic behavior for a cryptic animal) and had a strange habit of doubling back onto hard surfaces where their trail could not be followed.[60]

But the trail remained hot because the tracks kept showing up. Understandably, the tracks were generating some publicity, and, at one time or another, Bob Titmus, John Green, Roger Patterson, and Peter Byrne were present during one phase or another of the proceedings. By "proceedings," I refer to the fact that tracks were not the only evidence accumulating in Bossburg. One individual claimed to have captured a live Bigfoot and holding it prisoner in an abandoned mine shaft at some undisclosed location outside of town. This man, Joe Metlow, was entertaining various offers to sell information or the beast itself, later disclosing that if the Sasquatch hunters couldn't afford the whole package, he had a Sasquatch foot cooling its heel in a freezer that might fit within the pursuer's limited means. Patterson, Green, and Dahinden battled each other as much as Metlow in trying to get access to either the breathing Bigfoot or the iced-down remnant, but nobody ever laid eyes on either prize.[61]

There was even more to come. Marx had been strangely disinterested in the Metlow affair but instead had been out finding traces of the Bigfoot's passage at fairly regular intervals. Then, nearly a year after the first prints had been spotted around the town dump, Marx got a call that either a car or train had run into the crippled Sasquatch, and his instincts told him that this was his opportunity to get some film of the elusive Bigfoot now that it was hobbled beyond its existing handicap. Marx got the movie and briefly enjoyed fame equivalent to Roger Patterson's. Hunter and Dahinden's account of the film and its aftermath is brutally forthright.[62] Green endorsed the film initially, though he would later reconsider. Peter Byrne secured a copy of the film, to be placed in safe deposit, in exchange for paying Marx a monthly retainer. Now having a financial stake, Byrne conducted his investigation into the circumstances of the filming and discovered a number of inconsistencies with the account of the filming and the film itself. Having found the film site, Byrne was able to determine that old cripplefoot turned out to be not 9 feet tall but under 6, and Ivan Marx's credibility was plummeting fast. The fact that Marx had been spotted shopping for furs in Spokane beforehand[63] was not helpful either.

The shenanigans at Bossburg do not establish that the tracks themselves were fake. Krantz and Napier died being convinced of the tracks' authenticity, despite the events that undermined the serious question that the tracks posed. Napier could not imagine that there existed a sufficiently twisted mind to manufacture such a hoax. Incredulity, however, is a weak substitute for argument. Napier can be forgiven for his charitable view of humanity, but the creation of a hoax on the scale of Bossburg requires only (1) the knowledge that foot pathologies exist; (2) the ingenuity to create enlargements of such pathologies; and (3) the willingness to spend very modest amounts of time planting tracks. Nothing more special than this is required. The question of motivation is even simpler: money and fame have launched innumerable scams in human history, and the ledgers from Bossburg suggest this was precisely what was going on. Peter Byrne lost a few thousand dollars, Marx at one time was offered $25,000 simply to verify the authenticity of his film, and Metlow got offers of over $50,000 for a Bigfoot that no one ever saw.[64] A confidence trick is still a trick, even if it is hatched at the town dump.

The diversions provided by Metlow and Marx do not address the critical question of the tracks themselves. The two alternatives are that a crippled Sasquatch was living in greater Bossburg or someone with a fair degree of ingenuity and a keen sense of human gullibility pulled off a masterful deception. Who was the architect and how many were in on it is not relevant in the end, although the possibilities on this front are finite. The claim that the prints could not have been faked, though, is based more on hope than on data. What about the tracks or their circumstances make a hoax impossible?

The Bossburg tracks enjoy high status in the inventory of Bigfoot evidence in part because they have been validated by the three professional anthropologists who have looked into the matter fairly closely. For Napier, the mere presence of pathological details was sufficient to convince him that a living foot made the tracks. Krantz's follow up to the event was somewhat more involved in that he went to the trouble of reconstructing the anatomical implications of the pathology. The kicker for Krantz was that the foot displayed proportions that, in his view, couldn't have been sampled from a human population.[65] On this point, Krantz and Napier are actually in total disagreement. Napier's assessment of the normal Bossburg track is that it is essentially human in shape, but not in size.[66] Krantz implies, by his interpretation of the deformed tracks, that the proportion of the normal foot must be different from that of a human (if not, the foundation for his argument collapses). Anthropology's current Sasquatch advocate, Jeff Meldrum, endorses Krantz's interpretation up to a point[67]; he offers that the tracks "warrant evaluation."[68]

Krantz staked his professional reputation on his inference that the Bossburg tracks betrayed a uniquely proportioned foot skeleton that only made sense from an understanding of allometric principles, which, he insisted, no hoaxer could possess. Is Krantz's idea of relating footprint form to skeletal proportion scientifically defensible?

Michael Dennett was the first to put a dent in the crippled prints' legitimacy.[69] It was really nothing more than an anatomical observation that threw into doubt the basis for Krantz's reconstruction. The leverage of the calf muscles, attaching to the back of the heel via the Achilles tendon, depends on the position of the tendon from the tibiotalar joint, where the shin meets the ankle. It is the position of this joint that is critical to Krantz's reconstruction, and, as we have noted, Krantz reconstructed the position of this joint from the crippled print's anatomy. Dennett, however, made the mundane but critical observation that the tibiotalar joint makes no direct contact with the ground in walking, therefore establishing its position with precision from a footprint is apt to be tricky.[70] Of course, if the position of the talus could be established, it can be reasonably assumed that the location of the overlying tibiotalar joint could be established with a fair degree of accuracy. But a simple consultation with an anatomy textbook reveals that this, too, is unlikely, because the talus—in normal function—is elevated above the ground and makes no direct contact with it, as the calcaneus and various ligaments hold this bone in place to form the keystone for the arches of the foot.

We will give Krantz the benefit of the doubt here, as there is a scenario in which—in theory—the position of the talus could be established. But it bears emphasizing that at no point in his argument does Krantz actually articulate the following. When the arches of the foot collapse, which can occur for a variety of reasons, a typical outcome is "subluxation" of the talus. This is podiatrist's jargon meaning simply that the normal mechanisms that keep the talus elevated have failed, and the bone slips to a position where ostensibly it is in more direct contact with the ground during walking. Bigfoot is, after all, rather famous for its flat-footed prints. Perhaps the crippled Bigfoot's talus was just where Krantz said it was, and he really could infer this from the twisted imprint of its deformed foot.

The question becomes a very simple one, and it should have been the first one Krantz posed prior to his analysis: how easy is it to reconstruct a foot skeleton from a foot imprint? Certainly we can tell about where the calcaneus lies and the bones of the toes are, but can the location of each joint be narrowed down to a precise and reliable estimate? Krantz's model of Sasquatch foot anatomy depends on it. If we know where to look, can we really tell how much leverage the Achilles tendon has?

Krantz deserves credit for trying to take some apparently credible evidence and see if it made sense on anatomical and biomechanical grounds. But the inference of foot anatomy from a mere imprint of its plantar surface (the sole of the foot) is, in reality, a losing proposition. I discovered this during a memorable year I spent teaching lower limb anatomy at the California College of Podiatric Medicine in San Francisco in 1999. This narrow topic might seem to be the kind of thing that could be covered over perhaps a few weeks or a month, but at CCPM this was a full-year course: four hours of lecture and three hours of lab a week for twenty-five weeks. Both my students and I learned more about legs and feet than we ever thought possible, or for that matter, necessary.

As any veteran of gross anatomy can attest, the learning really happens in the lab rather than in the lecture hall. One thing dissection teaches you is that, despite the pattern that always emerges when you examine the human body, the big revelation is the variety of variations that exist within those patterns. Every sole of each foot on every cadaver looks pretty similar: rounded heel, five toes, wider at the front than in the back. But the outward appearance of the foot actually says very little about what lies deeper, not only in terms of tendons and ligaments but also in terms of the subtleties of the bones as well. Certainly one can tell where the back of the calcaneus lies or even where the metatarsal heads give way to the phalanges, but that is about all one can deduce with certainty from the sole of a foot, much less its footprint.

How striking this was I discovered while consulting a clinical orthopedic volume on children's foot disorders. Typically, these volumes include pictures of the feet themselves and accompanying radiographs. In one figure, a patient's right and left feet were radiographed, revealing one foot having a stunning malformation of its skeleton. What was really striking in this context, however, was the adjacent picture of the soles of the feet, photographed from below with the patient standing on a transparent glass plate. The feet, despite the gross difference in their underlying skeletons, were nearly mirror images of one another, except for some shortening in the affected foot. There was no hint of any underlying pathology from the footprints.[71]

Of course, there are pathologies of the feet that are manifested in footprints, but the point here is that there is no necessary correspondence between the exact position of the foot bones and the tracks left by a foot. Certainly the cripplefoot's imprint is telling us all was not well with its possessor, but moving beyond that inference to pinpointing the location of the overlying ankle joint is scientifically indefensible. Krantz didn't bother to test his own technique. The idea that individual footprints reveal the precise locations of the underlying foot bones is invalid.

The problem with Krantz's argument is simply this: there was no demonstration at the time, nor has there been since, that a foot skeleton can be recreated out of a footprint with any degree of certainty. Investigation that has been done on this question suggests that footprints are simply not good indicators of underlying anatomy.[72] Krantz correlated the bumps on the lateral aspect of the foot with two anatomical joints, the calcaneocuboid and cubometatarsal (named for the bones contributing to their formation). Why these joints are implicated in forming these bumps is never explained. It is equally plausible that nearby sesamoid bones or any number of soft tissue pathologies could produce the same effects in a track and these would influence the skeletal reconstruction.[73] In any case, there are no data out there that lend any credence to Krantz's reconstruction.

Henner Fahrenbach has argued that genuine Bigfoot tracks are disproportionately wide in comparison to scaled-down human feet,[74] and this interpretation could plausibly be applied to the Bossburg tracks (we assume here that Napier's assessment of the same evidence—that the tracks are human-like in proportion—is simply wrong). It would seem that if this were the case, the hoaxing scenario of simply enlarging a human deformity would be out of the question. This is the linchpin of Krantz's argument that the tracks could not be faked: they are not simply blown up versions of adult human feet, normal or pathological. But this does not mean that there is not a human source for oddly proportioned footprints after all.

All the talk of shape and proportion in the Bossburg tracks is in reference to adult human feet, which do appear to be somewhat narrower than the average Sasquatch print, especially at the heel. Infants, however, have feet that differ from adults in precisely this way—they present a foreshortened foot outline that can appear relatively wide at the heel. This appearance exists despite the fact that the relative proportions of the foot bones, which are incompletely formed in infants, are about the same as in adults.[75]

The implication to the Bossburg mystery here is perhaps anticlimactic, but relevant nonetheless. An enlargement of an infant foot outline would produce an oddly proportioned print with reference to an adult human foot. But how would a potential hoaxer find suitable replicas of infant foot pathologies? In fact, finding images to serve as Sasquatch templates is astonishingly easy. There has been a large clinical literature on malformation of human feet since the mid-nineteenth century; as most of these sources are concerned with corrective treatment, the majority of images in these sources are of infants and juveniles prior to medical intervention. There are literally dozens of books, each with scores of drawings and photographs, that illustrate all types of pedal deformities. At the time the Bossburg tracks were made, there were hundreds of convincing templates for Bigfoot tracks, normal and deformed, sitting in the stacks of the public and university libraries of the State of Washington. All a hoaxer had to do was have the wherewithal to scale them up, and he or she did not need to know one iota of anatomy to do so.

Advocates are fond of pointing out that René Dahinden, who was on the scene for much of the time when the Sasquatch was active, once counted a trackway that sported a full 1,089 prints.[76] The implication of this figure is that a hoaxer would have had to put in some serious mischief overtime to plant that many tracks, and he or she would have to be logging these hours while escaping detection, assuming nobody else was in on the joke. How much time we are talking about depends on how the tracks were made. In all the accounts of the Bossburg Bigfoot, the only mention of depth of the tracks is that Dahinden thought that the soil was more deeply impressed by the crippled foot rather than the normal one.[77] No reports from the incident talk about impossibly deep imprints or superhuman stride lengths; the one item arguing against a simple hoax is that the tracks appeared to step over a 43-inch, tightly strung barbed-wire fence twice during the jaunt.[78]

It is reasonable to suppose, if we entertain the possibility of a hoax, that the most efficient way to do so would be via the boot-on-the-fake-foot technique: that is, creating the Bigfoot illusion by walking around with the offending feet attached. The size of the feet would make walking a little problematic but by no means impossible; swim fins, after all, do not immobilize people on land. The size of the feet might actually slow you down considerably but it would still be quite feasible to produce forty–forty-five prints in this manner in a minute's time. What this works out to is that Bigfoot or the hoaxer could have produced the 1,000-print trackway in well under half an hour!

But what of the issue of the barbed-wire fence? The assumption by Krantz is that even a tall person could not simply step over such a fence; this is a fair supposition, as there aren't many people out there with a 4-foot inseam. But neither Bigfoot nor a hoaxer would need to: barbed-wire fences stop cattle but are not as good for stopping people. Scaling barbed-wire fences is only marginally hazardous for the experienced, and anyone who has climbed over a few knows that a tightly wound fence is an easier one to negotiate than a decrepit one. The problem is not the fence but an assumption of lack of resourcefulness on the part of the hoaxer.

For the sake of argument, let us envision that following a robbery, a suspect makes his getaway on foot. The forensic examiners analyze the crime scene the next day, find footprints, and notice that the footprints stop 3 feet in front of a 6-foot barbed-wire fence and begin again 3 feet on the other side. You will surely agree that the forensics crew is not going to conclude that the suspect possessed a 6-foot stride and simply stepped over the fence. The footprint evidence permits this interpretation, but it does not logically compel it.

Is there circumstantial evidence from Bossburg that allows us to dismiss the whole affair as a prank on a grand scale? Marx's handiwork with the movie puts him near the top of the suspect list in some people's eyes,[79] but the film could have been made to exploit a situation that its director had nothing to do with. This is, perhaps, a charitable interpretation.

Kenneth Wylie suggests that the perpetrator was one Ray Pickens from Colville, Washington.[80] Wylie closed the books on the Bossburg case when he learned of an interview Pickens did with the BBC, apparently confessing to fabricating tracks. This would apparently wrap up the affair; the only problem, however, is that the interview is alleged to have been made in 1968, well before the tracks made their debut at the town dump.

Over thirty years have elapsed since the crippled Sasquatch began sampling the Colville trash for evening meals.[81] The evidence that emerged from the events that followed comprises a film that no one deems credible and innumerable footprints from which a single set of casts survives. The argument that the footprints could not be fabricated is not compelling: their hoaxing may have involved a good deal of ingenuity and resourcefulness, but such a stunt was by no means impossible. What is beyond doubt is that the Bigfoot hunters were ultimately frustrated by the whole affair and that at least a few people had a good deal of fun, regardless of the reality of a Bigfoot tramping about the town.

A footnote to Bossburg is that the form of argument, rather than the force of the evidence itself, maintains the event as legitimate in advocate circles. Krantz's argument as to why the Bossburg prints represent Bigfoot's smoking gun is simply that nobody could have known how to fake those tracks. Krantz opined that Leonardo da Vinci might have had the ingenuity to dream this up, but he wasn't around in 1969.[82] The logic Krantz used here is not entirely sound. Basically, his thesis is that someone would have to possess such esoteric knowledge of anatomy and biomechanics that it becomes inconceivable that such an individual could fabricate a "correct" deformity from scratch. Yet, construction of a pathologically "correct" footprint requires only imitation, not a career's worth of anatomical training. Krantz's idea, however, continues to be endorsed in Bigfoot circles as the kind of evidence that skeptics have no answer for.[83]

BIGFOOT ON DEMAND

Beginning in 1982, Paul Freeman embarked on a remarkable career of tracking Bigfoot that would last over fifteen years. All the more remarkable was that he was finding evidence of a Bigfoot population well removed from the mountainous coastal habitat that is usually associated with Sasquatch activity. Freeman's status in Bigfoot lore is largely due to his most forceful supporters who, parenthetically, also endorsed the Bossburg prints. It is no exaggeration to state that without the endorsements of Grover Krantz and Jeff Meldrum, Freeman would have been forgotten as a small-time operator in the Bigfoot universe.

Freeman's signing on with the Forest Service was punctuated by a Bigfoot sighting. He also found tracks. A wildlife biologist by the name of Rodney Johnson and a veteran tracker with the Border Patrol, Joel Hardin, were dispatched to the scene to examine the evidence firsthand. Hardin makes his living tracking human quarry, and that quarry was usually interested in not being followed. Hardin thus, over the course of his career, had to learn a good deal more than simply following an obvious trail to excel at his trade. While Hardin was skilled at detecting signs of human passage, Rodney Johnson was more intimately familiar with animal spoor. It was, in retrospect, fortuitous that the Forest Service was able to get two different experts at the scene of the encounter. Johnson and Hardin suspected a hoax after looking things over.[84]

Grover Krantz would later cry foul because it was his understanding that Hardin was skeptical of the trackway before he actually arrived at the scene.[85] One wonders what an acceptable prior attitude would be. The fact that the two federal employees would consent to being dragged away from their normal duties indicates that they had not completely rejected the track's claim to authenticity a priori. Both Johnson and Hardin found that the context of the tracks did not match up to an encounter with a gigantic biped. The problems were numerous. The tracks seemed to start and end without indication of how the Bigfoot arrived in the area or departed the scene. The investigator's footwear was sinking more deeply into the soil than the prints of the alleged Sasquatch. The prints themselves were unaccountably free of the litter that covered the forest floor. The pattern of the friction skin, or dermal ridges, was incongruous: the ridges persisted where they would be worn down or absent in an unshod human. In sum, there were several reasons to suspect that the tracks were not what they were purported to be.[86]

Freeman would, nevertheless, continue to encounter Bigfoot in the ensuing years, in the form of sightings (some recorded on film), footprints, handprints, kneeprints, and hair. One would think that such skill would endear someone like Paul Freeman to the inner circle of Bigfoot researchers. But one of the great ironies of the Bigfoot subculture is that in claiming multiple encounters, one immediately falls under suspicion of perpetrating a hoax. René Dahinden, Bob Titmus, and Peter Byrne, all elder statesmen for the field during their lifetimes, found Freeman's successes to be suspect, and the volume of his evidence alone—regardless of quality—was enough to invite skepticism from researchers who were eager to resolve the Sasquatch mystery. Each of these veterans of the search would have dealings with Freeman and find his credibility wanting.

Barbara Wasson, aware of the publicity surrounding Freeman's finds in 1982, went to Walla Walla, Washington, to interview Freeman and his frequent sidekick, Wes Sumerlin. Wasson was a psychologist by training and practiced animal tracking as an avocation; thus, she would evaluate Freeman as an eyewitness and examine what sign there was to back up his story. She was not impressed with Freeman or his story; she told René Dahinden not to bother making the trip (see fig. 4.2).[87]

But Dahinden did find himself in the Blue Mountains late in 1987 when Freeman made a fortuitous discovery of a Sasquatch trackway. These prints were sunk deeply into the earth, and Dahinden shed his own footwear just to see what his feet would do in this particular substrate. While the depth of the prints was something he could not match, Dahinden was stunned to find that the dermal ridges on his feet and toes showed up very clearly in the soil, while the Bigfoot tracks had no such features. Preparing to photograph one of the tracks, Dahinden blew on one of the toe impressions to clear out some soil that had slipped into it. In doing so, he displaced some dirt forming a margin of the track, where he saw the impression of a skin pattern *beneath* where the soil of the track itself had been compressed. This unexpected finding led Dahinden to conclude that "this skin pattern was made by someone patting down the dirt before pushing more dirt on top."[88] Later, he would examine the sequence of casts he made at the site and discover something odd: in sequence the tracks were left, right, left, and left. This represented either a clumsy oversight by a hoaxer or an apparent case of Bigfoot practicing hopscotch.[89]

Dahinden spent ten weeks in the Walla Walla area in 1987 and 1988; he considered none of Freeman's finds credible, adding that by his reading the local Bigfoot tracks were ridiculous in terms of their anatomical implications.[90] He later denounced Freeman in public forums.[91] Most Bigfoot advocates, deferring

FIGURE 4.2
René Dahinden with the cast of a Bigfoot track found by Paul Freeman in November 1987. Dahinden spent nearly fifty years in pursuit of Bigfoot and considered all Freeman's discoveries bogus. A skeptic in the advocate camp, he was never certain of Bigfoot's existence, despite being a staunch defender of the Patterson film. He told Michael Dennett (1988:8): "the longer it goes without one of them being collected, the less likely it is that they exist." Photo by Michael Dennett, used with permission.

to the experience and reputation of the elder researchers, followed suit and Freeman became *persona non grata* in many Bigfoot circles. That would seem sufficient to seal Freeman's reputation and banish him forever from the pantheon of Bigfoot heroes. Instead of being a champion of the cause, he was regarded as having cast a pall over the field.

Bob Titmus also happened to call on Freeman sometime prior to 1989 (the exact date is not known). Perhaps aware of Freeman's ability to conjure Bigfoot evidence on demand, Titmus remarked to Freeman his sense that a Sasquatch might be in the vicinity. Freeman drove off to investigate on his own and returned a mere twenty minutes later with news of a discovery. Titmus discovered that Freeman had, indeed, found a few Bigfoot prints. But Titmus, having done decades of tracking himself, determined that these tracks were of the variety that Joel Hardin and Rodney Johnson had discovered—

starting and ending without a trace, despite favorable conditions for following footprints. Titmus settled on a hoax being the likeliest explanation.[92]

Peter Byrne had his own experience with Freeman in Walla Walla that paralleled Titmus's experience.[93] He had phoned ahead to let Freeman know that he and a television crew were interested in seeing footprints. Upon their arrival, Freeman obliged by taking them to a trackway about 100 feet back from a road. About 100 footprints were found running along a ridge, but Byrne—having plenty of experience following animal sign from years of big game hunting—determined that the tracks started and ended abruptly with no other sign of the Bigfoot's arriving at or departing the ridge. Byrne sarcastically congratulated Freeman on his discovery of the first flying Bigfoot. Byrne does not believe that any of Freeman's evidence is credible.[94]

Still, Freeman enjoyed support from anthropologists Krantz and Meldrum, who endorsed Freeman's footprint evidence as compelling.[95] In fact, Freeman's inventory of prints would become a centerpiece of each scientist's argument for the reality of Bigfoot. For Krantz, the presence and the pattern of dermal ridges were totally convincing. In a *Newsweek* article, Krantz is on record that no less than forty fingerprint experts had signed off on the dermatoglyphic details as genuine.[96] Who these forty individuals are remains mysterious, although Michael Dennett toiled considerably to locate a handful of these experts who had indeed been consulted by Krantz about the tracks in question. The opinions of some of these experts turn out to be something less than ringing endorsements. Two fingerprint experts, George Bonebrake and Robert Olsen, suggest that the evidence does not permit an informed opinion as to authenticity. Two academics, Kazumichi Katayama of Tokyo University and D. A. G. de Wilde from the Netherlands, also point out that it is unlikely that one could distinguish Bigfoot dermatoglyphics from those of a large human.[97] In fact, without a known Bigfoot standard as a comparative yardstick, such a determination would seem to be, on logical grounds, impossible. What de Wilde reported to Krantz would seem to not qualify as a supportive opinion at all: the dermal ridges on the casts, de Wilde concluded, could not be distinguished from those of large people.[98]

Jeff Meldrum has staked much of his academic reputation on the evidence that Freeman has discovered. In Internet postings and in public lectures, Meldrum has defied anyone to create a foot prosthesis capable of producing the variations in footprints and toe positions found in the tracks discovered by

Freeman.[99] Dahinden's discovery of dermal ridges beneath the footprints themselves addresses the problem: the tracks need not have been fabricated by a prosthesis. As Bob Titmus noted with respect to the limited trackways that typified Freeman's finds, one does not need a fake foot to manufacture a fake footprint.[100]

Freeman is the academic advocates' best source for Bigfoot evidence, but, by virtue of his poor reputation among the nonacademic advocates, there is the need to explain why Paul Freeman was finding all the evidence in the Blue Mountains, while nobody else around Walla Walla seemed to be aware that a population of Bigfoot was hanging out beyond the city limits. Krantz's explanation was that Freeman was spending an "inordinate" amount of time and energy to the enterprise,[101] a claim that rings suspicious with Bigfoot advocate Daniel Perez. Perez established himself as a major player in Bigfoot circles with the 1988 publication of *Big Footnotes*, an impressive annotated bibliography of Bigfoot "and related beings." For bluntness, he fits perfectly into the Dahinden mold: Perez dismisses Freeman as "no woodsman" who had physical impairments that would not predispose him to be a successful Bigfoot hunter.[102] Krantz claims there were other folks finding evidence,[103] but he could only get this information secondhand. Thus, we don't know just who these people are.

Meldrum's position with respect to Freeman's involvement with Bigfoot is event-specific. He admits skepticism to certain sources of evidence[104] but argues that the footprints, in particular, are credible. It is clear enough from his media interviews and conference presentations that his view of the Freeman tracks is similar to Krantz's position on the Bossburg prints: the anatomical detail is too good, too subtle, and too functionally harmonious to be the product of a clumsy hoaxer.

Krantz also concedes that Freeman's association with evidence does not always inspire confidence. Freeman has submitted casts of handprints for consideration, and on one occasion what Freeman told Krantz about the circumstances of the find was different from the story Bob Titmus was told about the same item of evidence.[105] Dahinden notes that Freeman's discovery occurred only after Krantz provided Freeman with a handprint discovered by Ivan Marx.[106] Both Krantz and Dahinden find that there is strong resemblance between the handprints, but they believe this for very different reasons. Bigfoot hair has been recovered at sites associated with Freeman's investigations; these samples have since been positively identified as synthetic fibers.[107]

Freeman died in 2003 at the age of fifty-nine.[108] He was not the joker that Ray Wallace was and he did not quite have the directorial flair that Ivan Marx possessed. There can be little question, however, that Freeman was more than capable of hoaxes. He admitted as much on ABC's *Good Morning America* on October 29, 1987.[109] Michael Dennett noted that Freeman was a skilled artisan and it is believed that he once worked for an orthopedic shoe company.[110] Still, Freeman insisted that the materials that he provided to Krantz and Meldrum were the real deal, and the anthropologists contend he could not have possessed the expertise to fake the prints.[111] Krantz published an analysis concerning Freeman's discoveries in the Bigfoot-friendly journal *Cryptozoology*[112] that were later challenged on several points by René Dahinden and Michael Dennett[113] in published rebuttals. Meldrum, for his part, insists that the Freeman prints possess a dynamic signature of a living foot.

Meldrum recounted his examination of over forty footprints in his talk at the Sasquatch Symposium in May 1996. He described his arrival in Walla Walla as unannounced and was surprised to discover Freeman had found tracks that morning.[114] Meldrum did, however, admit to phoning Wes Sumerlin beforehand to inform him he was planning to visit Walla Walla. Sumerlin and Freeman had several joint Bigfoot encounters over the years, and certain symposium participants, including René Dahinden, questioned whether Freeman was unaware of Meldrum's impending visit.[115] Meldrum considers this and other Bigfoot track finds to be relevant to the study of the evolution of human bipedalism, on par with the famed Laetoli footprint discovery of 1976, which established that human ancestors were walking upright over 3.5 million years ago.[116]

The usual fallback to tainted evidence is that there is no motivation for hoaxing, since the instigators have nothing to gain. This argument presumes an understanding of individual motives. Freeman got two things from his work on Bigfoot that, for most people, are sufficient to keep them in their chosen occupation: fame and money. Krantz peddled Freeman's finds to *Newsweek*, and Freeman himself managed a network television appearance.[117] Meldrum was so convinced that Freeman's collection was worthy of study that he was arranging to purchase it for $2,000 in 1996.[118] These observations, in addition to the fact that Freeman actively pursued Bigfoot after 1982, suggest that he found the hunt to be a worthwhile endeavor.

BIGFOOT GETS MUDDY

The Marx movies (he made at least half a dozen) and Freeman's unparalleled success kept Bigfoot in the public eye but, on balance, did not further the cause for legitimacy. The Skookum Cast is Bigfoot's latest best hope. It is an impression of an impression, but its proponents proclaim it is compelling evidence. What the public and scientific community know about this evidence is largely confined to the Bigfoot Field Researchers Organization (BFRO) website,[119] the initial flurry of press, and a purportedly scientific television program.[120] The compelling nature of the cast is based on the following observations: (1) the size and shape of the indentations lie outside the human range; (2) the finer details reveal markings consistent with hair, dermatoglyphics (dermal ridges), and genitalia (testicular impressions are said to be present); and (3) a hair from the site that Henner Fahrenbach described as "Sasquatch" in origin[121] (how a standard for Sasquatch hair was established is not clear, and later attempts to extract DNA from hair samples recovered at the site were unsuccessful).[122]

The impression was discovered at the end of a BFRO expedition that had been dispatched to follow up reports of twisted trees (standard behavior for Bigfoot) and mysterious hair in this region of the Gifford Pinchot National Forest. It is fortuitous that expedition member Richard Noll was transporting large amounts of casting compound at the time, and, as luck would have it, a TV crew from *Animal X* was on a shoot with the BFRO when the discovery was made.[123]

The BFRO has offered their own scenario of the event that produced the cast.[124] The muddy roadside locale was baited with fruit with the specific objective of getting a Bigfoot to waddle through the mess and leave traces of its passage. But the Sasquatch did not walk up to the fruit, gather it up, and then walk off to enjoy the snack. Instead, it apparently chose to lie down in the mud first and reach across the puddle to gain its prize.

This scenario alone raises serious questions. My own sense is that a person's last inclination, when confronted with a problem of retrieving something from the center of a big pool of mud, is to lie down in the mess while collecting the desired object. I would choose to walk through the mud, whether I am unshod or have my Wellingtons on, and muddy my soles and not my whole person. Bigfoot did not choose to do this in the turnout at Skookum Meadow. Why?

The BFRO team suggested the chosen strategy was part of a behavioral adaptive complex peculiar to the Sasquatch.[125] Grover Krantz and Peter Byrne have both suggested that the relative scarcity of Bigfoot tracks, even around sites of Bigfoot activity, has a sound biological basis. Rather than pointing to the obvious possibility of hoaxing, what they suggest is that Bigfoot intentionally hides its tracks as a means of eluding detection.[126] How Bigfoot is supposed to accomplish this is something of a mystery. On the one hand, what makes the footprint evidence compelling is supposed to be the tremendous depth of the prints, betraying the massive weight of the animal. But what does Bigfoot do with this mass when it is trying to hide its tracks? How can it stop making tracks when it doesn't want to be followed? Does it double back to cover its trail? What does it do with the trail it created doubling back?

For the sake of argument, however, let us concede that Byrne and Krantz are correct, and somehow Bigfoot can disguise its sign when it needs to remain cryptic. The BFRO official explanation for the Skookum Cast is that the Sasquatch involved did not wish to leave the obvious sign of its presence by leaving its footprints all over the roadside. So it lay down in the mud instead. Ben Radford, science writer and managing editor of the *Skeptical Inquirer*, raised the not trivial issue that in laying down in the mud, the Bigfoot in question was leaving a very visible—and obviously discoverable—sign of its presence.[127] Why leave an imprint of your whole body when one of your goals is to remain undetected?

The Skookum Cast has been hyped tremendously by advocates inside the BFRO, but it has been in the form of an orchestrated media campaign rather than the presentation of any scientific argument. It is very difficult to debunk the cast systematically since no useful data have been made public. Endorsement by the scientific community has amounted to sympathetic sound bites from allegedly disinterested scientists on a Discovery Channel program.[128]

Ben Radford and I were able to question Meldrum in person about the Skookum Cast in 2002, and he was kind enough to allow us to examine some good quality photographs he had of the cast itself. I can only say that the cast must be decidedly more impressive in three dimensions than it appears in two. Ben thought the impressions were reminiscent of ink blots, and I could only make out what might be a heel impression. It could easily be an impression of a million other things. Radford attempted to see the original when he was in the

Seattle area; he was rebuffed by the explanation that access to the cast was only available to individuals with appropriate scientific credentials.[129]

Any claim that the Skookum Cast could not have been faked borders on the asinine. The initial claims for authenticity have not been followed up by any substantive analysis of what's actually shown in the plaster. As is typical with Sasquatch discoveries, the claim to authenticity is made first, with intimations that further research will bear the claim out. Three years after the fact, nothing further has been learned. The significance of the find would seem to demand publication of a detailed analysis. Given that no fewer than five individuals holding doctoral degrees in anthropology and cognate fields of biology examined the find, it is no longer permissible to excuse the absence of basic research into the evidence.

If a hoax was involved in making the Skookum Cast, who might be implicated is impossible to determine. The question of what would motivate a hoax, however, is answered by noting the huge publicity generated by the find. But one does not even need to entertain the possibility of a hoax to argue that what we have in the cast is not Bigfoot. As is often the case, the most withering critique of the evidence comes from the advocate camp itself.

Cliff Crook founded Bigfoot Central, a fairly small but visible organization devoted to "peaceful pursuit" of Bigfoot. Crook has been on the trail of Bigfoot since an encounter of his own in 1956 and is often embroiled in controversy. He stands accused of hoaxing Bigfoot photographs[130] and has himself argued that the Patterson film is bogus.[131] He was one of Krantz's most vocal critics among the Bigfoot fraternity.[132] Bigfoot Central's website contains a sensible and pointed critique of the Skookum Cast.[133] Crook begins from the observation that since there are elk hairs and elk prints all over the casting site, the first suspect to rule out as the cast's creator is that creature. Being large and hirsute, the elk possesses two of the outstanding characteristics that the cast impressions reveal. The "heel" is nothing more than the elk kneeling, and the elk's torso could also produce hairy imprints that, with a little suggestion, could be construed as an oversized primate (whether an elk or anything else could make the Skookum impression in a particular pose is irrelevant; there is no reason that the impressions attributed to Bigfoot had to be made simultaneously). The presence of elk prints and the absence of Bigfoot tracks around the site compels a careful consideration of his hypothesis—unless, of course, we insist that Bigfoot was hiding its tracks prior to the mudbath. Crook regards BFRO's interpretation as unbridled imagination. Other advocates agree that the cast represents an elk.[134]

Misidentification seems as likely a culprit here as Bigfoot. Daniel Perez echoes Crook's reasoning. The question Perez poses is "how did it get there?"[135] A body print without footprints does not sit well with him, especially considering other animal sign was clearly visible. Even Grover Krantz declined to endorse the cast.[136]

The hypothesis under consideration, that the Bigfoot phenomenon is entirely the product of human manufacture, cannot be ruled out when we examine the most celebrated cases. Even the best evidence for Bigfoot, on close examination, seems to be tainted or, at the very least, equivocal. The peripheral shenanigans surrounding many of these incidents should give us some pause in deciding whether there really are apes among us in North America. If we don't have the actual remains of Bigfoot in our hands, the only other way to demonstrate its existence is to rule out all possibility of human fabrication or misinterpretation. There is no question—in all of the cases reviewed—that a human could have been the creative force behind the evidence, assuming considerable ingenuity coupled with a lack of social responsibility. With respect to this observation, the hypothesis is on very secure footing. Thus far, the case for Sasquatch is not strong.

There are still questions to confront. Could fake footprints really fool competent anatomists? Is it fair or legitimate to explain away every last eyewitness account? Aren't Bigfoot scholars getting a cold shoulder from the scientific community without a fair hearing? These issues have to be tackled if the hypothesis that Bigfoot is a purely human enterprise will hold water. In addition, there remains the most compelling evidence of all: the advocates call her Patty, and she was taking a stroll along Bluff Creek when Roger Patterson made her a movie star.

NOTES

1. Stein (2001).

2. Nigel Barber (2002). Cold fusion controversy. *Encyclopedia of Ethics in Science and Technology.* New York: Facts on File. Accessed from the Facts on File On Line Reference Database, www.fofweb.com.

3. The analysis presented here is that of Feder (2002:60–81).

4. Green (1994:3). Binns (1984) also discusses the linkage of publicity with clusters of sightings in his study of the Loch Ness Monster.

5. Napier (1974:72–73).

6. Jeffrey (1980).

7. Sanderson (1961).

8. Krantz (1992:204).

9. Barnum (2000:348). This volume is a reprint of Barnum's 1855 publication.

10. Saxon (1983:xxix).

11. Johnson (2002). Accessed online at www.iridescent-publishing.com/rtm/ch1p4.htm.

12. Saxon (1989:284).

13. Green (1978:83–88).

14. Hunter and Dahinden (1975:49, 57).

15. Green (1978:112) reports that Ostman claimed that he told a few people after his abduction what had happened to him, and Green relates a third-hand account of someone hearing a story like this in 1933.

16. Bindernagel (1998) uses Ostman's account as data for inferring Sasquatch ecology.

17. Dennett (1988:7).

18. Wasson (1979:12).

19. Byrne (1976:23) suggests that the people following up on the Beck report did not find anything in support of the encounter, but this is at odds with Green's (1978:89–90) account based on reprinted news reports.

20. Green (1978:90, 91, 97).

21. Green (1978:90).

22. Byrne (1976:23–28); Green (1978:89–91; Dennett (1982).

23. Green (1980:241) opines that "the Sasquatch is not normally a dangerous animal" and (1994:64) that "they are nothing to be afraid of."

24. Byrne (1976:22).

25. Roosevelt (1893:254–255).

26. Green (1978:68).

27. Sanderson (1961:131).

28. Personal communication via audiotape, February 20, 1996. Dahinden maintains this attitude of the road-building crews persisted well beyond 1958 and was typical of the Bluff Creek area finds in the 1960s.

29. Coleman (2003:73).

30. Sanderson (1961:131).

31. Napier (1974:87).

32. Pyle (1995:188–189).

33. Coleman (2003:72) and Byrne (1976:104–106). Byrne doesn't name Wallace other than by description in his account. Byrne doubted the claim from the outset but indulged Wallace for the entertainment value. The captured Bigfoot was sustained on a steady diet of frosted flakes.

34. Coleman (2003:75).

35. Daegling and Radford (2003).

36. In a telephone conversation (December 19, 2003), Dale Lee Wallace indicated that his Uncle Ray used the feet periodically on road-building operations in northern California as well as the Mount Baker and Mount St. Helens regions of the Cascades. He believed that the pranks continued intermittently up until Ray Wallace became ill shortly before his death.

37. Chorvinsky (1993a, 1993b). Robert Pyle (1995) devotes considerable attention to Wallace and his role, however unwelcome by the advocates, in promoting Bigfoot. In a somewhat cryptic foreshadowing of his family's disclosure of his pranks, Wallace advised Pyle (1995:195) that searching for Bigfoot was a waste of time.

38. Dennett (1982).

39. Mullens (1979).

40. The BFRO took the lead in denouncing the story in cyberspace; see http://www.bfro.net/news/Wallace.asp. Among their visuals is a photograph of Jerry Crew holding up a track cast and comparing it to a photograph of one of Wallace's fake feet; the fake could not have made the cast shown. There are, however, published photographs of some other bogus feet of Wallace's that compare very favorably to Crew's cast (http://www.channel3000.com/news/1823767/detail.html, http://oregonmag.com/BigfootHoax.htm).

41. Coleman (2003:59–73).

42. Coleman (2003:75).

43. Egan (2003).

44. Green made his comments on the Bigfoot Field Researchers Organization website: http://www.bfro.net/news/jgreen_bluff_creek_tracks.asp.

45. Patterson (1966:36).

46. Napier (1974:104).

47. Napier (1974:109).

48. Napier (1974:101–113).

49. Napier (1974:105).

50. Napier (1974:112).

51. Emery (1981).

52. Byrne (1975:223).

53. Napier (1974:113).

54. Napier (1974:103–104).
55. Coleman (2003:114).
56. Feder (2002:268–269).
57. Krantz (1992:53).
58. Meldrum (1999).
59. Napier (1974:123).
60. Coleman (2003:128).
61. Hunter and Dahinden (1975:159–165).
62. Hunter and Dahinden (1975:168–170).
63. Hunter and Dahinden (1975:170).
64. Hunter and Dahinden (1975:163–170).
65. Krantz (1984:131–133).
66. Napier (1974:121).
67. Krantz (1999:298). Meldrum differs from Krantz in his interpretation of the "double-ball" seen in Bigfoot tracks. The significance of the double-ball is explored in chapter 6.
68. This is stated in Meldrum's presentation of his 1999 abstract.
69. Dennett (1994).
70. Dennett (1994:504).
71. Tachdjian (1990:2678). This image was reprinted in Daegling (2002).
72. Gatesy et al. (1999); this is dealt with further in chapter 6.
73. Daegling (2002).
74. Fahrenbach (1998).
75. Daegling (2002:37).
76. Hunter and Dahinden (1975:154).
77. Hunter and Dahinden (1975:156).
78. Krantz (1992:43); Hunter and Dahinden (1975:154–155).
79. I know of no Bigfoot investigator who considers the Bossburg film—or any other movies under Marx's direction—to be authentic images of Bigfoot. Even so, nobody has gone on record to state categorically that Marx faked the film. Of Marx's film exploits, Daniel Perez (2000c) noted dryly: "The Bigfoot community, however, was less than impressed with the movie footages."
80. Wylie (1980:211) mistakenly reports Colville as a California town.
81. Byrne (personal communication, October 21, 2003) clarified that the dump where the Sasquatch left its sign was not located in Bossburg itself.
82. In an interview with KXLY-TV in Pullman, Washington, in August 1992, Krantz said of the Bossburg tracks "I finally decided if somebody faked that and put all these subtle hints of the anatomy design in that, he had to be a real genius, an expert in

anatomy, and very inventive and original thinking. He had to outclass me in those areas and I don't think anybody outclasses me in those areas, at least not since Leonardo da Vinci, and I'm told such person, I'd say, is impossible, therefore the tracks are real." This quote appears with permission from KXLY Broadcast Group, Spokane, WA.

83. Gordon (1992:26) in the *Field Guide to the Sasquatch* suggests that the idea of fabrication of the Bossburg tracks is "absurd."

84. Dennett (1989).

85. Krantz (1999:79).

86. Dahinden (1984) and Dennett (1989:266–268).

87. Dahinden, in his May 4, 1996, Sasquatch Symposium presentation in Harrison Hot Springs, BC. In a letter to me (March 6, 1997), Dahinden confirmed that Wasson believed the tracks were faked.

88. Dennett (1994:502).

89. Dennett (1994:502).

90. Personal communication via audiotape, February 20, 1996.

91. Presentation at the Sasquatch Symposium in Harrison Hot Springs, BC, May 5, 1996.

92. Dennett (1989:267).

93. Personal correspondence, October 21, 2003; the exact date of this interaction is not known.

94. Personal correspondence, October 21, 2003.

95. Krantz's support for Freeman and his discoveries is articulated in his 1992 book *Big Footprints.* Meldrum has featured some of Freeman's discoveries in his 1999 and 2002 poster presentations at the annual meetings of the American Association of Physical Anthropologists. He also argued in favor of a set of tracks Freeman led him to in February 1996; he presented this argument at the 1996 Sasquatch Symposium in Harrison Hot Springs, BC, May 5, 1996. Meldrum also presents this discovery of Freeman's in a favorable light in his review of Vance Orchard's *Bigfoot of the Blues.*

96. Dennett (1989:264).

97. Dennett (1989:270–271).

98. Dennett (1989:271).

99. 1996 Sasquatch Symposium in Harrison Hot Springs, BC, May 5, 1996. Meldrum also argued the point at some length in postings on the Internet Virtual Bigfoot Conference, January 6, 1997 (the URL is no longer active).

100. Dennett (1994:505).

101. Krantz (1992:82).

102. E-mail correspondence, June 12, 2002.

103. Krantz (1992:82).

104. Personal communication, May 1, 1999, and in his May 5, 1996, talk at the Sasquatch Symposium in Harrison Hot Springs, BC.

105. Krantz (1992:49). See Krantz (1977c) for his anatomical interpretation of Sasquatch handprints.

106. René Dahinden revealed this in a 1994 talk at the Sasquatch Symposium in Harrison Hot Springs, BC.

107. Dennett (1994:501).

108. Perez (2003b); Dennett (2003).

109. E-mail correspondence from Michael Dennett, July 21, 2002.

110. Dennett (1989). In an e-mail to the author (April 9, 1999), Dennett said that Freeman denied ever working for a specialty shoe company (Dennett cited two anonymous sources in his 1989 story who indicated otherwise). When Dennett asked Freeman if he would agree to release his U.S. government file on employment history, Freeman declined to do so.

111. Meldrum opined in his May 5, 1996 Sasquatch Symposium talk that Freeman did not know "squat" about foot anatomy.

112. Krantz (1983).

113. Dahinden (1984); Dennett (1989, 1994).

114. He repeated this assertion in his review of Orchard's 1993 book *Bigfoot of the Blues*, posted on Bobbie Short's website [http://www.n2.net/prey/Bigfoot/].

115. In personal correspondence (June 28, 1996), René Dahinden expressed his view that Freeman knew Meldrum was en route and that morning went out and "discovered" new Sasquatch tracks.

116. Meldrum (2004); Leakey (1987).

117. Dennett (1989).

118. A letter from Meldrum to Ohio Bigfoot investigator Don Keating (September 4, 1996) outlines the arrangement. It is unclear whether the transaction ever took place, although the Oregon Bigfoot website (http://www.oregonBigfoot.com/gallery.php, accessed March 14, 2004) states that it did.

119. See www.bfro.net.

120. Sasquatch: Legend Meets Science, 2003, Whitewolf Productions. The program aired initially on the Discovery Channel.

121. Idaho State University press release, October 23, 2000.

122. Stated in the video production Sasquatch: Legend Meets Science, 2003, Whitewolf Productions.

123. Coleman (2003:21).

124. See www.bfro.net/NEWS/BODYCAST/index.asp.

125. See www.bfro.net/NEWS/BODYCAST/expedition_details.asp.

126. This argument has enjoyed many incarnations. Peter Byrne invoked it in an *Ancient Mysteries* production for A&E television in 1994; Buckley (1984) and Krantz (1992) also discuss the idea.

127. Radford (2002:31).

128. Sasquatch: Legend Meets Science (2003, Whitewolf Productions).

129. E-mail exchange between Ben Radford and BFRO founding member Matt Moneymaker from March 11, 2002, to June 11, 2002. Moneymaker's reason given to Radford is disingenuous; postings from December 1, 2003–December 5, 2003 to the Bigfoot Information Project's online *Bigfoot Forums* (www.Bigfootforums.com) establish that others without scientific credentials have been allowed to view the cast. Specifically, Bigfoot investigator George Karras notes that he saw the cast even though he has no particular expertise for analyzing it.

130. Personal correspondence from René Dahinden, December 19, 1995, and on the BFRO website (http://www.bfro.net/REF/hoax.asp).

131. Hubbell (1999).

132. Dennett (1994:507).

133. See www.angelfire.com/biz/Bigfootcentral.

134. Don Keating, who believes he may have filmed a Sasquatch in Ohio, subscribes to the elk explanation in an interview dated August 26, 2003 (www.Bigfootinfo.org/), as does Todd Neiss, an advocate by virtue of his sighting of three Sasquatches at one time (Perez 2003e).

135. Personal communication, April 28, 2003. See also Perez (2003a).

136. Barcott (2002).

5

The Patterson Film

The one piece of Bigfoot evidence that deserves consideration on its own merits is the film made by Roger Patterson on October 20, 1967. On this bright autumn afternoon, Patterson took about a minute's worth of footage of a bipedal creature along the banks of Bluff Creek in northern California. Whether a real Sasquatch or a person in a clever costume forms the grainy imprint on the celluloid, it is remarkable film.

The film is less than a minute long, and as a piece of wildlife photography the quality may be charitably described as poor. It is easy to understand why: Patterson was no nature photographer by any stretch of the imagination. He rented the Kodak 16 mm camera without knowing much more than the basics of its operation, and when the moment of filming Bigfoot arrived, he did not get a good look at his subject until it was perhaps 80 feet away from him. But he did get on film what he and his partner, Bob Gimlin, had come to see.

Most people seeing the film for the first time get the impression that something very odd is going on. The camera stays still only momentarily in a few instances during the encounter; the rest of the film is punctuated by a series of wild jerks and pans recording Patterson's pursuit of his quarry. When Patterson did manage to steady his hand somewhat, the gait of the film subject is apparent, and it is not the walk of a typical human pedestrian. The body is thickset, although not unrecognizable as a human form. The most widely circulated frame of the film shows the subject turning its head and massive shoulders toward the camera, facing it with an indecipherable expression as no detail of its physiognomy is clear. The film ends with the subject, now at a great distance from Patterson, continuing to walk decidedly yet unhurriedly into the forest.

Every Bigfoot buff remembers seeing the film for the first time. I was living in the Bay Area at the time and got to see it on television in an advertisement imploring me to get down to the local theater and see the whole thing on the big screen. For some Bigfoot aficionados, seeing the film would literally change their lives. Understandably, it created a huge stir in the Bigfoot community and aroused public interest as never before. Indeed, in the Bigfoot universe, things have never been the same since. It is arguable that had this movie never been made, the legend of Bigfoot would have ended up on the junkheap of American folklore, remembered but no longer embraced as a worthwhile legend. But the film was greeted with a substantial amount of press initially, and it became clear in the long run that if the film could survive critical scrutiny, it was destined to be the evidential anchor for Bigfoot. Media interest in the film persists, as Bigfoot documentaries replay the film several times a year on cable television. True believers still cling to the film as the most credible indication that something is out there, since at this writing thirty-six years have passed and definitive proof of a hoax has not surfaced.

How did Patterson and his partner happen to be in Bluff Creek on that particular afternoon? Their plan all along was to head down to the area from their homes in Yakima, Washington, to do a documentary film on Bigfoot.[1] This admission has struck the more cynical skeptics as more than just a little suspicious: renting a camera for the singular purpose of capturing Bigfoot on film and succeeding in short order is awfully lucky.[2] But in fairness, Patterson and Gimlin were not bushwhacking their way randomly through the forests. They had targeted the area because of its history of Bigfoot activity and—more specifically—there had been a rash of footprint discoveries the previous summer.[3] Anybody who knew anything about Bigfoot knew this was the place to look. Another common misperception is that the two men arrived in the area, made the film more or less immediately on making it into the drainage, and were off again in a matter of a day or two. It is more accurate to say that they were there a week before having their monster encounter.[4] Patterson's interest in Bigfoot was at least in part commercial: he wanted to make a lot of money on the film. Dahinden would always regard Patterson's success with some circumspection, since he knew Patterson's modus operandi: "with him it had to be a million bucks or nothing."[5] Patterson did have a genuine interest in the possibility of a monster unknown to science, but Bigfoot's allure for him was undoubtedly also financial. He had chronicled some of the more fantastic antics of Bigfoot in his 1966 book *Do Abominable Snowmen of America Really Exist?* This was a book designed to sell rather than educate—it wasn't pretending to be a balanced consideration of the evidence. It was a promotion.

In fact, the book foreshadows the film. Patterson himself illustrated the book, and his drawings—revealing considerable artistic talent—show the details that would eventually be seen in his film a year later. Of course, we can interpret this two ways: Patterson's film captured a real Sasquatch that reflected remarkably the details provided in previous eyewitness accounts, or Patterson knew what kind of creature would make a convincing Sasquatch. Patterson's capable artistry in 1966 is no proof of a 1967 hoax, but one cannot argue that the image captured on film was beyond anyone's imagination at the time.

The book didn't do very well in terms of sales, and Patterson, like everyone else, knew a film was going to generate a lot more interest than a mere book. The film itself was packaged for popular consumption by inserting it within a short feature on Bigfoot, which included footage of Patterson searching the drainage for signs of the creature. An outfit out of Salt Lake City called American National Enterprises distributed the film through one of their subsidiaries, Rainbow Adventure Films.[6]

The short feature had a very brief run playing to curious audiences (the extent of its distribution is, over three decades after the fact, uncertain), but for years the scientific community paid little attention. Certainly there was nothing resembling an institutional response to the film—as a group, scientists appeared, for the most part, rather uninterested. The few scientists who would speak for the record were blunt in their opinions.[7] The film was not going to rouse the curiosity of the universities for the same reason photographs of ghosts today do not prompt the formation of academic divisions devoted to the study of poltergeists. Science as an institution had its mind made up regarding Bigfoot before the Patterson film. It was part legend, part hoax, and the details did not matter. What was on the film was of no consequence to that conclusion. The film had to be a fake because there was no such thing as Bigfoot. Bigfoot enthusiasts felt stunned by the wholesale disinterest—even a cool reception to the film would have been welcome, since then there would be at least a grudging acknowledgment that something was going on.

There is some truth to the frequent charge in the Bigfoot literature that scientists would not touch the film simply because to be associated with Bigfoot was tantamount to academic suicide, unless you were approaching the subject from the perspective of a clinical psychologist. Eventually, however, some highly respected scientists with ample credentials would look at the film, study the details, and render a judgment. The film did not look like a cheap hoax afterward.

EARLY VERDICTS

John Napier, the world-renowned anthropologist, locomotion expert, and student of human evolution, broke with the ambivalence of his peers with his publication of *Bigfoot: The Yeti and Sasquatch in Myth and Reality* in 1972. Napier took a hard look at the Patterson film as well as the rest of the compendium of Bigfoot evidence. One could have hardly recommended a more qualified critic. A first-rate anatomist, Napier had published classic articles on human locomotion in the scientific literature. Napier dissected the film, blurry stride by blurry stride, examined all the information that could be had, and decided that, on balance, the footprints, the subject's stature, and its gait did not add up to a natural event. His verdict: a hoax. Nevertheless, Napier remained troubled by the film; by his own admission, his confidence that the film was a put-on was not unshakable. Of his repeated viewings of the film he said: "I could not see the zipper, and I still can't."[8] The anthropological community's disinterest was thereby legitimized.

The wholesale inattention given to the film by zoologists, anthropologists, and the like only reinforced the Bigfoot seekers' suspicions that the scientific community would not confront the possibility of an unknown animal of such large size. It was an embarrassing topic, however one approached it: if there was anything to it, why were the "experts" so late at recognizing it, and if it was a sham, one did not dare risk a carefully cultivated academic reputation by slogging through the woods chasing monsters. Within the Ivory Tower, it is perfectly legitimate for a folklorist to pursue unicorns; for a biologist, it is a foolish commitment of resources. Napier was a special case in that his professional reputation was rock solid and internationally recognized. Few of his peers would openly question his consideration of Bigfoot publicly.

Even the dedicated pursuers of Bigfoot did not necessarily embrace the film uncritically. René Dahinden recalls that his initial reaction to it was a mix of skepticism and disappointment: "It was such a small thing running across the screen."[9] Dahinden figured sufficient scrutiny would reveal the zipper, some buttons, a tell-tale seam. But as he watched the film again and again, he slowly recognized that the movement of what he has since referred to as "the creature" was decidedly unlike that of a striding person. In addition, there were details that one might not expect to find on a dime-store gorilla costume. Pendulous breasts? Muscles rippling with every powerful step? These were not features that were stock-in-trade in the costume shops of the 1960s. It *looked* like a real animal; did Patterson and Gimlin have the expertise to put this monster together? Dahinden did not consider Patterson a sophisticated man, at least not one who had either the expertise or the connections required to parade a creature like that in front of the camera. Dahinden was never 100% convinced the film was real, but he began to doubt seriously that the principals involved had the wherewithal to manufacture that particular film star.[10] Eventually, Dahinden tacitly endorsed the film when he purchased a share of the rights to it.[11]

By 1971, Dahinden had become fed up with the summary dismissal of the film by U.S. and Canadian scientists and he quite literally took the show on the road to the Old World where he hoped the film could be viewed without prejudice.[12] He was not entirely disappointed. Two stops on his tour, London and Moscow, were particularly noteworthy. Dr. D. W. Grieve, an anatomist with expertise in human biomechanics at the Royal Free Hospital School of Medicine, viewed the film repeatedly and offered a written report on his perspective as to the possibility that what was filmed was human or not.[13] That report highlighted another wrinkle in the saga of the film: at what speed was the movie taken?

The camera that Patterson had rented for recording the event was a Kodak K-100 16 mm camera. With this model it is possible to shoot at a variety of speeds ranging from 16 to 64 frames per second (fps).[14] Before the fateful encounter, Patterson had been shooting documentary footage of the area and had been filming at 24 fps. Checking the camera sometime after the excitement of the encounter, Patterson reports that the speed settings had been switched—to 16 fps. At what point the switch occurred, Patterson confessed, he did not know. The favored speculation among Bigfoot enthusiasts is that it happened at the moment Bigfoot stood up from its position by the creek and Patterson's horse startled and reared. As Patterson first spied his quarry, he reached into his saddlebag and pulled the camera out, without the usual care with which one would handle expensive equipment, and it is proposed that at this time the film speed was inadvertently switched.[15]

This seems a plausible scenario until the particulars of the model camera used are considered. Daniel Perez, in his self-published *Bigfoot at Bluff Creek*, notes that the construction of the camera is such that changing film speeds requires a very deliberate and specific action by the operator and is not likely to occur accidentally with, for example, wrestling the camera from its enclosure. Perez also effectively demolishes a second argument for determining film speed. Grover Krantz argued that by estimating the periods of swing of the film subject's arms and legs (he assumes these are constant for a given stature), one can confidently determine the film speed. Krantz concluded that this and other evidence points to the unavoidable conclusion that the film speed at the moment Bigfoot was filmed was 18 fps. Krantz's method of uncovering the "true" film speed apparently settles the issue.[16] There remains, Perez notes, a not insubstantial problem, however: this particular speed setting does not exist on the model camera in question.[17]

Why does film speed matter? Grieve couched his conclusions in terms of qualification about this variable.[18] Different camera speeds will affect estimates of subject kinematics (details of body movements through time) and subject speed. Human locomotion has a particular cadence to it, one that can be measured, quantified, and applied to other sources of data to see if they conform to a human pattern. What Grieve had to work with was a film of uncertain speed and information about the film subject's course of travel that had been measured—estimated, really—months after the actual event. Dahinden had pieced together what he could from landmarks on the film (trees, fallen logs) to estimate where the "creature" had walked over the creek bed. He measured everything that could be seen on the film and that was still recognizable at the film site.[19] What he didn't have were the footprints—the details of those had long been eroded away by rain, wind, and perhaps by some of the curious seekers who preceded his arrival. His estimate of the course of the film subject was probably close to what it had been, but it was far from exact, and Dahinden never pretended otherwise. The data Grieve had to analyze were therefore less than ideal.

What Grieve ended up doing was to take Dahinden's film site data at face value—he would assume, for the sake of argument, that the data were completely accurate. Rather than choose, based on little more than speculation, that one film speed was more likely than the other, he essentially evaluated the various possibilities. He came to two very distinct conclusions. If the film was shot at 16 fps, Grieve opined, then the movements of the film subject were completely incompatible with the human model with which he was familiar. On the other hand, he reasoned, a film speed of 24 fps revealed a film subject that certainly could be a human in a costume, but it was a person moving awfully fast in that case. Either way, Grieve's conclusions did not have the ring of unwavering skepticism that René had come to expect from an academic veteran. Grieve himself confessed to being perplexed and unsettled—not so much at the film—but at what it represented, given the tangible possibility that it was real.[20]

Dahinden's travels would also take him to Moscow, where the film played to the warmest reception it would ever enjoy in academic circles. The reason was hardly obscure: the Moscow Academy of Sciences boasted its own Institute of Hominology, which had as one of its aims the discovery of relict populations of what convention deemed "extinct" hominid forms. The ringleaders of the group consisted of Victor Porshnev, a professor of history, and two individuals schooled in biomechanics, Dmitri Bayanov and Dmitri Donskoy.[21] The group's response to the film was less measured than Napier's or Grieve's. To them, Patterson had filmed an unknown animal, and that fact bolstered their own convictions about strange human-like creatures residing in the remote and not-so-remote reaches of the Soviet Union. Donskoy gave his own assessment of the film, reprinted in numerous Bigfoot books and now viewable all over cyberspace. His assessment of the film was firm: this massive, muscular beast moved with a fluidity and strength that represented a real creature.[22] Donskoy could not be bothered to fiddle with the calculations that Grieve and Napier had made, his biomechanical eye saw something that made sense for a massive creature rather than a guy in a costume. Donskoy's pronouncements were welcomed in the community of Bigfoot seekers, but even this endorsement did not make inroads with the U.S. scientific establishment.

Donskoy's conviction seems born of faith rather than any particular observation of incontrovertible fact. His report is thoroughly subjective and devoid of any particulars of argument. His observation that "[t]he gait of the creature is confident, the strides are regular, no signs of loss of balance, of wavering or any redundant movements are visible"[23] hardly serves as a demonstration of validity—it corresponds to a walking person as much as to a hypothetical Bigfoot. Dahinden had managed to get a handful of experts to look at the film, but mainstream science would not get involved beyond the odd academic viewing, followed by reflexive dismissal.

Validating the film has been a frustrating enterprise for the Bigfoot advocates. The only legitimate way to prove the film is of a real Sasquatch is to demonstrate beyond any doubt that what Patterson filmed was beyond the ability of human fabrication. Research on the film has invariably, and correctly, taken this approach. If the film could not have been faked, then why listen to the skeptics?

One of the first arguments on the authenticity of the film was advanced by John Green.[24] Green noted that despite the poor image quality, you could see things on the film subject that seemed to rule out the possibility that Patterson and Gimlin had invested a few dollars in a gorilla costume. Whatever walked in front of that camera had bouncing breasts and displayed muscular movement beneath the skin. Most acquaintances of Patterson volunteered that neither he nor Gimlin were clever enough to put something that detailed together. John Green and Peter Byrne took the argument one step further. Who was talked to when is not exactly clear, but the film (or perhaps a copy) made its way to Disney Studios in Hollywood where the experts in house were asked, in some fashion, whether the film was real or not.[25] What the experts told Peter Byrne was that they didn't have the ability to duplicate the film with their technology.

It is very important to remember the date of the film. In 1967, we were still a few years away from *Planet the Apes* and *2001: A Space Odyssey*. Ape and monster costumes were not very sophisticated and apparently hard to come by (the same hokey gorilla costume recycled its way through such memorable shows as *Star Trek* and *Voyage to the Bottom of the Sea*).[26] While it is really impossible to discern the finer details of the Patterson film subject, it is not unreasonable to suggest that it is better than some of the tackier monster outfits that got thrown together for television at the time.

The types of special effects we enjoy today at the movies, where any image can be seamlessly matted into another, were not fully developed in 1967. In his quest to authenticate the film, Green offered the film for analysis to Canawest Films, Ltd.[27] The technicians there firmly concluded that what was filmed at Bluff Creek that day was, in fact, plodding through the sand—no trick of the trade available at the time could have dropped the walking Sasquatch into the autumn scene from the studio. What we see on the film was there.

The details of the conversation with the Disney techies become very important here, but we don't have transcripts of these. Disney was then, and still is, known as one of the pioneers in animation. The form of the question put to the Disney officials is critical. The questions "Could you produce this scene in animated form?" or "Could you go out in the woods and produce these images?" are very different in their implications. In the first case, the answer of "no" simply means that special effects could not fabricate that scene. In the second, it would mean that they could not have accomplished what Patterson had with all their resources. The critical question is whether a person or a machine could have been the entity filmed that day. What the Disney people said was that if faced with the task of making a Bigfoot feature, they would rather draw one than build one.[28]

It is safe to say that the robotics of the time were not up to the task, even if Patterson had procured millions to bankroll the job (René Dahinden unapologetically probed Patterson's personal affairs subsequent to the film and concluded Patterson had virtually no financial resources at the time[29]). That leaves the possibility that we have a man or a woman in a costume parading through the forest. A great deal has been made about whether a hoaxer would have been in on the job with Patterson and Gimlin or whether someone decided to put one over on the two seekers. For evaluating the film on its own merits, it is inconsequential. The possibility of someone hoaxing Patterson and Gimlin has been described as "literally impossible,"[30] on the grounds that the hoaxer would have put his life in imminent danger, given the two Bigfoot hunters' habit of carrying firearms with them. On the other hand, Patterson was on record as saying he was not going shoot a Sasquatch except in self-defense.[31] Who would be stupid enough to entrust two excitable thrillseekers to hold their fire in the event of an encounter with a monster? This is a fair rhetorical question, except that it ignores the possibility that the third party was an accomplice. That, too, is mere speculation. More ink has been devoted to character analyses of Patterson and Gimlin[32] than to the film itself, and many advocates use a peculiar logical algebra to support the film's authenticity: Patterson was too unskilled to have produced such a hoax, and Gimlin was too honest to be part of one.

THE FILMMAKERS EXAMINED

There is one aspect of motivation that seems beyond dispute: Patterson was in the Bigfoot enterprise for fame and fortune, apparently needing the latter more desperately.[33] Despite his energetic efforts in marketing the film, he did not make a killing financially. Bigfoot advocates emphasize that Patterson remained an active Bigfoot hunter up until his death in 1972 from Hodgkin's disease and that he never made another film of Bigfoot after 1967.

René Dahinden was no fan of Roger Patterson the person. Always suspicious under the best of circumstances, he was convinced by the Bossburg fiasco of 1969–1970 that Patterson was not to be trusted, when a bitter bidding war erupted over a trapped Bigfoot that no one ever saw. Dahinden subsequently dealt with Patterson for the same reason he engaged other Bigfoot hunters whom he disliked: his singular drive to solve the mystery compelled him to. Though he did not admire Patterson's modus operandi, he was impressed by the fact that, in his view, Patterson's recollection of the events leading up to and during the film remained consistent through countless retellings,[34] and no deathbed confession was forthcoming.[35] Patterson did say, after the reception to the film turned out to be less than rosy, that in retrospect he wished his rifle had done the shooting instead of the camera.[36]

For Dahinden, the film is the key to the whole Sasquatch mystery. It is safe to say that no one has thought more about the film in the thirty years since it was made. He has visited the film site on numerous occasions, toured overseas to show the film, and continued to encourage research into the film right up to his death in April 2001. That his efforts to spark scientific interest in the film were fruitless may have been the motivating force behind his relentless investigation of Patterson and his partner, the only living witness to the film, Bob Gimlin. This eyewitness has turned out to be the most celebrated of them all.

In Bob Gimlin, one could scarcely imagine a man more unlike Roger Patterson. His involvement in the Bigfoot phenomenon seems to be almost accidental; he hadn't been deeply involved in the search for Bigfoot before the movie was made and his role since has been his own endless accountings, generally consistent, of the events of that October afternoon. He returned to the forests of northern California in search of the creature in 1978,[37] but this venture was apparently uneventful and garnered no publicity. According to some, Gimlin is the piece of the puzzle that cinches the film's authenticity. The details differ somewhat depending on the teller, but it is certain that Gimlin never made any money to speak of from the film, and some accounts have him being squeezed out of any proceeds altogether.[38] The idea that he would be cut out of any royalties and elect to remain silent if the film were a hoax struck many advocates as too fantastic—ergo, the film is real. While this does not qualify as a scientific argument, it is worth noting that some of the most hardened skeptics speak of Gimlin in no less than glowing terms. Kenneth Wylie describes Gimlin as "almost too good to be true."[39] What Wylie referred to was his impression of Gimlin's remarkable transparency: the man was simply convinced that what he saw that afternoon in Bluff Creek was the real deal and yet seemed to be relatively unconcerned with the implication. This, Wylie surmised, was odd indeed: what makes the Bigfoot phenomenon so interesting is the life-changing nature of eyewitness encounters, but here is a man who participated in the most celebrated encounter of them all and he just didn't seem to care that much. Gimlin's indifference did not take the spotlight off him, though, and while he is somewhat reluctant to talk to the media,[40] he does make it to the occasional Bigfoot event.[41]

What light does Gimlin and his celebrated character shed on the film in particular or the idea of Bigfoot in general? Materially, he contributes nothing, if we truly embrace the principle that personal testimony alone is insufficient as scientific proof. What we can glean from the widespread admiration is that we cannot write off the phenomenon of the Sasquatch as the exclusive domain of showmen, eccentrics, and pranksters. Bigfoot "happened" to Gimlin and it seemed to bring him few rewards and abundant annoyance. Gimlin, it seems, never seriously entertained the possibility that he could have been hoaxed—he really thought what they caught on film was real.[42]

The two men's accounts of the event are generally comparable, although they differ is some details (Patterson thought the thing he filmed was 7 feet tall, Gimlin put it closer to 6).[43] The objection to their story that I've heard most frequently is not at all convoluted. In separate public talks on Bigfoot that I've given, I have been asked by university professors and eight-year-old children the same question: why didn't they just shoot the thing? Both men had rifles, and taking the creature's life would have settled the matter. The story goes, as I said, that both men had agreed not to shoot unless absolutely necessary if they eventually did have an encounter. As it happened, then, Gimlin had his rifle out and would have let fly if the beast attacked Patterson. But it didn't, and no shots were fired. "Patty" (the term of endearment for the film subject used by her more ardent supporters) walked off and Patterson and Gimlin had their film.

Take their story as you will, because whether true or not we will most likely never know. If Gimlin's sincerity is genuine, the account reveals two men who may have been incredibly naive in thinking that an amateur film would be sufficient to resolve the mystery. Perhaps Gimlin didn't shoot because "Mr. Sasquatch" may have been hanging around and wouldn't take kindly to the missus getting plugged. Alternatively, it is also plausible that they didn't shoot because it was their buddy who wears XXL from the Big & Tall Shop parading around the sandbar. Both explanations make sense in the context of the moment.

I have yet to correspond with anyone acquainted with Roger Patterson who thought he was above faking a film, but none of these people has ever suggested that Patterson faked anything in his years in the monster-hunting business. Is Patterson's reputation relevant to the issue? Ultimately, if the film's status is ever resolved, it will appear to be in retrospect. But for determining the film's authenticity, it alone cannot be decisive.

RUMORS OF HOAXES

The cult status of the Patterson film has provided endless fodder for the rumor mill. Several individuals have, at different times since 1967, either suggested that they were the fellow in the costume or that they knew who was. One of the more recent theories has appeared, appropriately it seems, in *Strange Magazine.* The editor of the periodical, Mark Chorvinsky, believes a Hollywood makeup artist named John Chambers was behind the hoax.[44] At first, the story's reliance on second- and third-hand sources appears to give it a weak foundation. The famous director John Landis "knew" about this, and every special effects guy Chorvinsky has spoken to attests to the film's bogus nature. Chambers had a closetful of costumes and monster suits, he worked on the Planet of the Apes films, he had been engaged in prior Bigfoot hoaxes—in other words, he is one man who at the time had the expertise to pull of a hoax of this nature.

What does Chambers say? Chorvinsky's initial reports related, regrettably (or perhaps conveniently), that Chambers was ailing and did not wish to be interviewed. In the past he had denied involvement, but in this tale of intrigue this denial only serves to encourage speculation that he has reasons to resist coming clean.

Bigfoot fans are, by and large, fairly easygoing folk, but the Patterson film is revered in the same way a patriot feels about the Constitution. Chorvinsky's story came out and it did not sit well, so Bobbie Short, a California Bigfoot investigator, decided to go straight to the source and managed to get an audience with Chambers. Chambers denied involvement, even going so far as to suggest that he could not have made the film costume.[45] How carefully he had ever studied the film and its subject is not clear. Chorvinsky has since argued that Chambers had an interest in not confessing, and correctly points out that the denial cannot settle the issue.[46] Chamber's death in August 2001 permitted correspondence between Chorvinsky and John Landis that had been "off the record" to become very much on the record. Landis had, apparently, been asked to clam up concerning Chamber's involvement—by Chambers himself—and respected his wishes. Chambers could not afford to have his role made public because, according to Landis, "I believe that he signed some kind of non-disclosure agreement."[47] No direct evidence exists that details any meeting of Patterson and Chambers, although Chorvinsky notes Patterson had made more than one trip to Los Angeles before making his film of Bigfoot. The readers are left to draw their own conclusion.

Chorvinsky claimed there were other connections to the Patterson film that deserved scrutiny as well. These were harder to dismiss and seemed circumstantially damning. In particular, the person of Ray Wallace had a degree of involvement that, for the skeptics at least, was more than a little interesting. Wallace, of course, claimed many Bigfoot encounters, from some of which he came away with photographic or cinematic evidence. The films and photos in terms of visual quality were no better or worse than your average Sasquatch portrait, but in the context of Wallace's colorful and fanciful narratives they never enjoyed wholesale endorsement. What Chorvinsky pointed out was that Wallace's presence in the Bluff Creek area had a pattern of association with Bigfoot activity. Chorvinsky's thesis was simple: Wallace was responsible for the legend. In connection to the film, Chorvinsky claims that sometime after Patterson arrived in Bluff Creek but before his famous encounter, he met with Ray Wallace. Patterson was making no secret of why he was there, and Wallace volunteered that there was a spot on the creek that was likely to provide a glimpse of Bigfoot.[48] That locality is, by Wallace's account, where the film was eventually shot.

Even skeptics familiar with the film and the events surrounding it are by and large unconvinced by the various and frequent claims of the hoaxer confessing.

The published accounts might name names and provide some tantalizing details of the nature of the "monkey suit" (ranging from a bearhide patchwork[49] to a revamped monster suit from the *Lost in Space* television series[50]), but in the end none of them answer an obviously critical question: can the hoaxer be placed at Bluff Creek on October 20, 1967? None of the claimants has yet to establish this, even if Ray Wallace could have sent them to the right spot. As I write this, a furor is erupting over the claim that one Bob Heironimus of Yakima, Washington, was the costumed figure that Patterson filmed (the circumstances are detailed in Greg Long's *The Making of Bigfoot*).[51] The rebuttal from the advocate camp has been predictable: it can't be true because no costume could be that good, the beast is too large and its arms are too long to be a person, and the walk is too bizarre for a human to adopt. Whether history proves Heironimus of Yakima right, we will see that this argument in defense of the film is wrong.

The question of why all these people claim to be involved is hardly mysterious. We are dealing with a central feature of the Bigfoot phenomenon: it provides a relatively safe means by which to get attention. Making up stories about Bigfoot doesn't ostensibly hurt anyone—the worst injury it imposes is some irritation. The same is not true about making up stories about your neighbors or the sheriff; those fabrications could get you sued or even sent up the river. When it comes to Bigfoot, generally the worst that can happen is that you'll be called a liar or a nut. But you will have had your fifteen minutes of fame.

There have been many more declarations that the film is fake than there have been arguments accompanying them. "It's a man in a fur suit" is not much in the way of a detailed rebuttal of the film, yet it is the most frequently encountered summation of the film by the more skeptical scientists who have viewed it. This terse evaluation should not strike us as surprising. It may be unsatisfactory, but it is perfectly consistent with the view that since the animal does not exist, the only other possibility is that some joker was having a good laugh out in the woods.

It is interesting that the negative opinions expressed about the film's authenticity have been propped up by rather vague points of argument. Kenneth Wylie's chief complaint was that the suit looked "baggy,"[52] while others have remarked on the "exaggerated"[53] gait of the film's star. These observations might be key to deciphering what is on the film, but these points need a more developed argument to make a persuasive case for human agency. Once again, without a more detailed line of reasoning, you can have these observations both ways. One man's "baggy suit" is another's "mat of hair overlying the buttocks." The "self-conscious" walk so clear on the film can be just as easily be phrased as a gait "absolutely nontypical of man."[54] The skeptics have not felt compelled to offer much of a detailed argument against the film; the burden of proof, rightly enough, should lie with the advocates. As this has been the case, however, the film has not gone away.

THE FACTS OF CONTEXT

There are innumerable accounts of the context of the film in the Bigfoot literature and those accounts are loaded with inconsistencies. In my view, the best source for details of the film and events surrounding it can be found in *Bigfoot at Bluff Creek*, a special edition of Daniel Perez's idiosyncratic periodical *Bigfoot Times*. Perez writes in a careening, shoot-from-the-hip style with frequent jaunts into hyperbole, but he is in some respects an ideal Bigfoot researcher because he takes few statements as given and is not above calling his colleagues liars if the facts don't jibe. Perez interviewed many of the principals involved in the aftermath of the film and published his report in 1992 to commemorate the twenty-fifth anniversary of the film. While Perez has lingering questions about some of the events surrounding the film,[55] he is unapologetically supportive.[56] In essence, Perez rhetorically threw down the gauntlet, marshalling the facts at hand to argue that after a quarter-century, the film was no closer to being proven a hoax than the day after it was made. At the same time, two comprehensive analyses of the film were emerging from credentialed scientists in the 1990s that would add teeth to Perez's thesis that the film deserved a closer look.

Bigfoot advocates have lamented that very little scientific study of the film has been undertaken. They are by and large correct, although there have been a smattering of such investigations since the film was made. These consisted of little more than qualitative assessments, ranging from Donskoy's uncritical acceptance based on the natural appearance of the subject to Napier's consternation over a peculiar combination of features defining the alleged Bigfoot. Up until 1992, a more appropriate complaint would have been that there had been no scientific efforts directed at the film that took up the issue from a purely quantitative (and ostensibly objective) standpoint. That is, the simplest way to solve the film is to measure how big the Bigfoot was, how long its steps were, how fast it was going, and, in effect, establish whether or not a human being could duplicate the dimensions and kinematics of the film subject. If the Bigfoot is too large to accommodate a human form—if it is walking too fast for a person and its gait is demonstrably nonhuman—then questions of Patterson's motives, Gimlin's complicity, and Ray Wallace's advice become completely irrelevant. This strategy was never lost on Bigfoot enthusiasts; the problem was that few of them had the expertise to extract the necessary data from the film. What was needed was somebody with expertise in anatomy and forensic sciences who could extract some objective measurements. Two such scientists would study the film in this fashion and come to a startling conclusion in separate publications in the 1990s. Neither argument would survive critical scrutiny.

Before we examine these studies, however, a digression on what we know and what we don't know about the film is in order. The location and time of the film check out—the film was made approximately when and exactly where it was claimed to have happened. Tracks were photographed and cast sometime around that time. Gimlin had a tape measure with him, and they measured 14.5 inches in length, with an average of 41 inches between prints.[57] The approximate course of travel of the film subject is known, the exact course of travel is not.[58] The film speed used at the time of filming is not known; the subject's speed is therefore uncertain.

The film is of poor quality. This is not a "fact," of course, but the following observation is: the size of the subject on the film itself does not exceed 2 mm in any frame.[59] This makes for a blurry image that is exacerbated in many frames by movement of the camera, which is never absolutely still. It is possible that a better-quality film of the scene that transpired would have settled the issue of authenticity rather quickly, but the strong positions taken by skeptics and advocates alike suggest that this is only wishful thinking.

The success of any attempts at data extraction from the film depends critically on the ability of the researcher to reconstruct several variables from the Bluff Creek site. These are variables of location: where the camera was and where the Bigfoot walked. When the historical circumstances of the film's aftermath are considered, it becomes clear that the determination of these apparently simple facts is fraught with problems. Torrential rains soaked Patterson and Gimlin the night after their encounter, prompting them to hightail it out of the drainage. They had apparently had the foresight to pick up some cardboard to cover the tracks when they returned from going into a nearby town to send the film out for processing earlier that evening.[60] It is surprising to many, and troubling to some, that when Bob Titmus arrived at Bluff Creek a week later, the tracks were described as being well preserved—sufficiently so that Titmus was essentially able to map the encounter as it unfolded the week before. The map clearly indicates that the bulk of the tracks were made within the margins of the creekbed, which prompted Ken Wylie to ask rhetorically: given the storm after the film, wouldn't this pathway have been subject to some erosion given its exposure to the elements?[61]

What happened in the weeks and even years after the film was to prove critical. The serious Bigfoot hunters would all make pilgrimages to the film site and collectively they began to recognize that it was going to be essential to reconstruct the precise circumstances of the filming to be able to judge the movie on its own merits. Data independent of the original film had to be collected. The quality of that data would determine the scientific value of the film. The labor that went into this data collection was considerable, but delays and oversights compromised the quality of data. In terms of reconstructing exactly what did happen, the film would be doomed.

Gimlin measured some of the prints and the distance between them the afternoon of the filming. He and Patterson cast some of the tracks. Bob Titmus would arrive to examine the film site on October 29, at which point he found an abundance of tracks remaining from the encounter. He made casts of ten consecutive prints and mapped the film site to reconstruct the details of the encounter. With footprints still visible, this map would provide essential data if and when the film was analyzed to determine quantitative parameters of the film. There was, however, a problem: Titmus mapped the site without the aid of a tape measure or yardstick.[62] The best he could have managed under the circumstances was an approximation of what had happened. Daniel Perez says that "Titmus' measurement, I am sure, was probably just a repeat or echo of what Roger Patterson told him when they met in Canada when the film was first shown in a public forum."[63]

In the summer of 1968, John Green visited the film site and performed the first quantitative reconstruction of the encounter. With him was Jim McClarin, who had been to the film site previously on November 5, 1967, and claimed the route of the subject remained clear from the residual tracks.[64] Green filmed McClarin as a comparative Sasquatch in an ingenious attempt to figure the original subject's size by superimposing his 1968 film on the 1967 original.[65] Fortuitously, the background of the original film contained trees in sharp contrast to the denser forest behind, and the foreground also contained high-contrast detritus in the creek bed. Green found it a small matter to position his camera so that the back and foregrounds matched up with the images from the previous autumn. By the time of Green's arrival, however, only a few residual depressions of some of the cast footprints remained, and no trace of the Bigfoot's passing was visible over the area of the critical part of the film.[66] Retracing the path of the original subject was therefore based largely on McClain's memory of his visit several months before. While Green obtained a film that bears a surprising resemblance to the original, he admits that lining up the films precisely is, in his words, a "fussy business," and that "there is little likelihood that Jim walked exactly where the Sasquatch walked."[67]

There would be other, more involved attempts to establish the dimensions of the film site in the hopes of eventually determining the dimensions of the film star. By the time René Dahinden first got to the film site in 1969 and Peter Byrne went in 1972, all traces of the original encounter were gone.[68] Even so, Dahinden would map the film site exhaustively in the hope that the information would some day become relevant; he would end up visiting the site over half a dozen times. On one occasion, Dahinden timed the people with him as they walked his reconstructed path of the film subject in an attempt to resolve the issue of speed—both of the alleged Bigfoot and the film in the camera.[69] Peter Byrne would revisit John Green's strategy of lining up images and having a subject retrace Bigfoot's path; he had his subject holding a measuring rod to ease calibration of the two images. Like Green, Byrne willingly admits that the precise positioning of cameraman and film subject could not be determined.[70] While Dahinden's and Byrne's data collection were another step removed from the original event, there was ostensibly a body of data from different sources that could resolve some things about the film. By 1992, when the first serious scientific study of the film was being published, the film site was overgrown to the extent that it was unrecognizable as the place of the 1967 film.

THE FILM IS ANALYZED

Grover Krantz went firmly on record and declared the Patterson film genuine in his 1992 book *Big Footprints*. Krantz was not the first anthropologist to consider the film (nor was this his first public comment on the subject), but this was, some twenty-five years after the fact, the first endorsement supported by a systematic dissection of it. Krantz examined the film frame by frame and offered two specific arguments in favor of the film's authenticity.[71] First, he argued that the body proportions of the film subject are outside the range of human populations and could not be achieved using a human in a costume. He also argued that the gait is sufficiently distinct from that of living humans to dismiss the possibility that a person could reproduce the movements of the film subject.

Krantz based his size estimates for the film subject from two independently known parameters, foot length (determined from prints and casts) and stride length (measured by Gimlin after the event). He also argues that there is a known quantity from the film itself, that being the distance of the camera to the subject in one of the film's more celebrated frames. Krantz's source for this is the map drawn by Titmus a week after filming, which, we recall, is one in which we can have little confidence as far as accuracy is concerned. Nevertheless, Krantz uses the Titmus reconstruction and his own reading of the movement of the subject in the film itself to draw his *own* map of the proceedings, which differs from the Titmus original in several respects. It is exceedingly unlikely that his specified distance of Patterson to the erstwhile Bigfoot is accurate for the frame in question; fortunately, Krantz needed this parameter as a check on only one of his measurements, so it is not crucial for most of his analysis. It does, however, betray a confidence in reconstructing the filming environment that is far too optimistic (see fig. 5.1).

Sparing the reader the details of calculation and computation (these are detailed fully in his 1992 book), Krantz has the subject's walking height perhaps a shade above 6 feet (given the subject's slightly stooped posture; standing the beast bolt-upright might add as much as 6 inches) and on this metric alone the film subject is obviously not inhuman in size. The body proportions, say Krantz, are entirely a different matter. This part of Krantz's analysis (which relies heavily on the original accuracy of the Titmus map) yields an interesting result. The height of the creature is within the human range, but the width of the chest (over 18 inches across), given that height, is completely unexpected. This finding seemed to embolden Krantz to the point that a hoax was now completely out of the question: "I can confidently state that no man of such stature is built that broadly."[72]

FIGURE 5.1
The Bluff Creek film site in August 2001. The clearing over which Patterson's Bigfoot walked in 1967 is largely overgrown. The original context of the film is no longer recoverable from the site itself, compromising any attempts to reconstruct the events of the film. Photo by Daniel Perez, used with permission.

That should settle the issue, it would seem. Two issues demand our attention. The first is whether Krantz's reconstruction of the positions of Patterson and Bigfoot were accurate: it is a fair question especially considering that he never visited the film site.[73] He had no way of knowing the accuracy of the Titmus map. The second issue is whether Krantz's confident assertion should be taken at face value. He was a credentialed anthropologist after all, who knew quite a bit about human variation and anatomy.

It was a slow afternoon in New Haven when I decided, for lack of anything better to do, that I would verify this claim. I headed off to Yale's Science Library and began searching various databases. Having found what I wanted, I spent a few minutes in the stacks tracking down the *Anthropometry Sourcebook*, a thick book containing a comprehensive assortment of measurements on the human body from a number of populations. Pulling the large volume off the shelf, I found statistics on height and a measurement called the "interscye," which is an armpit-to-armpit measurement and gives you an idea of how wide a individual's chest is. Conveniently, this measurement is taken across the back, in the same way that Krantz was compelled to measure it on the film since the subject was heading away from the camera. For this variable, I had before me a set of data on over one thousand individuals, not a very big sample compared to all the people running around but big enough to establish how bizarrely Patty was shaped. I was astonished in poring over the tables, but not because it was dawning on me that a flesh and blood Bigfoot had been caught on film. Instead, I was dumbfounded that Krantz, who was a respected scientist at a major research university, could have been so sloppy in making such a bold claim. If no human existed of the dimensions Krantz gives, then about 5% of members of the German Air Force were in need of zoological reclassification.[74] The "impossible" dimensions of the film subject were anything but. The numbers were clear: if that was a Sasquatch, then it had the body proportions that can be found in people walking around today. I left the library considerably annoyed and I became deeply skeptical of the remainder of Krantz's argument.

What remained of that argument was the subject's gait. Anyone who has seen the film notices that this isn't the look of an average person out for a stroll. The subject doesn't have much of a bounce to the step, the knees flex excessively, and the hip does not extend behind the body quite as much as what one is used to seeing. The most concise way to describe it is as an understated Groucho walk from an old Marx Brothers' movie. We are not witnessing on the film a typical human stride. Krantz took this observation one step further; he suggested that the motions of Patty could not be imitated by a person—any person.[75] It was not the first time a scientist had claimed the locomotion seen on the film was not that of a human form. But my recent experience with the reliability of Krantz's confident assertions compelled me to investigate further.

On this point, however, I was out of my league. While I have a basic understanding of primate locomotion, kinematics—the dynamic study of motion—is far from my strong suit. A simple trip to the library was unlikely to bear fruit in this case; I needed to get a locomotor expert to look at the film and then persuade the same expert to go on the record about it.

I ended up sending a videotape copy of the film to an expert on human locomotion, Dr. Daniel Schmitt of Duke University. I knew Schmitt from graduate school and convinced him that he owed me a favor. While not excited in the least at the prospect of embarking on Bigfoot research, he consented after some badgering to offer an opinion. He had some vague recollection of the film from his youth, but I didn't tell him anything else about it because I didn't want to bias any opinion he might offer after studying the film. I simply asked him to look at the walk.

He had been videotaping people walking for a long time before he saw the film, and he has countless hours filming nonhuman primate locomotion as well. Schmitt was, in some sense, the ideal person to look at the film, because so much of his research involved extracting reliable locomotor data from photographic images. One part of his research involved asking people to walk in atypical fashion in order to simulate the kinematics of certain fossil hominids, human ancestors whose bones suggested that their movements at the hip and knee were considerably different from our own. In the process, he convinced several volunteers to be filmed doing the scientific equivalent of Groucho Marx walking (see fig. 5.2).

As it turned out, when Schmitt viewed the Patterson film for the first time, he looked at a gait that he had seen before—in his own laboratory. He called with an assessment: this is the way people walk when we don't allow them to extend their knees or hips fully. I asked him what that implied about the film, and his answer was sensibly noncommittal, though his tone betrayed some sarcasm: "either this is a person trying to walk funny, or Bigfoot walks in a manner that is more or less identical to people walking this way." The gait was human in the sense that people could produce the walk seen in the film. In scientific literature it is known as a "compliant gait," and it has several predictable attributes: the knees never extend fully, the excursion (the range of motion over a single stride) of the thigh from the hip differs from a normally walking person, and the hips, shoulders, and head don't bob up and down from step to step. The observation of the fluidity of movement in the film subject is a direct consequence of the compliant gait. Krantz was wrong again. There were aspects of the gait, however, that still required explanation, if we accept that there has been a reasonable reconstruction of the context of the film. These are the apparently mystifying speed of the film subject and its fantastic stride length.

Perhaps it was just dumb luck in choosing my collaborator, but Schmitt's research was also telling in an unexpected manner with respect to the film. As I noted before, Dahinden—in one of his trips to Bluff Creek—timed various

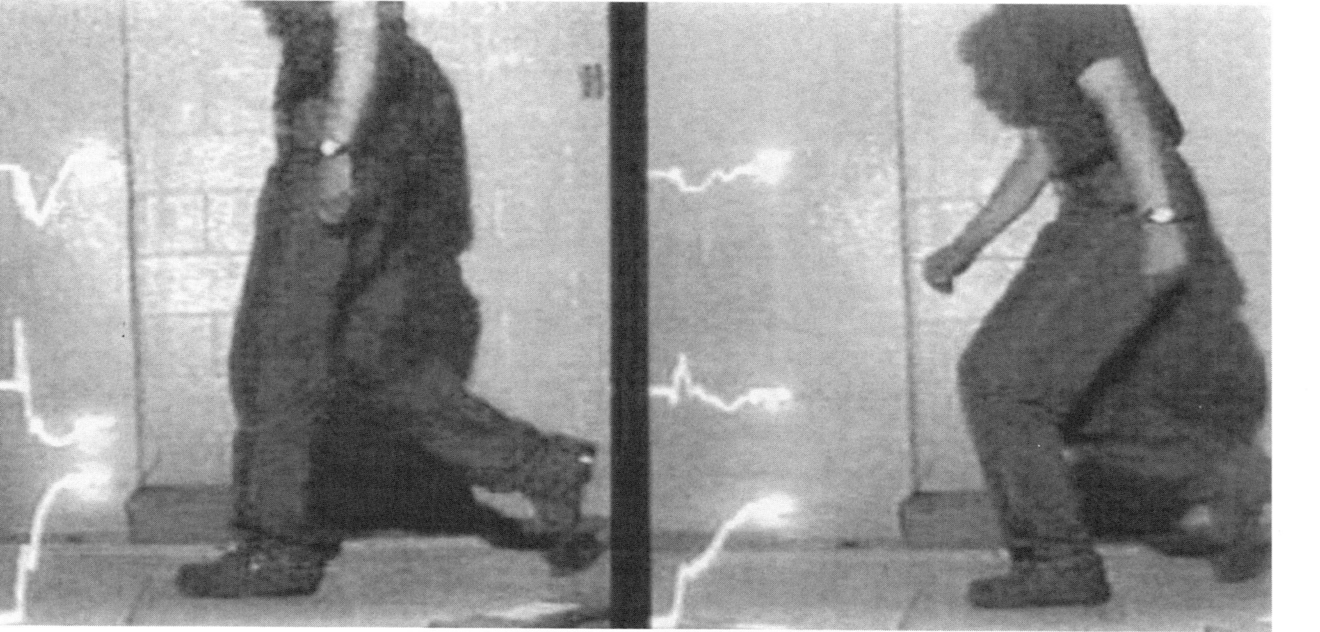

FIGURE 5.2

Normal (left) and compliant (right) forms of bipedal locomotion. The tracings on the left of each image represent different components of ground reaction force: side-to-side (top), braking/propulsion (middle), and vertical (bottom). Among the differences in the force profiles is that the vertical component of force—presumably instrumental in producing foot impressions in soil—is lessened in a compliant gait. The compliant gait is reminiscent of the locomotion shown by subject in the Patterson film. Supposed peculiarities of subject speed, stride length, and posture are all reproducible by a human being employing this type of locomotion. Images courtesy of Daniel Schmitt.

people walking along the reconstructed course of travel along the creek margin. Their walking speeds were then recorded and Dahinden compared these to the velocities figured for the film subject. I say "velocities" because the number you come up with depends on the film speed, which in this particular case is unknown. If the film speed Patterson used was 24 fps, Dahinden found that no one in his group could match the speed of the film subject.[76] At slower film speeds, the people could keep up with Patty as far as what the numbers said. I decided to see for myself how this worked out with my own sample of people. I measured out Dahinden's estimate of the length of travel of the film's Bigfoot on a basement hallway of the Yale Peabody Museum, and, armed with a stopwatch, collared unsuspecting graduate students on the way to a seminar. Regarding me with that look of dawning realization that their professor had finally gone off the deep end, they nevertheless consented to pit themselves against Bigfoot's brisk pace. Here, on the smooth tile floor, the students faced no obstacles of uneven terrain, sticks, or mushy sand. But in the world of Sasquatch walking in a film shot at 24 fps, they, too, could not keep up.

Now, of course, the way out of this problem is simply to claim that the film speed wasn't 24 fps. But it is one of two possibilities, and I thought it an interesting quandary if you have a beast moving too fast for a mere human. This enticing dilemma was not to last, however. Now that I had convinced Schmitt to look at the film, I recruited him to do some quantitative work on it, reasoning with him that by actually considering the film he was already a bona fide Bigfoot investigator, so if he was in for a dime he should stay in for a dollar. I told him about Dahinden's discussion of velocity and film speeds and the fact that I could verify the result independently. Wouldn't that mean, if the film speed was 24 fps, that we would have some explaining to do? Not really, Schmitt explained: by adopting the particular kinematics of the Groucho walk, the film subject, be it Bigfoot or some joker, would be putting themselves in a position to move very quickly.

What Schmitt had found with his human subjects doing the strange walks was that they could travel much *faster* walking in this bizarre fashion. I found this hard to believe, since if this were the case, why wouldn't people walk with bent knees and hips all the time? Why cover half the ground in twice the time? The catch was, Schmitt said, that you could travel faster but you become exhausted after only a minute or two—walking with the knees and hips bent entails much greater muscular effort than the normal striding gait of humans, where we basically turn our legs into stilts and let gravity do our work for us. As far as energy expenditure goes, the Groucho walk is a bust. But it really is faster: the top velocities in Schmitt's human volunteers (3.8 m/s) aren't just comparable to the film subject's (2.8 m/s), they are well beyond it! In truth, the figure for the subject over the course of the movie is rather imprecise, as the film speed (even if it was set to 24 fps) could vary from the setting by some amount in a given camera, and the distance traversed by the subject is only an estimate with some error as well. In any case, even though the compliant gait of the film subject allowed it to maximize its speed of travel, this Bigfoot (be it real or imitation) was not setting any land speed records. So far, the arguments that body proportions or the subject's gait and speed were not human cannot establish that this celluloid Bigfoot is the genuine article. Ergo, the impossibility of a hoax has not been established.

There remains one variable, not easily established from the film itself, that also deserves scrutiny in the context of compliant walking: stride length. The stride of the subject (measured from, for example, left heel to left heel, so as to complete one full locomotor cycle) from measurements at the film site is from 280 to 305 cm.[77] This figure is beyond the ability of normal human walking with the possible exception of some very tall people. In a compliant walk, however, the altered kinematics of the gait produce a predictable change, so that stride length necessarily increases in quite dramatic fashion. To drive home the point, Schmitt and I measured our normal stride length with the length found when adopting a compliant gait, which worked out to about a 35% increase. More interesting in the context of the film was that our compliant stride lengths (288 and 293 cm) were equal to the apparently incredible length of Bigfoot's stride.[78] The compliant gait, one that humans can learn in a matter of minutes, was turning out to explain a number of curiosities of the film that had before seemed to defy explanation.

Krantz's study of the Patterson film did not suffer from errors in computation or even lapses in reasoning; in fact, it represents a laudable effort to extract as much information as possible from a very poorly documented situation. The problem was not with the analysis itself but the reckless conclusions that followed from it. Krantz was simply too confident: since the body proportions were unusual, it wasn't human; since the walk wasn't typical, a human could not imitate it. Both propositions, in retrospect, were indefensible.

In 1992, however, the Patterson's film staunchest defense had yet to begin. It would not come from within an academic institution; instead, it would emanate from two obscure institutions, Progressive Research and the North American Science Institute (NASI). Bigfoot research organizations are strange entities, and are not all created equal. John Green summed up the phenomenon with the observation that "there's nothing stopping people from calling themselves anything they like" and forming an organization that can have as little as one member or a financial support base that supports several full-time staff.[79] The two organizations involved with the Patterson film occupy these extremes. Progressive Research was based in New Westminster, British Columbia, was started by Chris Murphy as a clearinghouse for Bigfoot books, posters, casts, and Canadian postage stamps featuring the monster.[80] While Dahinden was apparently an informal consultant to the company,[81] it is unclear whether the organization was anything other than an institutional title for Murphy himself. Before founding the company sometime in the mid-1990s, Murphy had worked for what was then British Columbia Telecom.[82] Murphy has published a number of articles in support of the Patterson film, with one noteworthy exception related below.[83]

NASI is as close to a real research organization as the Bigfoot community has ever seen. It essentially replaced The Bigfoot Research Project (TBRP) that had been run by Peter Byrne from 1992 until 1997. The project ended in 1997 and reemerged instantaneously as the North American Science Institute, in the same location in Hood River, Oregon. The only thing that seemed to have changed was the man in charge: Byrne was out and replacing him was Jeff Glickman, who had been a consultant with TBRP during Byrne's tenure. NASI apparently inherited TBRP's paid full-time staff, dedicated office space, vehicles, and thousands of dollars worth of computer and remote-sensing equipment. What prompted the titular change was never publicly disclosed, although it seemed that all TRBP data were ceded to NASI. Peter Byrne confirmed to me that NASI operated under the same benefactor, and that the widespread belief that TBRP was bankrolled by the Academy of Applied Science of Concord, New Hamphire, was incorrect.[84]

Jeff Glickman had been commissioned by Byrne to analyze the film[85]; he was seemingly the ideal man for the job. A board-certified forensic examiner, Glickman had started his own company, Photek, which specialized in image enhancement and reconstruction.[86] One of his specialties was removing visual noise from photographic images; as he put it to me, what he tries to do with a picture is reconstruct the exact conditions that existed when the picture was made.[87] Glickman was hired to do more than just clean up the Patterson film. Byrne had photographic data from the film site, better data than Krantz had utilized, and he wanted Glickman to do a definitive quantitative analysis of the film subject in addition to searching the image for tell-tale seams or zippers that would expose a hoax. The process would take years; by the time Byrne closed TBRP, the analysis was still ongoing.

NASI's doors closed soon after the publication of Glickman's report in 1998, after which, in the manner of a hired gun, he vanished completely from the Bigfoot scene. Murphy continues to be active in Bigfoot circles but has dropped the Progressive Research moniker. With the demise of their respective organizations, the works of these authors are harder to track down, although one can find them through various Internet repositories of Bigfoot evidence.[88]

What Murphy and Glickman did, in the spirit of Krantz's chapter on the film in *Big Footprints*, is offer an explicitly quantitative approach through measurements, calibrations, standardizations, and calculations that replace subjective impressions with cold hard numbers that should not change with one's mood or sense of bravado. Krantz's study illustrated that this approach was long overdue and a welcome form of argument, and at first glance Murphy's and Glickman's studies provided a seemingly solid case for the film's authenticity. The logic underlying these analyses was straightforward and convincing. Since the film star is no longer on the set, she cannot be measured directly. But she did leave footprints, and many of the props that adorned the Bluff Creek stage were still there years after the filming. So the idea that both Murphy and Glickman hit on was that Patty's size could be known if there was something else in the film that was a known quantity. This quantity could then be measured on the film and then any dimension on the Bigfoot in the frame could be scaled appropriately. In theory, the problem of "how big" could be solved.

Murphy used two different sources of calibration for the film subject. The first of these is the subject's foot (the width of the heel, ostensibly known from the footprints) and a long piece of wood (ca. 25 inches long) recovered from the film site. It is argued that the subject steps directly over this stick in the film.[89] Glickman used a different source for his calibration: an individual holding a very tall measuring stick at the film site (photographed by Peter Byrne in 1972), presumably standing in the same spot as the film subject. It is a simple matter to use these known parameters to calibrate each film frame and then proceed to extract quantitative data. Even though they relied on different objects to calibrate the film subject's girth and stature, both Glickman and Murphy come up with identical numbers. Whether the stick, the foot, or the measuring pole is used as the calibration instrument, the stature remains constant—that film's Bigfoot was breathing rarefied air at a dizzying altitude of 7 feet 3.5 inches above the sands of Bluff Creek. Glickman used the calibration data to go a few steps further: through a series of involved steps (some of which he does not reveal), he decided that the subject weighed over 1,900 pounds,[90] with a barrel chest (an astonishing 83 inches around) that would leave Charles Atlas feeling inadequate. The NASI report did not have to assert that the film was genuine. The numbers spoke for themselves: this could not be a person in a costume.

Here, at first glance, appears to be a triumph of the scientific method. Singular observations don't count for much in science, as recent claims of cold fusion demonstrate. If you can find something out that no one else can, then your interpretation of an event is flawed or your method of finding things out isn't what it's cracked up to be. Replication of results is absolutely critical for a claim to be scientifically valid. If you can arrive at the same conclusion via different methods, so much the better. Perhaps Glickman and Murphy have solved the film. They looked at the same event. They measured different things from the event. They got the same answer.[91]

Scientific practice—let's be honest here—is also all about mistakes. Knowledge advances principally by someone pointing out that someone else has made a mistake, either in observation or in theory. One seemingly mundane source of mistakes is measurement error, in which you think you have established that something is of length X and weight Y when in fact it isn't. Measurement error is ubiquitous in scientific endeavors, and it can have many causes. The scale you are using could be biased. You might expect a certain answer and subconsciously convince yourself that you haven't measured something correctly until you get that answer. You might want to record the same thing on two individuals but you end up measuring it differently on them. You cannot hope to eliminate measurement error, but you can try to get a sense of how good your measurements are. There is a reason scientists will measure the exact same thing more than once.

So what does this have to do with Patterson's Bigfoot? We are dealing with estimates in this case, and estimates can be like guesses. There are educated guesses, and there are wild guesses. What Glickman and Murphy present us with are guesses of a sort, estimates, based on something we *know* to assess something that we don't know. But what we know about footprints on the Bluff Creek sand, sticks over which Bigfoot steps, and precisely marked measuring staffs is only half the story. What also must be considered is what we know about the circumstances of the film, and I am not talking about Patterson's ulterior motives. These "circumstances" are mundane details such as camera position, the film subject's course of travel, and the precise orientation of sticks and feet relative to the camera lens. These details seem trivial, but consideration of these can enable us to decide whether a precise figure such as 7 feet 3.5 inches is an educated guess or merely a wild one.

I only became interested in the minutiae of camera positions and object orientations after a long conversation with Dan Schmitt about measuring things on film or videotape. Schmitt was convinced that the NASI report was on shaky footing with its estimates of subject stature. In the Vertebrate Movement Laboratory that Schmitt runs at Duke's Medical Center, he measures images of moving primates to document how they use their limbs when moving on the ground or in the trees. With computer software that allows you to click and measure anything on an image, this does not sound like a particularly daunting task. But I soon learned that there are a number of ways to measure something very "definitively" and give you an absolutely wrong answer. Glickman's report stated that the measurement error of his film analysis was on the order of a few centimeters—nothing to make the Bigfoot's size fall within a human likeness—but the methods of measurement underlying this error was not included in the report "for the sake of brevity."[92] If Glickman's error is that small, then the guy-in-a-costume hypothesis can be dismissed once and for all.

Schmitt and I had, to this point, dealt with the problems in Krantz's analysis. What about the measurements Glickman came up with? Don't those make the whole discussion of gait irrelevant? After all, I reminded Schmitt, this guy is a forensic examiner. Schmitt countered that Glickman is in the business of doing is cleaning up images and that there is every indication that he is very good at it. But there is a huge difference between enhancing an image and extracting quantitative data from it. Schmitt recounted his own difficulties in making his point: "I've been measuring primates off of films for years, and there are hundreds of mistakes you can make. I know this, because I've made them. There is no way any of these guys know how big that thing is."

We set out to do something very simple: establish what the minimum errors are in the context of the Patterson film under the assumption that at least some parameters of the event can be reasonably estimated. What we had going for us was that, unlike the October afternoon in Bluff Creek, we could do all of our filming in the laboratory, where we could measure objects in the flesh and on film, knowing every detail of camera and object position for each analysis. In effect, we would be estimating the absolute minimum error that would be present in Murphy's analysis and in Glickman's report.

We basically did three experiments. First, we compared how well something the size of Glickman's calibration object (a marked staff from Byrne's 1972 photo) would compare to Murphy's use of the subject's foot dimensions to estimate someone's height. Second, we looked at what errors resulted from having a calibration object out of plane (closer or further from the camera) to the intended object of measurement. Third, we looked at what would happen if the optical axis of the camera (i.e., which way the lens was pointing) was off-kilter to the plane in which the calibration object and the measurement object were positioned.

It is fair to say that as we embarked on these analyses, neither one of us was predisposed toward authenticating the film. Schmitt was anxious to get on with his own work and make his foray into Sasquatch research as brief as possible, and I was steaming over the passive noncooperation I was getting from NASI and Murphy with respect to recreating their methodology.[93] Understanding this, we agreed that we needed to insulate our findings from our own influence. So we disqualified ourselves from taking any measurements; we would take the pictures and get five volunteers to do the calibrating and the measuring. We did not tell the volunteers what we were up to. We simply asked each of them to measure a calibration object and store the data. We then had a different volunteer use the calibration data (the value of which they were not privy to) to estimate stature. This procedure blinded us to the outcome until the analysis was over; we had to live with the results the volunteers provided.

Our first test was to look at how well different calibration standards would fare in predicting my height. We did this under perfect conditions: the lighting was excellent, I was merely 5 meters from the camera, my image was clear because it filled a large fraction of the frame, and the lens of the camera was perpendicular to myself and the calibration object, which we positioned in the same plane (i.e., at exactly the same distance from the camera lens). No one analyzing the Patterson film has such luxuries; thus, we can state that these errors are the absolute minimum that would be involved in measuring the 1967 subject. We first measured Murphy's chosen standard of subject heel width. How well would my heel predict my true height? In the real world (to make extra sure we measured my height just prior to the analysis) I am about 6 feet 4 inches not slouching. By Murphy's criteria, I was suddenly over 8 feet tall (a 28% error). We estimate if he had used foot length, that error would have been as low as 3%. Using a 2-meter standard corresponding to Glickman's technique, we obtained an error of less than one percent. Glickman's method was working thus far. Why was Murphy's standard such a miserable failure? The answer has to do with the intrinsic quality of the image and how well you can detect borders and edges in it. In a particular film frame, it may be that the grain of the image (or the pixel size in a digital photograph) is such that you can't measure anything under 5 mm with much confidence. That threshold of clarity is going to apply to the edges of objects as well. The reason Glickman's standard worked so much better than Murphy's had to do with their absolute size. An intrinsic absolute error of a few millimeters in a large object is going to yield a small proportional error. This intrinsic error that relates to image quality is exactly the same in a small object, but in this case the error contributes to a greater proportion of the estimate (see fig. 5.3).

For our second procedure, we used a calibration object (myself) to estimate the height of an 180 cm object (we used a mounted skeleton in Duke's anatomy lab). In this case, we wanted to use a distance from subject to camera that was on the order of what Glickman was dealing with in the context of the 1967 film (80 feet). It's worth repeating here that we do not know what this distance really was: nobody measured it until the tell-tale signs from the event were gone. In any case, when the object and I were in the same plane, even at 80 feet away, using me as a calibration object, the "unknown" object's height was estimated within 1% of its true height. If, however, I left our unknown where it was and moved just 3 feet closer to the camera, the object apparently shrank by 4%. If I was further away from the camera than the object, it would get bigger (see fig. 5.4).

What is essential to realize here is that the problem isn't just that the calibration object and the unknown object are out of plane relative to the camera: what

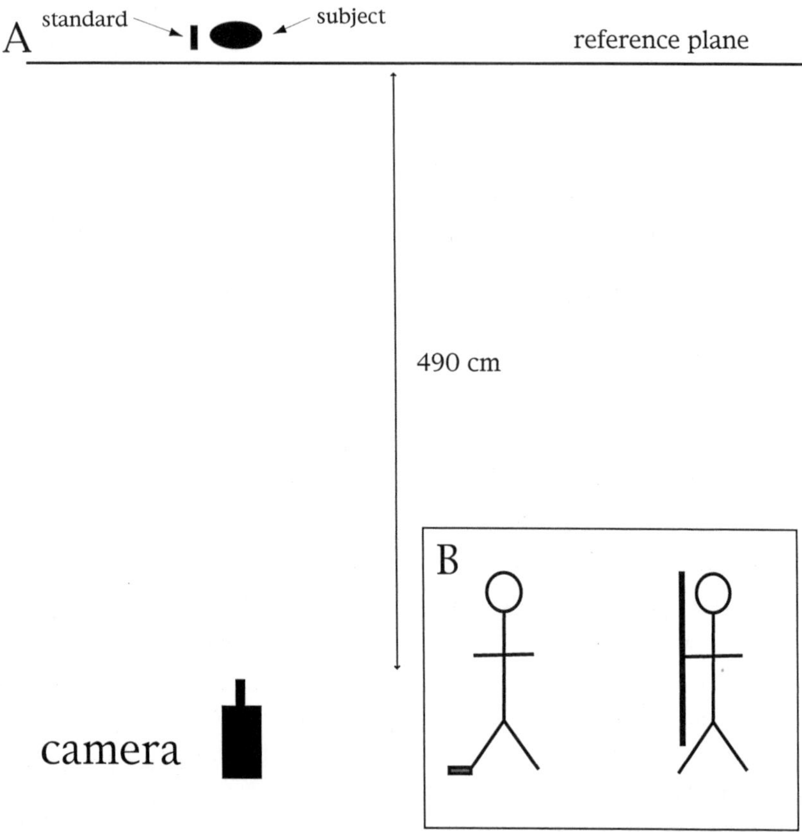

FIGURE 5.3
The ideal context for measuring unknowns from photographic images. (A) Some scalar standard (a known quantity) will accurately estimate subject dimensions only if the two objects occupy the same plane perpendicular to the camera lens. (B) The size of the standard is also critical to the accuracy of estimated dimensions. A foot (left) is more unreliable than a 2-meter standard (right) because of intrinsic measurement errors associated with image quality. Even under ideal circumstances, measurement errors exist. The Patterson film suffers from problems of image quality, uncertain camera position, and unknown subject positions. From Daegling and Schmitt (1999), with permission from the publisher.

kills the reconstruction effort is that the out of plane error is undetectable on the film. Byrne's 1972 photo allows for the superimposition of the background and foreground details with images from the 1967 film. Fallen logs in the foreground can be aligned; dead trees in the distance can be matched up. Bigfoot walked between them in 1967, and Byrne's companion walked between them

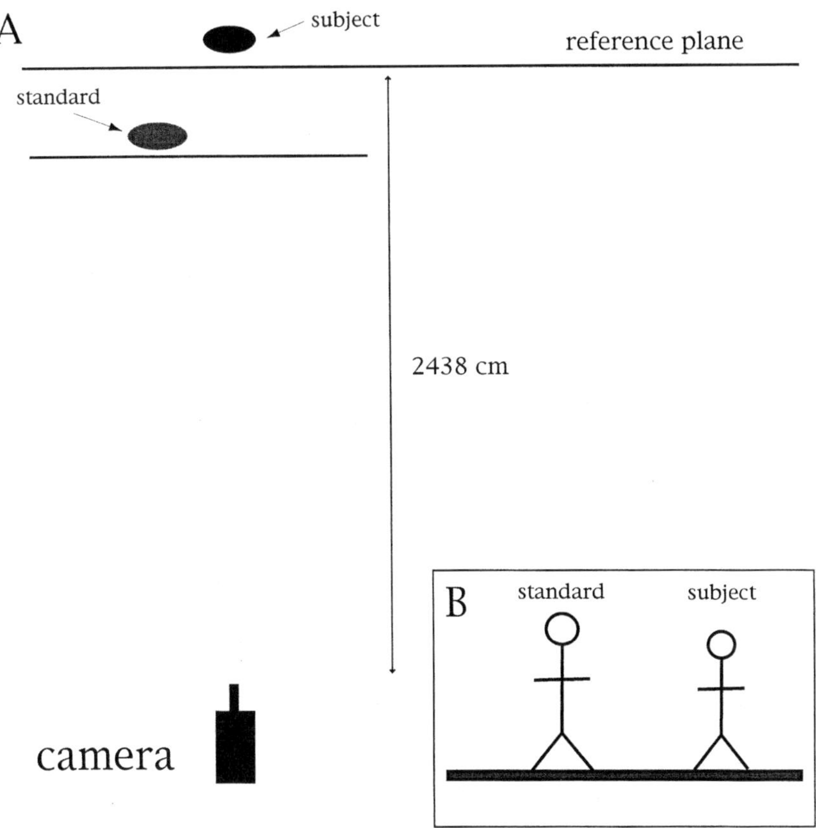

FIGURE 5.4
(A) When calibration standards are used to estimate an unknown object, errors mount if the two are out-of-plane with one another relative to the camera lens. (B) The presence of off-plane errors cannot be detected in a two-dimensional image unless the exact positions of standard and subject are independently known. The standard may be bigger than the subject, or merely closer to the camera. Supporters of the Patterson film argue that the superimposition of foreground and background detail correct for the problem, but the location of the subject relative to the superimposed objects has never been established. Superimposition only establishes the coincidence of standard and object in two dimensions, but calibration requires knowledge of location in three dimensions. From Daegling and Schmitt (1999), with permission from the publisher.

some five years later. Byrne's photo seemed to show that you can superimpose a known standard on an unknown Bigfoot.

As noted before, both John Green and Peter Byrne expressed reservations about how accurate such a procedure would be. Their caution was well founded. The superimposition that NASI hitched its analysis to cannot distinguish between the two possibilities that (1) Bigfoot was gigantic versus (2) Bigfoot and calibration object were out of plane with respect to one another as far as Patterson's camera was concerned. The film and the photo are two-dimensional representations and accurate measurement in this context requires knowledge of position in three dimensions. That information does not exist anymore. Glickman could not fix this problem then and nobody can now.

There is no way to distinguish whether the object is really large (or small) compared to the calibration standard, or if that standard is simply off-plane. The only way to know this is if you have a second standard whose position is known (and at that point, you do not need the first one anymore). This is where the piece of wood from the film comes in. René Dahinden collected the wood as a souvenir some years after the film was made,[94] and it is argued that the film subject steps over this very stick. The stick's length is obviously now known, and the fact that Bigfoot steps over it means that problem of calibrator and unknown being coplanar is solved. At that moment, the known parameter and the unknown one are exactly the same distance from Patterson's camera. Whether the wood fragment is the identical object seen on the film is, of course, very much an open question, but it does not matter in the final analysis. The stick presents its own problems that our third experiment exposes.

In our third experiment, Schmitt and I simply evaluated a special case of a calibration standard and unknown object being out of plane. This involved lining up the things to be measured in a defined plane but then tilting the camera at an angle so that the lens was not perpendicular to the "intended" reference plane where the objects were lined up. This, in effect, creates the same problem as our second test, because the standard and the unknown are not exactly where they are purported to be, at least where measurement is concerned. There is no way to know the extent of this problem in the Patterson film at all; in any case, it depends on what object is doing the calibrating and what frame is being analyzed. For our purposes, we looked at what a rotation of the lens by a mere 5 degrees would do to a set of objects 80 feet from the camera. In the case our volunteers analyzed, the calibration standard missed the true dimension of the unknown by 8%.[95] This figure will change as things get further from the camera, if a zoom lens is used, and if image quality is otherwise compromised, but the point is that some error is there (see fig. 5.5).

This means that the piece of wood does not solve the problem of measurement error. Murphy measured the length of the fragment and used this in the

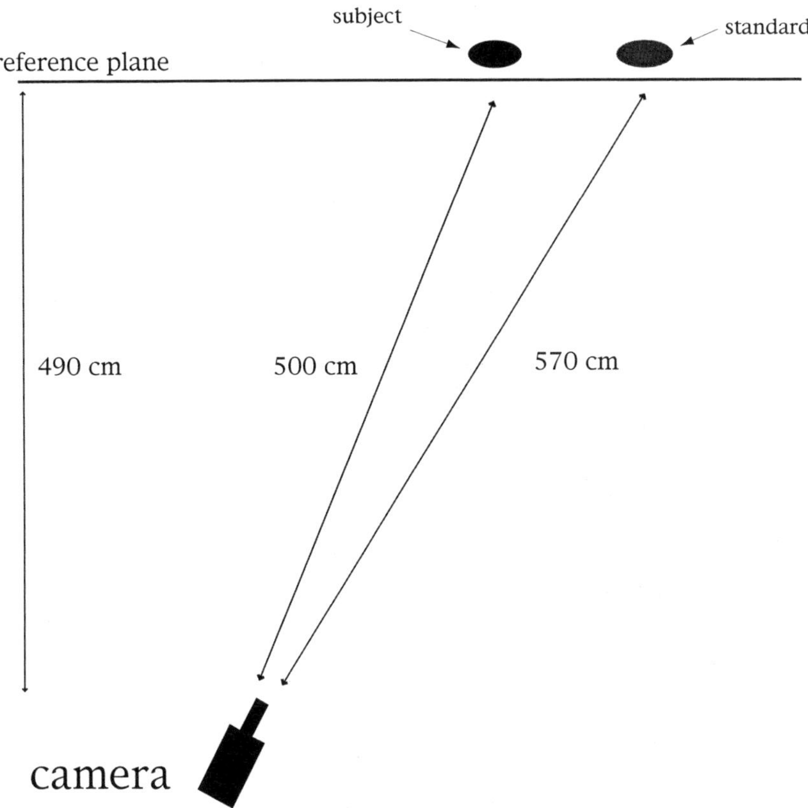

FIGURE 5.5
If the optical axis of the camera is not perpendicular to an intended reference plane, a calibration standard will not accurately estimate an unknown subject's dimensions. This is a certain, but inestimable, source of error in the 1967 Patterson film. In this example, the camera is about 25 degrees off-angle. The minimum error expected if the standard and subject are assumed to be coplanar would approach 15%. Figure is not to scale.

film to arrive at an identical answer for stature yet again. This stick's length was parallel to the ground in the film, but if the calibration was to be valid, then both ends of that stick had to be the exact same distance from the camera. That is a piece of information that nobody knows; Dahinden did not measure or photograph the wood when he collected it.[96] Consequently, the orientation of the wood with respect to Roger Patterson's camera is unknown. All we can reasonably say is that it was not edge on, since in that case it would not have been recognizable as a stick of some sort. That is as far as we can take it. A camera lens being off-angle to a stick is the same thing as the stick being off-angle to the camera. If the desired dimension of that wood is not precisely perpendicular to the camera, then any use of it to estimate the film subject is going to make her very much larger than she really is. The length of the wood on the film is assumed to be the same as what it measures today, so that if it is at all obliquely disposed to the camera, the whole world in that frame is going to get a lot bigger. You can prove this yourself with a ruler, a camera, and your cat. It is a small matter to get a kitty to the size of a lynx.

What we did in conducting three separate experiments was try to isolate the effects of different sources of error. In the context of the Patterson film, these sources will be compounding—each source of error makes the resulting estimate worse. Our conclusion was simple: there is no justification for giving a precise estimate of the size of its subject, whatever that estimate is. The bottom line is that the thing in the Patterson film might be 8 feet tall, it might be 5 feet tall, but nobody is ever going to figure that out. There is a minimum of information that must be known outside of the film to estimate anything within the film, and it is intellectually dishonest to pretend that we have it.

The results of our experiments, together with a critique of Krantz's views on the film, were published in *Skeptical Inquirer* in 1999.[97] The Bigfoot community has only recently acknowledged the argument.[98] Loren Coleman actually lists the article in the bibliography of his 2003 book *Bigfoot!*, but in the text itself he parrots Krantz's claim that it would be very difficult for a hoaxer to be able to duplicate the gait seen in the film. Glickman's study, given its fantastically favorable results, has eclipsed Krantz's earlier work and remains de rigueur among the advocates, except with respect to its weight estimate (see chapter 6). Chris Murphy abruptly withdrew his support for the Patterson film in bizarre fashion early in 1999.

Murphy had just published a series of articles for NASI's newsletter in 1998 regarding the context of the Patterson-Gimlin film, in which he repeated the claim that the film subject's stature had been verified by independent means.[99] Then Murphy and longtime Bigfoot researcher Cliff Crook shocked the Bigfoot community by announcing to the media that they had discovered a "fastener" around the waist of the film subject, thereby establishing the film as fraudulent.[100]

The claim was debunked swiftly. Murphy discovered the bell-shaped fastener by enlarging a color image of a frame of the film. His original, however, was a color plate from a book (at least a third-generation copy), and his mode of enlargement was an office copier.[101] Henner Fahrenbach, a staunch advocate, subsequently demonstrated that the resolution claimed by Murphy was, in effect, impossible given the methods used and the physical condition of the emulsion.[102] In fact, Murphy might have realized that if only he had read the initial issue of *NASI News* the year before, where the issue of resolution limits on the film was thoroughly discussed.[103]

The print and Internet media were only too happy to air the firestorm created by the discovery of the fastener. Dahinden denounced Crook and Murphy as clowns out for revenge.[104] The recent history of the three men made vengeance seem a plausible motivator.[105] In Dahinden's view, Crook was guilty of foisting bogus photographs on the Bigfoot community and the media.[106] Forever intolerant of idle speculation, Dahinden had also bristled at reading Murphy's assessments of the Patterson film. The NASI connection added to his displeasure (at this point in conversations with me, he referred to the organization as Not Another Stupid Idea) since he had been disappointed by Glickman's report. In any case, by debunking the film Murphy in effect repudiated the calibration methods he originally championed for reconstructing the film subject's stature.

Attempts to measure something definitive from the film persist. The latest defense of the film was prompted by Greg Long's claim in *The Making of Bigfoot,* in which the man in the suit is purportedly identified. Long's accusation that the film was a hoax engineered by Patterson enraged the Bigfoot community, and in response John Green resurrected an argument for the film's authenticity from thirty years before. What Green told the Bigfoot community was a dressed-up version of his 1968 observation that the film subject's arms are too long (in proportion to its legs) to accommodate a human form.[107] Meldrum drafted a supporting statement hailing Green's insight as a watershed event in the analysis of the film, remarking that the unusually long arms were apparent in a routine viewing of the film.[108] That the upper limb is abnormally long is not obvious, however, as the arms of the subject hang as low as one would expect for a human being walking with bent knees and with the trunk pitched slightly forward. Green concurs in observing that "her body is also very long, so her arms do not appear to hang very low."[109]

Green correctly proceeds from the assumption that while exact measurements from the film are impossible, it is theoretically possible to measure the length of the limbs relative to one another. This is only permissible, as Meldrum notes, if the limb segments (upper arm, forearm, thigh, and lower leg) are oriented perpendicular to the optical axis of the camera. The relative measures will be distorted to an unknown degree if this is not the case, and there is no justification for stating that this contingency is ever satisfied in the movie, given the fact that the orientation of Patterson's camera and the route of the film subject remains unknown. Still, Meldrum argues that for the Sasquatch in the movie the proportion of the upper to lower limb is between 80 and 90%, while this ratio in people averages only 72%. Given that the limb segments in the Bigfoot's arm appear normal, a prosthesis would seem to be out of the question.

I tried to see for myself how reliable these relative measures might be and took three frames from the movie where the arms appear to be reasonably positioned (i.e., perpendicular to the camera) to see if the proportions of the forearm to arm were consistent. In the most famous still from the movie, frame 352, the forearm is only slightly longer than the upper arm segment (around 10%). In frame 61, depending on where exactly you decide the shoulder and elbow joints are (it is by no means obvious), the forearm is up to half again as long. For frame 72 I get numbers in between. The point here is that the estimates are all over the map, yet in each frame I have no basis for inferring if one or both limb segments is rotated out of the desired measurement plane. The situation for the lower limb is even worse; since the knees are bent throughout the film,[110] and as the subject is walking away from Patterson (at some oblique and unknown angle) the thigh and lower leg segments are undoubtedly rotated out of the plane of the film. Consequently, lower limb length—expressed in either absolute or relative terms—cannot be reliably ascertained. In other words, the same problems involved in trying to get absolute measurements from the film creep into the measurement of relative proportions.

But perhaps Meldrum's numbers make all this imprecision irrelevant if there is such a huge gap between Bigfoot's limb proportions and those of humans. The problem here, however, is that measurements of limb proportions (based on either skeletal or anthropometric measures) utilize discrete landmarks on bones or bodies and the Bigfoot data are necessarily estimated from amorphous surface features on the film subject. The landmarks needed to obtain a reliable estimate might indeed be present on the film subject, but they are not discretely visible on the film. In fact, experts schooled in anthropometrics will tell you that these landmarks are best located through palpation (i.e., locating by touch) rather than by visual inspection. Trying to locate the landmarks through a fur coat in a lousy film is a losing proposition.

Even if we accept Green's reasoning and Meldrum's numbers, the strange limb proportions of the Patterson Bigfoot could be explained as an incidental effect of a costume. Donning a fur suit—whether from a costume rental outfit or a more sophisticated one sewn together from horsehide—necessarily elevates the height of the shoulder (with or without padding) and at the same time lowers the crotch toward the knees. The effect on limb proportions is obvious if you measure the costumed human as a normal anatomical specimen: the arms will appear a tad long but the legs will look positively stumpy. The unusually long trunk that Green insists is portrayed in the film is also an expected effect of a costume.

CREDIBILITY OF THE FILM STAR

While the film's authenticity cannot be established, even the skeptic must concede that a smoking gun has yet to be found. There remains the question of how the film was done. Could Patterson, or anyone else, have engineered a hoax of such complexity? What about the bouncing breasts, the rippling muscles, the crest on the skull that on close examination appear undeniable? The advocates insist these details are consistent with primate anatomy but not with a joker in a furry costume. If the Patterson film were made today and hawked as the genuine article, it would stand almost zero chance of acceptance, given the ease with which images can be technologically altered or simply fabricated. Yet Patterson's book establishes that, at the very least, he could have conceived it. The combination of features seen in the film subject is in one sense anomalous: the breasts indicate the subject is a female, but the conical shape of the top of the head is a male characteristic. This odd shape is due to the presence of a pronounced sagittal crest, a raised ridge of bone on the top of the skull that provides a site of attachment for large chewing muscles. The presence of this ridge in a female primate is not only shocking, it is unprecedented.[111] In modern primates, those species that exhibit the sagittal crest are relatively few, and in those that do, it is only the males that have this feature. What is a female Sasquatch doing with this feature? The advocates will tell us that we should not presume to know what a Bigfoot should look like.[112]

There is one particular frame of the film that, when scrutinized, is also entirely inconsistent with known principles of primate anatomy. Frame 72 shows the film subject from the rear, with the left foot entirely clear of the ground (see fig. 5.6). The subject is at an angle to the camera, such that the viewer can see the foot in profile. The heel is clearly seen to project backward from the shank of the calf, such that rather than taper to the end of the heel, the Achilles tendon appears to insert far forward on the heel. Grover Krantz and Jeff Meldrum have both concluded from their analysis of tracks that Bigfoot has an unusually elongated heel bone relative to humans.[113] There is a biomechanical rationale for this: by lengthening the heel bone, the leverage of the Achilles tendon increases about the ankle joint which serves to enhance its bearer's ability to move and support a large mass. This was central to Krantz's argument over the significance of the Bossburg tracks. It might be a perfectly reasonable adaptation to expect in a giant biped. Does the film independently support this, at least for the frame in question?

Roger Patterson knew nothing of this when the film was made: it would be years later that Krantz would offer his interpretation of Bigfoot's unique foot skeleton. But the projecting heel does not serve as vindication for the anthropologists' hypothesis; it is more sensibly interpreted as a glaring anomaly in a film that is almost right in the other details. A lengthened heel bone gives you the needed mechanical advantage only if the Achilles tendon inserts at the very back of the heel. This is the pattern in living primates, ourselves included, regardless of locomotor specialization.[114] The Patterson film subject departs from this condition because the Achilles tendon appears to attach far forward on the heel, where the adaptive advantage of having an elongated heel bone in the first place is completely lost. This anatomical configuration is not only unprecedented, it makes no biomechanical sense at all. The advantage that the long heel bone confers to Bigfoot, by Meldrum's and Krantz's rationale, is negated by the condition we see in the film. What is seen does make sense, however, if the point is not efficiency in locomotion, but rather getting a human subject to appear as if it is something else. A prosthesis explains what is seen in the film; evolution, by contrast, cannot make sense of it.

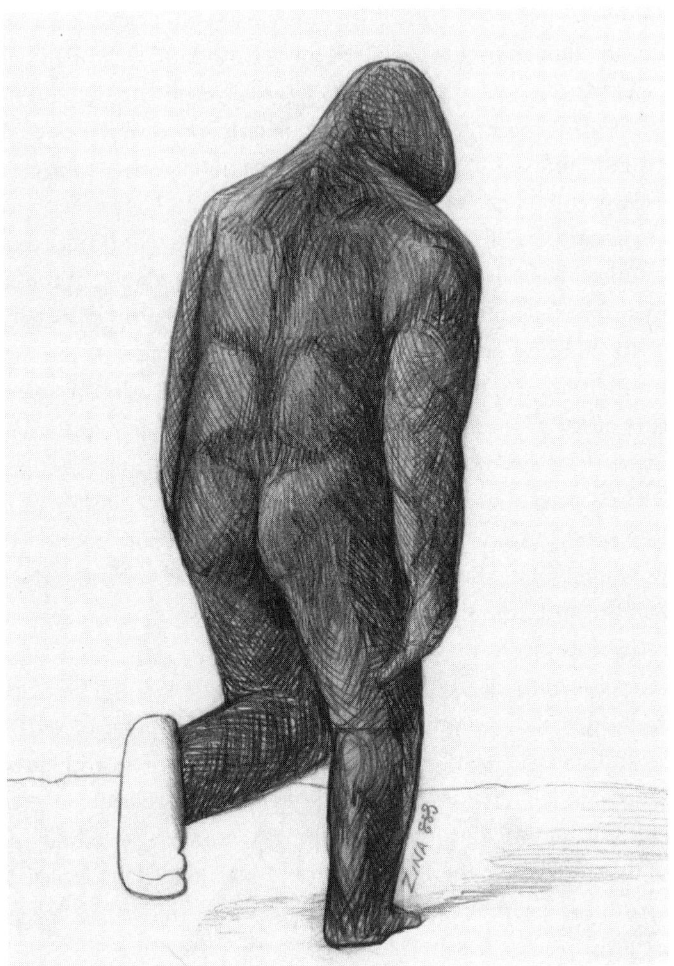

FIGURE 5.6
Artist's reconstruction of subject from frame 72 of the 1967 film shot by Roger Patterson. The bent-knee, bent-hip gait of the film subject can be visualized. Contrary to statements of Bigfoot researchers, this gait is easily reproducible by human subjects. The kinematics of this compliant gait have been thoroughly studied over the last fifteen years. Note the projecting heel of the subject's left foot. The shank of the calf extends into the foot unnaturally, well forward of the back of the heel where the Achilles tendon normally inserts in primates. The two competing explanations for this observation: (1) the configuration of the Sasquatch heel is unique among primates, or (2) the foot is a prosthetic device worn by a human subject. Drawing by Zina Deretsky.

Bob Gimlin has always claimed that he saw muscular movements beneath the skin of the film subject as it walked away from him. Dahinden has repeatedly emphasized that such movements are visible on the film, although the jerkiness of the footage makes it very difficult to tell. One of Jeff Glickman's initial tasks in examining the film was, in effect, to stabilize the footage. I was able to see this aspect of Glickman's work first hand in New Haven in 1996; what he did was to line up the same registration points on different frames so as to line up consecutive images in the same orientation. The result was impressive; after this process the effect of Patterson's shaky grip was all but eliminated. A clear image of the striding subject was possible; the graininess of the image persisted, but the subject was no longer jumping about from frame to frame.

Looking at the film after this manipulation, one clearly sees what Gimlin and Dahinden insisted was there all along: when the subject's foot hits the ground, what appears to be the mass of the quadriceps muscle on the thigh quivers unmistakably. The dynamics of the movement correspond to what we expect to see in a living flesh and blood biped. This observation does not really extract the film from the realm of hoax, however. It may simply mean that if this was a costume, it was a very good one.

The skeptics must deal with this fact of the film; it does not portray a poorly fashioned suit. Dahinden talked to several people involved with film costumes and special effects, and his conclusion from these various conversations was that the hair must have been glued onto the body of a would-be hoaxer. This would obviously require a long investment of tedious labor, and the act of disrobing from this costume would presumably be unpleasant if not actually painful. Glickman emphasized to me that spandex was not around in 1967, so that attire was not an option for a would-be hoaxer.

I concur with Dahinden that gluing hair onto skin seems an unlikely scenario and I concede Glickman's point on spandex as well. There are, however, alternative ways in which the effects seen in the film could have been produced by something other than Bigfoot. Michael Dennett suggested to me that one can produce the effect of soft-tissue movement in a costume by placing bags of water beneath the apparent skin. Certainly the inertia of the thigh when the foot contacts the ground is such that the effect produced would be comparable to what is seen on the film. A second possibility came to me when reminiscing about childhood skiing trips in the 1960s. We did not have polypropylene thermal underwear back then but relatively heavier cotton long johns that sported a miniature waffle design to trap body heat. As children will grow from year to year, I would find that the long johns I had worn on last year's ski trip were of a size considerably less suited to my body proportions on the current one. Yet, there was sufficient give in the cotton so that I could wriggle my way into them and achieve a very snug, if uncomfortable, fit. It hardly seems beyond reason that a set of long johns, a size or two too small, could be squeezed on to a muscular frame and given a nice fur coat to boot. Given this premise, an individual walking along in such a getup would certainly show the effects of muscular activity almost as faithfully as if the person were naked.

A balanced consideration of the evidence suggests that it is simply rash to declare that the Patterson film is beyond fabrication. It cannot be proven that the film subject is too large for a person; one of the two people who were there thought it was at most 6 feet 2 inches.[115] The gait of the film subject, in terms of both speed and kinematics, is not typically human but is easily duplicated by human beings. Despite claims to the contrary, no particular expertise in biomechanics would have been required to produce what is seen on the film. Perhaps the most important observation of all is that Patterson imagined—and drew—the very likeness of what he would eventually film. Someone did not need to dream up a costume in 1967; the template for the movie was publicly available in 1966.

CREDIBILITY OF A STORYLINE

Even the story surrounding the film might give us cause for suspicion. Daniel Perez, among the staunchest defenders of the film's value, has lingering doubts about the events surrounding the movie.[116] In short, the timeline between when the film was allegedly shot, shipped out for processing, and viewed for the first time in Yakima, Washington, was astonishingly short: a mere forty-eight hours perhaps. Other emerging details, coupled with a curious lack of information on some apparently mundane items, throw into doubt the idea that the narrative surrounding the film is entirely accurate.

The film was shot at 1:30 PM.[117] According to René Dahinden, the light and shadows for that time of year at the film site establishes this as a reasonable window.[118] Patterson and Gimlin left the creek that afternoon, but not immediately after the film was made. Gimlin tried in vain to follow the film subject, but managed to follow spoor for only a few hundred feet. Patterson then took the extraordinary step of changing film in the camera to take footage of the footprints on the sandbar. He did this by getting beneath a poncho, switching rolls, and securing the motion picture from the daylight. Apparently after casting some of the tracks and filming the procedure, Patterson and Gimlin finally left the creek and headed back to civilization. Before reaching the town of Orick, however, the men stopped at a friend's place for a visit and shower. From Orick, the two are thought to have driven to Eureka, a little over 25 miles away, where they arranged for the film to be shipped out by air courier. There is no documentation of any kind as to who this courier was. They continued on to Willow Creek, where they phoned Al Hodgson sometime after 6 PM and told him about their adventure. Patterson and Gimlin would return to their camp in Bluff Creek that night, but not before speaking to someone at the *Eureka Times-Standard* around 9:30 PM.[119]

The tale got a front-page story the next day without anyone having seen the film, and, to Perez's consternation, no one seems to know whose name belongs on the byline. A reporter by the name of Andrew Genzoli is generally credited, since he had been the writer behind past Bigfoot stories carried by the paper. Perez asked Genzoli's widow in 1995 if he had been responsible for the piece, and she was doubtful: stylistically it was not a good fit, and she had no other recollection that he had been involved. Patterson is quoted in the article as saying he first saw the creature at a distance of 80–90 feet (and it is unlikely he got much closer); interestingly, Patterson is able to describe very well what the subject looked like in the article, right down to features of the face that are barely discernible in enhanced and enlarged images of the film that nobody had yet seen.[120]

At some point on Saturday, October 21, Patterson's brother-in-law, Al DeAtley, took possession of the film from the air courier to arrange for processing. Incredibly, DeAtley cannot recall where the film was processed.[121] After this point, Perez told me, "there is no chain of custody." Development of the Kodachrome film was at that time a proprietary process guarded by Kodak, and no one in Seattle was apparently so equipped. Nobody knows where the film was developed, or for that matter when, but by early Sunday afternoon, Dahinden, Green, and Patterson were watching the film in DeAtley's home. Patterson would try to promote and sell the film in his few remaining years, but he was so sloppy in doing so that at some point the original copy was not returned to him. The original film is lost: the best copies of the film are all second generation.

These details might only mean that Patterson was careless in handling the film but did succeed in getting it developed in a mere day and a half after it left his hands. It is certainly possible, but the time line suggests to Perez that "you have to have more time [to] do all that was claimed."[122] Patterson was under tremendous pressure to get a marketable film[123]: a warrant had been issued for his arrest for nonpayment for the rented camera and Dahinden established that Patterson was for all intents and purposes broke at the time.[124] Perez is appropriately cautious about what the information and lack thereof means with respect to the film's aftermath, yet the implications are clear. All of the problems of timing disappear if the film is shot a few days or hours beforehand. If that is the case, one has to wonder what other details of this story are wrong. As monsters go, nobody breeds intrigue quite like Bigfoot.

NOTES

1. Green (1978:116); Coleman (2003:82).
2. This has been one of Michael Dennett's principal objections to the film's authenticity, stated in a letter to Peter Byrne dated January 29, 1995.
3. Hunter and Dahinden (1975:111–115); Green (1978:116).
4. Murphy (1998a:6).
5. Hunter and Dahinden (1975:119).
6. Peter Byrne, in an e-mail to the author on July 16, 2003.
7. Montagna (1976) opined in a *Primate News* editorial: "simply stated, Patterson and Friends perpetuated a hoax."
8. Napier (1974:94).
9. Perez (1992:17).
10. In a personal communication via audiotape (February 20, 1996), Dahinden indicated that despite his opinion that Patterson was irresponsible and unethical, he believed the possibility of a hoax was remote.
11. How much Dahinden paid for Gimlin's share of the rights remains unestablished (Perez, e-mail correspondence, March 12, 2003), although one report gives a figure of $10 (this from Scott Forslund's 1983 article "The Nature of the Beast" that appeared in *Pacific Northwest Magazine*). The article can now be accessed online at Bobbie Short's Bigfoot Encounters website: http://www.n2.net/prey/bigfoot/articles/forslund.htm. According to Wasson (1979:34), Gimlin transferred his rights to Dahinden on September 25, 1978; according to Forslund, it was four days later.
12. Perez (1992:15–16).

13. Grieve's report was never published as a stand-alone article in a scientific journal but has been reprinted several times in the Bigfoot literature (including as an appendix in Napier 1972).

14. Perez (1992:21).

15. Krantz (1992:94).

16. Krantz (1992:94–97).

17. Perez (1999b).

18. Napier (1974:221).

19. Personal communication via audiotape (February 20, 1996), and his presentation at the Harrison Hot Springs Sasquatch Symposium, May 6, 1995.

20. Napier (1974:222).

21. See Bayanov, Bourtsev, and Dahinden (1984) for a summary assessment of the Russian group's findings.

22. Hunter and Dahinden (1975:199–202).

23. Quoted in Markotic and Krantz (1984:227–228).

24. Green (1971:52–56).

25. Peter Byrne, in an e-mail to the author, September 8, 2002, indicates that he personally talked to the Disney people. Green does not name Byrne as the contact. Green followed up with the Disney Studios in 1969 (1978:129).

26. See http://critics.emphasys.net/Reviews/star_trek_original_v23.htm; http://www.tvtome.com/tvtome/servlet/EpisodeGuideSummary/showid-592/

27. Green (1978:129).

28. Green (1978:129).

29. Personal communication via audiotape, February 20, 1996. Greg Long (2004) has also established Patterson's limited financial means.

30. Green (1971:56).

31. Perez (1992:9); Krantz (1992:121).

32. See, for example, Wasson (1979:65–80, 82–85) and Long (2004).

33. Mark Chorvinsky (1997), Some thoughts about the Patterson film on its thirtieth anniversary. *Strange Magazine* website (www.strangemag.com). Greg Long (2004) details Patterson's obsession with Bigfoot as an object of income.

34. Personal communication via audiotape, February 20, 1996.

35. Wasson (1979:67).

36. Pyle (1995:269). Peter Byrne conveyed this information to Pyle.

37. Wasson (1979:82–83).

38. In an e-mail dated March 12, 2003, Daniel Perez reported to me that Gimlin claimed he never made a cent from the film.

39. Wylie (1980:179).

40. Coleman (2003:83).

41. Wasson (1979:86–96); Perez (2003f).

42. From an interview with Gimlin videotaped by John Green on March 29, 1992. The transcript is posted on the Bigfoot Encounters website (http://www.n2.net/prey/Bigfoot/).

43. Krantz (1992:96).

44. Mark Chorvinsky (1996), The Makeup Man and the Monster: John Chambers and the Patterson Bigfoot Suit. Accessed online at www.strangemag.com; the article first appeared in *Strange Magazine* 17.

45. Short (1998).

46. Mark Chorvinsky (2003). The Makeup Man and the Monster Part 2: Denials and Secrecy. *Strange Magazine* 22 (published online at http://www.strangemag.com/strangemag/strange22/chambers22.html).

47. Chorvinsky (2003).

48. Mark Chorvinsky (1997), Some thoughts about the Patterson film on its thirtieth anniversary. *Strange Magazine* website (www.strangemag.com).

49. Bigfoot prankster Rant Mullens suggested this in Dennett (1982).

50. Mark Chorvinsky (1996), John Chambers, *Lost in Space*, and the Patterson Suit. Accessed online at www.strangemag.com.

51. Gargas (2004).

52. Wylie (1980:181).

53. Napier (1974:89).

54. Napier (1974:89) regarded the gait as suspicious, while Donskoy (Bayanov, Bourtsev, and Dahinden 1984:232; Hunter and Dahinden 1975:192) saw the same movements as those of a genuine, but nonhuman, subject.

55. Perez (2003d).

56. Perez (2003j).

57. Perez (e-mail correspondence, February 3, 2003) believes that Gimlin had a tape measure with him, but Gimlin later claimed in a 1992 interview with John Green that he did not have an instrument to measure the prints. A transcript of that interview is on Bobbie Short's *Bigfoot Encounters* website (www.n2.net/prey/bigfoot/).

58. Bob Titmus drew a map reconstructing Patterson's and the film subject's movements during his visit to Bluff Creek. At the time, he did not have a tape measure or other mensurational device (Perez, e-mail correspondence, February 3, 2003). Krantz revised Titmus's map based on his analysis of the film, but never visited the film site prior to this revision (Dahinden, correspondence with the author, December 19, 1995).

59. Krantz (1992:93); Chorvinsky (2003:8).

60. The details of where the film was shipped from have never been clear, and Gimlin is uncertain on the point (Wylie 1980; Perez 1992).

61. Wylie (1980:187).

62. Daniel Perez, e-mail correspondence, February 3, 2003.

63. Daniel Perez, e-mail correspondence, February 3, 2003.

64. Perez (1992:21).

65. Daniel Perez discovered that on McClarin's November 5 visit earlier that year, one Richard Henry had filmed McClarin following the route of the film subject. This film was never used in subsequent analyses, and its whereabouts are unknown. From personal correspondence of Perez to the author, July 7, 2003, and Perez (2003i).

66. Green (1978:123).

67. Green (1978:124).

68. Personal correspondence with the author, July 17, 1995. In this letter, Dahinden states that he did not get to the film site until two years after the fact and that he could see no residual tracks at the film site.

69. Perez (1992:21).

70. Byrne (1976:124).

71. Krantz (1992:87–124).

72. Krantz (1992:118).

73. Dahinden, personal correspondence with the author, December 19, 1995.

74. Krantz gives the subject height as 198 cm and chest width as 46.5 cm. In a sample of over 1,000 men, the 95th percentile height is 187.5 cm and chest width is 49.6 cm. The only way Krantz can argue that Bigfoot is uniquely proportioned is to posit that taller people have absolutely narrower chests (Daegling and Schmitt 1999:24).

75. 1992:115.

76. Perez (1992:21).

77. Perez (1992:12).

78. Daegling and Schmitt (1999:23).

79. Green (1978:152).

80. Advertisement of the organization's products appeared in *NASI News* over its short publication run.

81. Coleman (2003:109).

82. Perez (2003h); Murphy (1998b).

83. Murphy (1998a, 1998b, 1998c).

84. Byrne related this in a letter to me dated October 21, 2003. The Academy of Applied Science was only involved, Byrne indicated, in terms of lending its name to the enterprise. The true benefactor was a single individual who wished to remain anonymous (Tod Deery, e-mail correspondence, December 8, 2003). This led several

sources to erroneously conclude that the academy was footing the bills (Pyle 1995:263; Goodavage 1996a; www.unknownmag.com/issue5-2.html).

85. Personal communication from Peter Byrne, October 21, 2003.

86. See www.photekimaging.com.

87. This conversation took place on November 12, 1996, in New Haven, Connecticut.

88. As of this writing, the complete text of the NASI report can be found at www.netcomuk.co.uk/~rfthomas/papers/nasi1.html or http://www.photekimaging.com/Support/support.html. Murphy's study was never published in print but was posted on the Internet Virtual Bigfoot Conference and summarized in *NASI News* (vol. 1). The IVBC is no longer actively maintained and Murphy's work is no longer accessible online.

89. The wood was recovered not at the time of the film but years later. The precise position of the wood in the film cannot be known with certainty. For the sake of argument, however, I assume here that it is known.

90. Glickman (1998:13).

91. The true independence of the estimates is unknown. Glickman and Murphy corresponded before the public release of the NASI report (Glickman 1998:35), such that the possibility looms that one party knew the other's results before the analyses were finalized. I first heard Glickman use the 7 foot 3.5 inch figure on November 12, 1996, when we met in New Haven—two years preceding the official report release in 1998. Michael Dennett indicated in a June 28, 1998, e-mail to the author that NASI staff member Tod Deery recalled (to the best of his recollection) that Murphy's results were reported after disclosure of Glickman's estimate. Murphy was using the 7 foot 3.5 inch figure on Internet postings to the Internet Virtual Bigfoot Conference as early as June 1996.

92. Glickman (1998:12). The report stated that Glickman could be contacted for "complete information." I wrote to request this material, but never received it.

93. My inquiries to NASI about specifics of methodology were not answered. When I asked Murphy for clarification of his methodology, he suggested in an e-mail message (January 28, 1998) that it was more appropriate for me to discuss his methods with Jeff Meldrum than himself. His rationale was that Meldrum was aware of his methods and was also in a better position to explain it to me given that we had similar backgrounds in anatomy. He also claimed Meldrum had used yet another technique for estimating stature and those numbers compared favorably to his own. Meldrum has not endorsed the NASI figures, and in a June 24, 1996, posting to the now defunct Internet Virtual Bigfoot Conference, Meldrum is sharply critical of Murphy's methods.

94. E-mail correspondence from Daniel Perez, February 3, 2003. Perez believes the date of recovery was 1972.

95. Theoretically, this error should be smaller, but this was our average empirical error (as measured by our volunteers).

96. Correspondence with the author, May 26, 1998.

97. Daegling and Schmitt (1999).

98. Jeff Meldrum e-mailed Schmitt and me (January 29, 2004) to alert us that he was publishing a rebuttal to our argument. He provided us with text to review and suggested that we consider recanting our statements. After cordial but frank exchanges among the three of us, we thanked Meldrum for the courtesy but declined to renounce our findings. Meldrum charged us with poor scholarship and careless research, including charges that the interscye dimension was incomparable to Krantz's measurements of the film because it is normally measured with a tape measure rather than a rigid ruler (Meldrum preferred a measure taken across the front of the chest, while Krantz measured this width across the back). The Bigfoot Field Researcher's Organization, in an online posting in May 2004 (www.bfro.net/news/challenge/home.asp), concedes our point on the impossibility of precise measurements while simultaneously endorsing Glickman's study as superior on the basis of his forensic expertise and access to a first-generation copy of the film.

99. Murphy (1998b).

100. Hubbell (1999).

101. Coleman (2003:105).

102. H. Fahrenbach (1999). Graphic case closure on the Crook-Murphy "Bell" story. Posted on www.bfro.net.

103. Fahrenbach and Glickman (1998).

104. Hubbell (1999).

105. Coleman (2003:108–109).

106. Personal correspondence, December 19, 1995.

107. Green's statement is posted on the Bigfoot Field Researcher's Organization website (www.bfro.net/news/challenge/green.asp). The original argument was made in the first edition of Green's *On the Track of the Sasquatch* in 1968 and may be found in Green (1971:55,73).

108. Meldrum's statement is appended to Green's at www.bfro.net/news/challenge/green.asp.

109. Green (1971:55).

110. Green (1971:55).

111. Napier (1974:89–90), among others, has made note of this odd combination.

112. See Green (1978:130–131) and Krantz (1992:119).

113. Krantz (1992:54–63); Meldrum (1999).

114. Osman-Hill (1955:47, 177; 1957:26, 34, 156).

115. Krantz (1992:98); this was Gimlin's estimate.

116. The ensuing discussion is based on an interview with Perez on April 28, 2003, with support from other sources provided where indicated. Perez has also written of his concerns in *Bigfoot Times* (Perez 2003d, 2003g, 2003i).

117. Perez (1992:2).

118. Personal communication via audiotape, February 20, 1996. Long (2004:434) has argued that the film was shot as early as late August 1967.

119. Perez (1992:13).

120. Anonymous, *Eureka Times Standard*, October 21, 1967.

121. Perez (1992). Despite having, at one time, a financial stake in the film, DeAtley remains agnostic concerning the film's authenticity: he said he never raised the question because he did not want to know the answer (Wasson 1999).

122. Perez (2003g:2).

123. Chorvinsky (2003).

124. René Dahinden, personal communication via audiotape, February 20, 1996.

6

Further Musings on Footprints

A skeptical critique of the Bigfoot phenomenon would be a much tidier endeavor were it not for the undeniable fact that the monster in question leaves footprints all over the place. If the skeptical position is to be entertained, how do we account for the tracks? The advocates' collections of casts of these footprints mean that we cannot dismiss the phenomenon as mere hallucination. Misidentification of the tracks is an insufficient explanation as well: I will happily concede that the Patterson footprints, the Bossburg tracks, Jerry Crew's finds, and Paul Freeman's fantastic inventory are not misidentified tracks of grizzly bear, black bear, or any other catalogued animal. We can thus reduce the argument on tracks to an either-or proposition: Bigfoot made them or people made them.

The skeptical position with respect to the footprints is simple: they are hoaxes, deliberately planted to further the case for Bigfoot. What motivates this activity is the subject of the final chapter. In this chapter, I want to progress further along this line of argument to address a few loose ends that need to be dealt with before Bigfoot can be relegated to the status of legend rather than animal. I submit that the footprint evidence is impressive only in volume but not in detail. It is testament to human ingenuity and mischief rather than to the presence of an undiscovered species.

One point often emphasized by advocates is the startling remoteness of the locations where Bigfoot tracks are found. The Bluff Creek region of northern

California is a favorite example. The question of how a hoaxer could get into such a region to leave his or her mark answers itself: if a person can get to a locality to examine Bigfoot tracks, then another (or the same) person has the ability to get to that place for more nefarious purposes. The claim that trackways extend into regions where a human tracker cannot follow also fails on its own logic: if you can't follow the tracks where Bigfoot ran up the densely forested canyon wall, how do you know the tracks extend all the way up or down a slope that is "covered with heavy underbrush"?[1] If the claim is going to be made that the inaccessibility of Bigfoot tracks makes them real, then we are assuming that nobody—including climbers, athletes, or even simply highly motivated individuals—cannot get to such areas *by any means.* The impossibility of human involvement in creating these tracks requires some sort of demonstration. If the advocates have done that kind of investigation, they haven't publicized it. They merely assert that it is impossible.

The argument that Bigfoot evidence is frequently found deep in inaccessible wilderness and thus could not be the product of sophomoric human engineering is not substantiated. Bluff Creek might be in the middle of nowhere, but that doesn't make it inaccessible. We can assume that Ray Wallace's road-building operation was not airlifted into place at the start of construction; as the road was built, the crew obviously had a way into work that did not require a mule train. Bigfoot made itself known by walking on the road that Wallace's employees were in the process of putting together. Patterson and Gimlin were on horseback when their furry movie star made her cameo appearance, but driving to the film site was by no means impossible: a passable road existed a mere 15–20 feet from the film site.[2] Patterson and his partner were less than a day's trip from the nearest town since the two managed to drive out of the creek bottom that afternoon, send the film out for processing, and then return to their camp the same evening.[3] The Bossburg Sasquatch rarely ventured far out of town and was not leaving any sign in the surrounding wilderness from whence it presumably came.[4] Examination of various investigators' dealings with Paul Freeman suggest that much of his evidence was within a stone's throw of where one could park a motor vehicle.[5] Bigfoot might, in fact, make its home deep within the American and Canadian wilderness, but the footprint evidence does not compel this conclusion. If Bigfoot is real, and its footprints are the likeliest sign we have of its reality, then this fantastic animal makes frequent visits to the fringes of civilization.

The sheer number of tracks found is impressive, but they combine to make fewer separate items of data than we might surmise. The issue isn't how many tracks can be counted but how many track events are really independent from one another. Every true student of Bigfoot knows that, in December 1969, something left a trackway of 1,089 prints that looked far too big to be human near Bossburg, Washington. In August 1967, John Green counted 590 tracks on Blue Creek Mountain, only a few miles from both the famous tracks of 1958 and the location of the Patterson-Gimlin movie, which would be made two months later.[6] If we are to treat these prints as data, we might be tempted to say that we have 1,679 pieces of evidence in support of Bigfoot, but subscribing to the principle of independence we have far less. Instead of a thousand pieces of evidence, we have but a handful. Common sense tells us that, given that the left prints all looked the same and the right prints all looked the same, the tracks in Bossburg were made by either a hairy ape or a skilled forger and that one of the two made the whole series. On Blue Creek Mountain, not all the tracks were the same size. Green describes there being three sets of distinguishable tracks. However many tracks individual #1 made, however, none of these were independent in the statistical scientific sense, because the same agent produced them. One print from this individual, if authenticated, is as good as a thousand. There are, thus, in this example, only four data items if we subscribe to a protocol of independent scientific sampling. Unfortunately for the advocates, this does not also mean one track is just as good as twenty, because the plausibility of hoaxing goes up as the number of tracks go down.

Rant Mullens, Ray Pickens, and Ray Wallace (through his next of kin), with their confessions of running through the woods with fake feet strapped to their boots, effectively ended all argument that the size of Bigfoot tracks ruled out their fabrication. What advocates continue to stress, however, is that the depth of the "authentic" tracks makes the possibility of hoaxing sufficiently remote to conclude that a very heavy animal made them. It is, at first glance, an intriguing possibility: if we have a string of a thousand tracks and they are sunk into the ground 3 full inches and the distance between the steps exceeds what an NBA star could accomplish, isn't that sufficient to rule out a human agent? It might be, but we should consider the problem in more detail.

If I were to strap a pair of 18-inch wood feet to my shoes and run for 100 steps on the beach, I could measure how deeply those prints sank into the sand and calculate the average. I would also observe that some of my prints sank more deeply than others and that the dimensions of all 100 prints were not identical. If I were then to take off the wood feet and run along in my regular shoes for another 100 steps, what would I find? First, I would find it easier to run because I wouldn't have to bend my knees and hips so much to keep from tripping on the wood feet. The dimensions of my footprints would still differ from print to print, as would the amount my feet would sink into the sand. But, on average, my footprints would now be deeper than they were when I was wearing my Sasquatch shoes.

This is not a particularly bold prediction. Some basic physics, familiar to advocate and skeptic alike, leads us inexorably to this conclusion. Thanks to Isaac Newton, we know that $F = ma$, which for our purposes means that the force (F) with which our foot hits the ground is going to be the product of how heavy we are (m for mass) and the acceleration (which in this case is actually deceleration) with which the foot comes to rest (a). Running is going to create a deeper impression than walking because the deceleration of the foot (the change in its velocity over time) is much greater.

It might seem like velocity is the immediate culprit here, but this is not really true. If you get hit with a Roger Clemens fastball, the force of it is what hurts you and the 90-mph velocity isn't to blame; it's that short time span that elapses between the time the ball first contacts your skin and the time it takes to stop completely. If you could magically lengthen that interval to ten minutes, you wouldn't feel a thing.

The depth of a print is dependent on how much pressure your foot imparts to the ground and how compliant the substrate is (compare dried concrete and mud). Pressure, or stress, is the force (F) divided by the area over which it is distributed. The area we are concerned with in this example is that of the sole of your normal shoe versus the sole of your Bigfoot track. Since the Bigfoot track has a greater area, the force you exert (which depends on your mass, or body weight) is dissipated over a larger area and the pressure is thereby less. This principle explains why snowshoes keep you on top of the snow, while wearing just boots causes you to sink deeply with each step.

What all this means is that, all things being equal, a big foot will not sink as deeply as a small one into a given type of soil. You would need to add proportionally more mass or acceleration to the equation to increase the force enough to also increase the depth. Thus, if you go into the business of faking Sasquatch prints, your fake feet will sink less deeply into the soil than your unshod foot unless, of course, you have had the foresight to make your phony feet out of a particularly heavy material, or—as the Wallace heirs claim—you use a moving vehicle to provide the punch necessary to impress the tracks deeply. It is this understanding that prompted rejection of some of Paul Freeman's earliest finds. Bigfoot is by all accounts really heavy, so much more than us that it is a foregone conclusion that Sasquatch tracks will always be deeper than any nearby human footprints. Everyone close to the phenomenon has understood this since 1958.

It is important to remember that acceleration is a major part of this equation. Neither Bigfoot nor a potential hoaxer has the option of altering its weight while making tracks, but both can alter the impact—the acceleration—with which their feet strike the ground. Increasing the impact of prints—by leaping, stamping, or getting some help from the inertia of vehicles or other heavy equipment—is one way a hoaxer can make an impressive track where someone taking a normal step next to the imprint would barely leave a mark. In the same vein, if Bigfoot is to successfully hide its tracks (which it must be doing a good deal of the time), one has to envision this beast literally tiptoeing about the forest (though not just on its toes), delicately placing its feet perfectly flat on the ground with each step, moving with such deliberate slowness that traveling a mile would be a literal day's walk. Eyewitness accounts do not describe such behavior.

The depth of Sasquatch prints is often awe inspiring. Certain impressions, it is reported, so far exceed anything a human, shod or unshod, can produce that there seems little point in arguing that a person could have made them. Yet few investigators have seriously pursued the question of whether an animal the description of Bigfoot is capable of producing such tracks—that is, how big an animal would be required to sink footprint impressions so deeply?

It is a difficult question to answer, because there are so many unknown variables after the fact. The data are all anecdotal: a human foot did not come close to matching what Bigfoot allegedly did, but we don't know the size of the human's shoe, what they weighed, or in some cases, how they tried to imprint their feet. Bigfoot tracks from the same event can vary in size. Moreover, what a difference in depth means in a given case is dependent on the condition of the ground and the properties of the foot (or shoe) that made the tracks—in hard-packed soil footprints might not show up at all; in mud, it is another story altogether. These factors mean that a direct assessment from a single Sasquatch event isn't usually possible.

We can do a series of thought experiments and arrive at some reasonable generalizations. I'll proceed from the following assumptions, which should not be controversial to the advocates. First, Bigfoot has a flat foot. This means that the pressure it exerts on the soil is more evenly distributed across its sole than in a human foot, which is usually arched along part of its length and width. If we use the Patterson film to argue that Bigfoot uses a compliant gait, then we can also conclude that the dynamics of the Sasquatch stance phase (the way in which the foot contacts and then leaves the ground in walking) are also different than the human pattern. People don't walk flat-footed in that the heel strikes the ground first, and only then does the weight of the body get transferred toward the front of the foot (the big toe in particular). In a compliant gait, the pressure exerted by the foot is dispersed more evenly across the sole because the heel-strike and toe-off of normal human bipedalism is of a different variety—and the greater dispersion of pressure will be more pronounced in a flat foot.[7] In using a compliant gait, Bigfoot also has an extended period of "double-support"; that is, a greater proportion of the stride cycle involves both feet on the ground compared to a striding human. This, too, will tend to decrease the overall pressure imparted to the ground. Finally, what we would really like to know is how hard Bigfoot presses its foot into the soil when it walks, and this is something that is difficult to get a handle on. What we do know from studies on people is that when a compliant gait is used, the initial impact of the heel is higher but the peak force on the ground is actually lower.[8] What the interplay of these twin observations do for footprint depth is yet to be thoroughly investigated.

Taken collectively, these observations suggest that even though the Sasquatch foot may be twice the size of a human one in terms of area, the overall pressure it exerts on the ground might be a mere fraction of a person's. What is the expected difference in the depth of their footprints in terms of numbers? Obviously, we cannot say, because we do not know how much the Sasquatch weighs.

If we work backwards from anecdote, however, we can get a ballpark figure for Bigfoot's weight and simply ask if it is reasonable. In one interview concerning the Patterson film, Bob Gimlin remarked that some of the tracks left at the scene sank a full three and a half inches into the ground.[9] In a separate interview,[10] Gimlin states that he walked his horse, which he estimated weighed 1,400 pounds loaded, right next to the Bigfoot tracks (no mention is made of how deep these particular tracks were) and that the horse's tracks did not sink as deeply as the Bigfoot's. In addition, Gimlin said he jumped off a tree stump 3 or 4 feet off the ground and landed on his high-heeled boot to try to match the depth of the tracks. Gimlin recalls that he was close to matching the track depth. Patterson apparently took footage of part of these operations in the aftermath of the film, but that film has since been lost.[11] One aspect of Gimlin's testimony enjoys some support in that, in separate visits to the film site shortly after the movie was made, both Lyle Laverty and Bob Titmus observed that human footprints did not come close to matching the 1-inch depth of the giant tracks.[12]

Gimlin is on record saying that his horse had a shoe about 5 inches in diameter. That works out to a hoof area of about 20 square inches, which does not even account for the fact that a shod horse is using a fraction of that area. He also states that he was walking his horse slowly at the time, so that at any given moment two or perhaps three hooves were impacting the soil. Measuring the area of one of the more distinct Bigfoot prints from the film site, one arrives at a value of 83 square inches.[13] If we make the reasonable assumption that, because they sank more deeply, the Sasquatch tracks were made by pressure greater than the horse's hooves, we can come up with a very conservative measure of its weight by using simple algebra: horse weight / hoof area = hoof pressure, and Bigfoot weight / track area = foot pressure. If we grant that at a given time three of the horse's hooves are in contact with ground, then hoof pressure is the horse's weight divided by the collective area of the three hooves: 1,400 pounds / 60 square inches = 23.3 pounds per square inch. Assuming hoof pressure < foot pressure, by substituting terms we can estimate that, using Gimlin's horse as a comparative yardstick, the Bigfoot Patterson filmed must have weighed in excess of 1,900 pounds! If we allow that our calculation of hoof area is too generous (likely as noted above), that number goes up: for example, if we allow that the contact area is only one-half the hoof area, then the Bigfoot filmed in 1967 weighs at least 3,800 pounds.

Actually a figure of 1,900 pounds has been posed for the film subject before—in the 1998 NASI report. But this figure is at odds with the favored estimates of up to 800 pounds,[14] and its reliability has been questioned by skeptic and advocate alike.[15] The figure is so fantastic that most advocates do not invoke it as persuasive evidence today. On the other hand, Gimlin's observations suggest that the depth of the tracks along Bluff Creek cannot be explained by a beast that weighs merely 800 pounds.

Since Gimlin said that his horse tracks did not match the depth of the Bigfoot prints, the figure of 1,900 pounds is a low estimate. When Gimlin jumped off the tree stump, his boot heel came fairly close to matching the Bigfoot impressions, which provides a more robust estimate of the weight implied by the tracks. But the problem is now one of dynamic pressures rather than static ones. That is, up to this point we are treating horse hooves and Bigfoot tracks as passively displacing the soil by virtue of body weight alone, without any extra impetus on the part of the animals. This is aptly termed a static analysis, which gives us only a rough idea of what is truly going on in a dynamic situation of stepping in and pushing off of the soil. It provides a seat-of-the-pants estimate, so the figures given above are only in the neighborhood of being accurate.

With Gimlin jumping off the tree stump, we now have to figure out what effect that has on the ground, in that he has given gravity 3 feet to add an impulse to his mass. If he concentrated the load on his boot heel the pressure imparted to the ground was tremendously large. We do not know what size boot heel Gimlin had, but he describes it as a high-heel one, presumably of the cowboy variety. I borrowed a set of such boots (size 10 ½) from a colleague and scanned and digitized the heel to get a rough idea of the impact area we're talking about—about 5 square inches. The calculation for estimating the force of impact is not involved, but it requires a number of assumptions about how he landed and the condition of the soil. Even so, whether the soil was the consistency of mud or concrete, we would always find that the impact force is several multiples of Gimlin's body weight.

The principle involved in arriving at an impact force and, ultimately, print depth, is the conservation of energy: when he left the tree stump, Gimlin began the conversion of his potential energy to kinetic energy, from which we can figure out Gimlin's (and his boot heel's) impact on the soil. Once we know this, and we specify how elastic the soil is, we can arrive at an estimate of how deeply his heel could sink in.

I consulted with an engineering colleague for help in defining the appropriate calculations. Andy Rapoff and I had collaborated on several projects involving how mechanical stresses affect bones, and in these I relied on his greater expertise in theoretical mechanics for developing our computational methods. In this instance, I provided him with the data that were available and simply asked him how we could figure out what might happen if Gimlin and Bigfoot jumped off the same tree stump. Of course, in the film it is clear that the subject was simply walking along rather than jumping off tall objects. No one has measured Bigfoot's impact force while it walks, but we can reasonably estimate what should happen if a flat-footed hairy giant jumped off the same tree stump that Gimlin did.

The math involved amounts to some straightforward algebra, with the necessary variables for estimating depth being the mass of the participants, the height over which they fall, the acceleration due to gravity (a constant), the area over which their impact is distributed, and a range of estimates for the stretchiness or compliance of the soil.[16] We solve the equation separately for Gimlin (165 pounds at the time[17]) and the alleged Bigfoot (800 pounds proposed for the film subject), with soil properties, height of their fall, and gravity being the same for each comparison (we did a series of these for different soil properties). The area of impact for Gimlin's boot heel (5 square inches) and Bigfoot's sole (83 square inches) provide the last bits of information needed to figure out how deep the two individuals are sinking in relative to one another.

When we compare the depth estimates for Gimlin's heel versus the Sasquatch print from the film site using a range of values for the soil compliance (encompassing the consistency of mud to brick and beyond), the results are surprisingly consistent: Gimlin's boot print imprints almost as deeply as the film subject's entire foot in this virtual experiment. Across a wide range of soils, we find that Gimlin's imprint sinks to over 90% of the depth of the prints made by the monster that Patterson filmed.

This is not good news for the advocates. Gimlin did say that his heel nearly matched the Bigfoot track depth, but that observation is presumably a comparison of tracks made by the film subject ambling along the creekbed, where much of the time both of its feet are on the ground supporting its weight. Our calculations suggest that only by jumping off a tree stump and landing on one foot could Bigfoot exceed Gimlin's imprint, and of course we see Bigfoot doing no such thing in the film. The only way that Gimlin's narrative of the film's aftermath makes sense is if the film star was fantastically heavy.

The bottom line is this: a boot heel, with Gimlin in the boot, should be able to provide a static pressure of somewhere around 33 pounds per square inch without any effort. If the filmed Bigfoot weighed 800 pounds, the static pressure is not even 20 pounds per square inch. If we insist on Glickman's weight estimate of 1,957 pounds, the static pressure is still below 25 pounds per square inch. It is not at all clear that the flat-footed Bigfoot should be leaving deeper tracks than Gimlin's boot heel (regardless of him jumping off of tree stumps) and that this thing's footprints should not be dwarfing Gimlin's horse's impressions. We superimpose on this problem the advocate's assertion that Bigfoot's sole has a flexible fat pad from 1 inch to 5 inches thick,[18] and the findings at Bluff Creek are even more mysterious. A hard rubber or leather heel and a horse's metallic shoes ought to have no trouble matching the depth created by a gigantic compliant foot, given the numbers that we are working with.

None of the above calculations establish beyond doubt that the tracks at the film site are bogus; ideally, we would have to know the exact nature of the impact forces that Gimlin (or his horse) produced walking along the creekbed, how compliant the Bigfoot's heel and foot was, and at what angle it contacted the ground—under the best of circumstances, the measurement of such variables is very complicated.[19] We have no hope of recovering the necessary information, as Daniel Perez notes "in the entire movie sequence, when studied carefully, never do we see the subject making a foot track in the sandbar."[20] In theory, Bigfoot's compliant gait imparts overall ground forces that should result in shallower prints than in a striding human, although the impact of the heel in a compliant gait should leave a deeper impression.

But these observations proceed from the assumption that the feet of people and Sasquatches are similarly proportioned to the rest of their bodies, and, according to one advocate, this is not the case. Henner Fahrenbach, in his 1998 statistical treatment of Bigfoot data, suggested that an unshod human might be expected to leave tracks of comparable depth to a Sasquatch foot in a given substrate.[21] He based this inference on his thinking that Bigfoot feet are relatively large in proportion to other parts of the body, and would thereby exhibit less pressure on the ground despite imparting greater overall force. Fahrenbach's observation by itself suggests that great depth of Sasquatch prints should not be a typical finding. His assessment is blunt: "contrary to popular belief, plantar pressure in even large sasquatches does not appear to range exorbitantly beyond human values, as one would reasonably expect from anatomical considerations."[22]

John Napier had a difficult time reconciling the footprints with what he saw on the film (based in part on some information that was later shown to be erroneous), such that he concluded that "the footprints must be fakes or the film is."[23] If we take the data from the advocates themselves, take their statements at face value, and simply follow the logic through, Napier's statement is not easily dismissed. There is reason to doubt that the Bigfoot seen on the film made the tracks described by Gimlin and others. In any case, people finding Bigfoot tracks ought to be able to match the depth of the prints, unless every Sasquatch out there weighs thousands and thousands of pounds.

Other investigations of print depth support this conclusion. One set of tracks from the Blue Mountains outside of Walla Walla, Washington, was investigated by veteran Bigfoot researcher Erik Beckjord in conjunction with the U.S. Forest Service.[24] These tracks were found by Paul Freeman in June 1982. Within a day of the tracks' discovery, the Forest Service brought a truck to the site. Having fashioned a steel plate matching the dimensions of the tracks, the investigators placed the plate beneath a jack that was raised to support the rear end of the truck. In three separate trials, the steel plate could only impress half as deep as the mysterious tracks, despite the fact that the rear of the truck weighed 3,100 pounds. What conclusions should be drawn? Beckjord does not entertain the idea of a hoax, but instead suggests that, perhaps being constructed of metallic materials, Bigfoot is not a normal zoological species. The suggestion that Bigfoot builds its tissues from the higher end of the periodic table is a novel concept, but the initial conclusion—that the tracks were not made by a conventional animal—is entirely plausible.

Krantz acknowledged that for the depth of some discovered tracks the Bigfoot's weight must exceed 2,000 pounds.[25] As this estimate would have Bigfoot dwarfing a good-sized polar bear, one wonders how a hoaxer could accomplish such a feat. For a trackway hundreds of yards long, it would seem unlikely that this could be done in a short period of time. Even for the cases reviewed above, however, the documentation of track depth is always anecdotal: there has been no systematic documentation of track depth over any significant distance or challenging terrain. Attempts at demonstrating that a particular depth is beyond the scope of human fabrication are rare, and those alleged demonstrations (e.g., in the context of the Patterson film noted above) have nagging problems. From my point of view, such research, if conducted and documented carefully, could pose a serious challenge to the skeptical position, but to date, the advocates have provided only dismissive assertions that no explanation suffices for the depth of prints other than Bigfoot. We have already noted the immediate problem with this line of thinking: it requires an insanely large weight for Bigfoot. The counter to this argument—that if the giant Sasquatch could not do it, then how could mere humans—is specious because it ignores human ingenuity. Donald Baird of the Princeton Museum of Natural History points out that a motivated human can create a very convincing trackway displaying inhumanly large strides and tracks of impressive depth by using a mallet and stake to drive templates into soil and bagging his own feet with forest litter to disguise the human sign.[26]

The various accounts of Jerry Crew's discoveries are cases where the anecdote is impressive, but the clincher of documentation and full investigation never materializes. In arriving at the scene of the Wallace road building operation in 1958, those investigating the tracks, including John Green, were disappointed that of the hundreds of tracks that the nighttime visitor had made in the recent past, very few remained for scrutiny.[27] Secondhand accounts put the depth of the tracks at a full 2 inches[28]; impressive indeed, although it isn't clear that anyone bothered to do any type of investigating to see how hard it would have been to duplicate the impressions. In any case, the problem of access to heavy equipment doesn't exist at the scene of a road-building operation, and the possibility that some of the equipment could have been recruited in the track-making effort can't be ruled out.

John Green knew this all too well, so he diligently reported that Bob Titmus found some more impressive tracks along the sandbar of Bluff Creek itself—far removed from bulldozers and road graters but still only a few hundred yards removed from the camps of potential practical-joking road crews. Green measured some of the tracks, noting that the impressive depth of 1 to 1.25 inches in the few tracks that remained compared favorably to his own scant imprints.[29] Only by jumping off a log could he get his heel to sink in as deeply. While conceding that fakery wasn't impossible, since he couldn't figure out the means Green discounted the possibility. A more sober conclusion would be to rule out a simple scenario of an unburdened individual ambling along the road with fake feet.

In order to consider other possibilities, it would be necessary to know more about the trackway itself. However, in this particular context, Green doesn't remark on how extensive the tracks were. In the case of single tracks or abbreviated trackways, the advocate position is weak indeed. Dahinden and Titmus have independently asserted that producing tracks without fake feet is quite feasible over short distances where there are a limited number of prints.[30] Producing alarming depth of prints is in such cases unproblematic.

If a person could not excavate to a certain depth in a given soil, certainly Bigfoot's capacious sole would not be up to the task.

Another aspect of the Crew discoveries that is remarked on is the dramatic distance between the prints, indicating a remarkable stride ranging from 4 to 5 feet[31] all the way up to 10.[32] The lower numbers aren't at all impossible for a tall person to duplicate with a little contortion of the hips and knees.[33] Ten feet is another matter, but those researchers visiting the site reported no such thing, that bit of fantastic evidence having been grated over in the name of progress in transportation.[34] Planting tracks from a moving vehicle obviously removes the mystery as well.

An impossibly long stride is a frequent motif of Bigfoot stories, so it is worth considering how problematic this observation is to the skeptical position. For the sake of argument, let's drop the complaint that the claim of the stride lacks documentation and also consider that the tracks are not found along a road. No less than Grover Krantz provides the skeptical position with an out.[35] He recalls an incident where Bigfoot apparently made its way up a steep incline with a distance of 8 feet being traversed from heel to opposite heel. It would appear that no person could put on a set of fake feet and accomplish this. Krantz reports, however, that the culprit came clean about his ingenious but simple deception. It seems a rather limber high school student put the fake feet on backwards and bounded down the slope to record a remarkable incident of Sasquatch athleticism.

This incident is a perfect example of the greatest mistake the advocates have historically made: underestimating the resourcefulness and determination of the hoaxers. Even the dimmest of confidence artists knows that for a shell game to work, the chump being hustled has to be distracted away from the point of deception. This is no less true for an effective Bigfoot hoax. You will recall that one anomaly that Joel Hardin noted in tracking Paul Freeman's Sasquatch was that the monster did not leave any sign of entering or leaving the short stretch of watershed where the prints were found. The question naturally arises: If Bigfoot shows no sign of entering or leaving an area, how does a hoaxer enter or leave, himself, without leaving a sign? It is a valid question, but not particularly problematic. In the act of producing Bigfoot evidence, a hoaxer cannot help but leave indications of his or her presence, but disguising these indications is by no means impossible. Brushing away one's own sign is a tedious but certain way of eliminating obvious clues to chicanery, and tossing a few twigs or other forest floor detritus over the dusted-off ground effectively distracts inquiring eyes from investigating further. One can envision obviating these procedures by simply tying a jumble of boughs to the bottom of one's feet while fashioning a convincing trackway by hand: the natural act of stepping over one's prints at different angles would leave a jumble of impressions that would be as amorphous as the surrounding earth.

In practice, however, such involved procedures would probably be overkill. Any footprint discovery that is unusual quickly gets overrun by curious investigators and the original context of the find is obliterated in short order. The important point is that most hoaxed footprints are deemed phony without mention of ancillary signs of the hoaxer's presence. That observation suggests that if some prints can be declared phony on their own merits without reference to other signs of human involvement, it stands to reason that hoaxers know effective means to disguise their own presence.

It boils down to the ability of the investigator to distinguish a legitimate track from a bogus one. The fact that no agreed-on standard exists against which novel Bigfoot tracks can be compared is not lost on most advocates. This lack of an unambiguously authentic track demands a level of agnosticism on the part of the investigator. Bob Titmus, who may have seen more tracks in his life than any other investigator, was clear in his conviction that no claim to authenticity could be made for a single print regardless of context or documentation.[36] This is an admirably skeptical position from someone who claims to have seen Bigfoot on two occasions.[37]

Deciding what constitutes a legitimate set of tracks is a very subjective endeavor. Consider the case of three people who went to the Patterson film site in the weeks after the movie was made. Each offered Daniel Perez decidedly different opinions of the tracks at the site. Bob Titmus was impressed: "Nothing whatever here indicated that these tracks could have been faked."[38] On the other hand, Richard Henry expressed "mixed emotions" about the event recorded by the tracks, since he stated that "I could not find [tracks] where they started" and the sequence of footprints looked "symmetrical and mechanical."[39] Lyle Laverty, who may have been the first person to see the tracks after Patterson and Gimlin had departed, was intrigued enough to take some pictures of the strange footprints. But he, too, has expressed some skepticism based on the proximity of the film site to a road and on his own experience in the months preceding the film: he had heard the tales of the disturbances on

Wallace's operation, but he had never seen any tracks at all that he couldn't explain until Patterson and Gimlin had come and gone.[40]

How does one recognize a real Bigfoot track? The simple answer is one can't, but two of my colleagues in anthropology disagree. Both Krantz and Meldrum have argued that the possibility of a hoax can be ruled out for certain footprints because no hoaxer could possess the requisite knowledge of correct anatomical details for an animal sporting the size and dimensions of Bigfoot.[41] These details might be the dermal ridges or the underlying foot skeleton betrayed by the particulars of the track. The premise of this argument is flawed, if not irrational, on two counts. The first problem is that these credentialed academics lay claim to a specialized body of knowledge that no layperson could possess. This is dubious on logical grounds, as we explored in chapter 4: the argument assumes that fabricated tracks cannot be interpreted as having anatomical consistency. These scientists' willingness to see biomechanical complexity where none may exist is not the fault of the track.

The second problem with their argument is that the confirming data for the model are assumed rather than known. The claim that the foot makes perfect sense for an animal the size and stature of the Sasquatch is all well and good, but it presumes that these are known quantities. The subject of the Patterson film has had its weight estimated as being between 350 pounds (Patterson's) and just shy of one ton (Glickman's). Which weight is perfectly harmonious with the footprints the subject left alongside the creek in 1967?

These objections may be trifling in the end because there are more direct problems of interpretation. I've noted this before at some length, but it bears repeating here because it renders the anatomical models, however detailed and elegant, irrelevant: *the exact form of the pedal skeleton cannot be reliably inferred from the shape of a footprint even under ideal circumstances.* Yes, you can tell where the heel bone is and where the toes begin in a given footprint. But you cannot reliably infer the position of the anatomical joints and the relative length and width of the foot bones from footprints alone. This would seem to be all the more difficult considering that one hypothesized adaptation of the Sasquatch foot is that the sole is cushioned by a soft-tissue pad that is perhaps several inches thick.[42] Regrettably, Krantz is no longer alive to defend himself on this point, but Meldrum has the background and expertise to conduct a controlled, double-blind study of the efficacy of inferring joint position from footprints. Without these kinds of data, no one is obligated to give credence to this model of the Sasquatch foot.

Meldrum's arguments bring up another point about Sasquatch footprints—the latest wrinkle in the history of efforts to prove that the tracks defy all explanation save one. He notes that some Bigfoot tracks leave pressure ridges in the soil.[43] Pressure ridges are exactly what their name implies: mounds of soil thrown up by the dynamic forces that a foot imparts to the ground during locomotion. At the Bluff Creek film site, at least one of the tracks displays a pressure ridge near the middle of the footprint—an apparently different pattern from that of a normal human print where the primary pressure ridge occurs nearer the front owing to the typical "toe-off" thrust of human bipedalism.

As it happens, Bob Titmus cast ten consecutive footprints from the film site a little over a week after the event. These prints show all manner of variation in their details.[44] What the allegedly anomalous pressure ridges and variability in the tracks mean is a matter of perspective. According to Meldrum, the variation (which is not quantified in any way) is evidence of a living, flexible foot that is functionally distinct from the rigid construction of the arched human foot.[45] This latter insight is gleaned from the strange pressure ridge in one of the Patterson film site tracks: Meldrum interprets this as evidence of a "midtarsal break" that betrays flexibility in some of the foot's anatomical joints that human beings simply do not possess.[46]

There are, however, alternative explanations that Meldrum does not explore (or, if he has explored them, he has not published the supporting data). Minor differences in soil composition, compaction, and humidity could account for much of the variation in the tracks cast by Titmus (for the sake of argument here, we will allow the casting process to be faithful and perfect—a generous allowance). Soil condition is well documented to have an immense impact on the form of animal tracks, so much so that the condition of the ground on which an animal walks can obscure and distort both anatomy and interpretation of locomotor dynamics.[47]

That a midtarsal break can be reliably inferred from footprints is therefore a dicey proposition, especially if such inferences involve casts of tracks rather than the tracks themselves, which are one step further removed from the event.[48] Even so, if we suspend skepticism about what the footprints can tell us, the argument about Sasquatch tracks being hard to fabricate still does not hold up. If the structure of the midfoot differs between Bigfoot and people, and if the pressure ridge seen in the one Patterson footprint can be specifically attributed to this condition, it follows that people should be unable to reproduce this pattern while walking. In fact, while conducting our research on the effects of striding versus compliant walking, Dan Schmitt and I discovered that by adopting a compliant gait, one could produce pressure ridges at very different locations in different footprints. If people can produce this pattern yet do not have midtarsal flexibility, the Bluff Creek track in question cannot be used to argue that Bigfoot has this condition, much less that the tracks must be authentic. Meldrum's model may be internally consistent, but it has yet to be corroborated in the real world where feet meet dirt (see figs. 6.1 and 6.2).

In public presentations, René Dahinden was ruthless in his criticism of Krantz's interpretation of footprint evidence, and, after hearing Meldrum defend some of that evidence, he indicated he would have nothing further to do with Meldrum.[49] This was only partly attributable to the fact that the two held the status of the Ph.D. types that Dahinden scorned. What really set Dahinden off was his impression that the two scientists thought that they couldn't be fooled. He knew that in a field of inquiry where deception was part and parcel of the endeavor, arrogance was a recipe for disaster. Once you became convinced that you couldn't be fooled, you could be fooled all the time.

FIGURE 6.1
Footprint from 1967 film site at Bluff Creek. The pressure ridge in the middle of the footprint has been argued to indicate a unique anatomical configuration of the Sasquatch foot. Photo used with permission from Lyle Laverty.

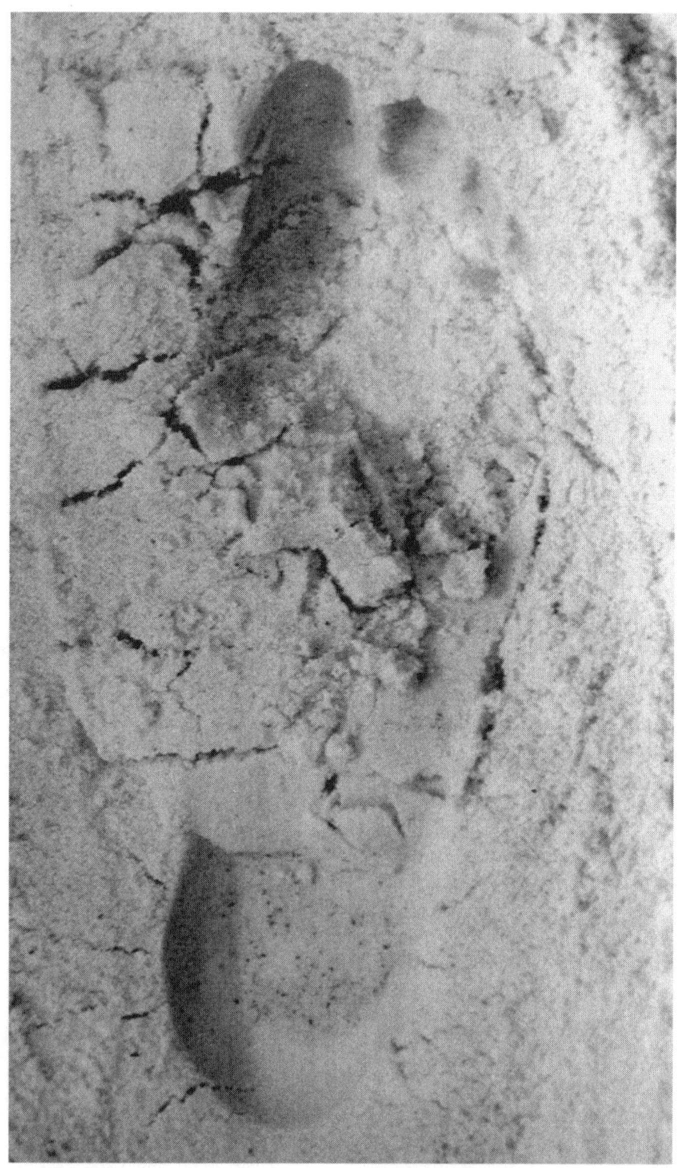

FIGURE 6.2
Human footprint resulting from compliant gait. This track displays a pressure ridge near the middle of the footprint. Consequently, the form of the Bluff Creek footprint is not evidence of a unique anatomical configuration of a Sasquatch foot. The form of the pressure ridges depends more on soil conditions than the anatomy of the feet in question.

In an odd departure from the norms of scientific practice, Krantz admitted to deliberately withholding information with respect to his research on Bigfoot. He claimed to have identified two features of Sasquatch prints that allowed him to rule out hoaxing.[50] In other words, Krantz claimed to have the ability to authenticate Bigfoot tracks. However, to circumvent future fabrication, Krantz decided he would tell no one just what these features were. In the context of Bigfoot this position is certainly understandable, but in so doing, Krantz could make no legitimate scientific claims. His proposed criteria for pronouncing tracks genuine could not be tested or evaluated by his peers or anyone else.

Or so it seemed. In 1990, Krantz received a cast of a track from, of all places, southern Indiana. Despite the unlikely point of origin, this track satisfied his two authenticating criteria, and Krantz cited Bob Titmus and some law enforcement personnel as supporting his conclusion that the track was genuine.[51] He declined to discuss the circumstances of the find and noted that the sender was anxious to put the experience behind him, had moved away, and could not be reached.

This claim would be Krantz's undoing. Michael Dennett was as surprised as anyone that Bigfoot could be eking out a living among the woods and cornfields of the Midwest and decided in 1994 that some follow-up investigation was in order.[52] Titmus reported that perhaps he wasn't quite as confident in the track as Krantz had represented, and when Dennett located the fingerprint expert in law enforcement that Krantz had cited, that official would not admit to being positive about the track being all that it was cracked up to be (see fig. 6.3).

After considerable effort, Dennett located a person by the name of J. W. Parker who knew all about the track.[53] Parker knew about the track because he had mailed the cast of it to Krantz; he knew even more about the track than Krantz thought because not only had he cast the print, he had fabricated the impression. It was a twenty-minute effort—an effort that, by Dennett's account, Parker now regrets having made. The hoaxer's motivation was one of simple curiosity rather than of malice; Parker thought Krantz's claim was interesting and wanted to see if Krantz could detect this particular hoax. Parker could not have anticipated that Krantz would feature this track in his next book as a trophy of his expertise.

In a published rebuttal to Dennett's stunning discovery, Krantz still declined to reveal his magic criteria of authentication.[54] Parker surmised it

FIGURE 6.3
Veteran Bigfoot researcher Cliff Crook with a track cast from Bloomington, Indiana, that passed Grover Krantz's secret tests for authenticity. Michael Dennett established the fraudulent nature of the track in 1994. Crook, despite having had a personal encounter with Bigfoot, denounces the Patterson film as a hoax and argues that the Skookum cast depicts a kneeling elk rather than a reclining Sasquatch. Photo by Michael Dennett, used with permission.

might have been any number of things: a phony scar, the imprint of a toenail, the walnut shell fragment for a little toe, or the planting of dermal ridges here and there. Krantz's rejoinder to Dennett was nothing less than bizarre. He insisted he had never endorsed the track as genuine, at least in so many words (what he did say in his 1992 book was that it satisfied his two secret criteria, that it was "tangible evidence," and "the best evidence" he had from east of the Rockies).[55] In addition, Krantz insisted that he knew part of the track was fake all along but thought it unnecessary to bring up that detail in 1992.[56]

Speaking at a Bigfoot conference in Harrison Hot Springs in May 1996, Dahinden embarked on a long and withering *ad hominem* attack on Krantz's work in the field of Sasquatch research.[57] Much of the talk was vintage Dahinden diatribe, but the subtext was a lecture to the next generation of researchers: this is not an enterprise in which your credentials will lead you infallibly to the truth. Using Krantz as a counterexample, Dahinden suggested that suspicion and skepticism are critical qualities in the Bigfoot researcher. He invoked the infamous case of the Hitler Diaries.[58] The text was apparently convincing, and the exciting prospect of the handwritten entries being the work of the Fuhrer prompted many to embrace them as genuine. The discovery that the manufacture of the paper on which the diaries were written post-dated Hitler's death put an end to the affair. Referring to the Freeman tracks that Krantz so often marshaled in support of his arguments, Dahinden observed, "It is not the implications which are in doubt, but the authenticity."[59] At the conference, he was simply making the point that if the trackway itself was manufactured, the study of the dermal ridge patterns was a waste of time. During these same proceedings, Dahinden interrupted Meldrum's discussion of a Paul Freeman discovery to make the same point.

Dahinden's admonition—at the conference and in the years since—fell on deaf ears. The Bigfoot community has, of late, hitched its credibility to a fingerprint expert hailing from Conroe, Texas. Jimmy Chilcutt has a collection of over 1,000 prints of nonhuman primate hands and feet.[60] Chilcutt is not an anthropologist but does police work involving forensic identification using fingerprint evidence. Soon after seeing Meldrum on television in 1998, Chilcutt arranged to examine Meldrum's cast collection to evaluate whether the dermatoglyphics (dermal ridge patterns) could shed any light on the Bigfoot mystery. Chilcutt portrayed himself as disinterested and skeptical with respect to the evidence. After examining Meldrum's collection, however, he became firmly of the opinion that the Sasquatch is real.[61]

Chilcutt's reasoning, at first glance, seems unobjectionable. Dermal ridges on human feet possess a certain pattern; dermal ridges on ape feet have some features in common with humans and some features that are different. But the Bigfoot casts are altogether a different story, Chilcutt explains. These casts have ridge patterns that differ from those of both humans and apes: the primary direction of the ridges run longitudinally in the Sasquatch foot, rather than transversely (as in humans) or obliquely (as in apes).[62] Chilcutt also detected the presence of tiny healed scars that disrupted the dermal patterns in the casts in the same fashion as can be observed in living primate feet. And it wasn't just Freeman's discoveries that impressed Chilcutt: he detected some of the same features in the Blue Creek Mountain material and even in a track cast from Georgia.[63] Chilcutt believes, and not without reason, that his expertise in this area exceeds that of most biologists. Of the minutiae of details in the prints, he figures "someone would have to know a real lot about biology and dermatoglyphics to know that. Anybody that smart wouldn't be messing with fakes."[64]

Chilcutt has insulated himself from criticism by peddling his wares for the television cameras and the newspapers,[65] while having avoided a systematic presentation of his case in a forum (e.g., any of a number of scientific journals) where the data can be examined critically.[66] Still, there is no need to suppose that Chilcutt has not found what he claims. The question is whether his interpretation is correct.

In its structure, Chilcutt's argument is identical to those of Krantz and Meldrum: Sufficient expertise on the part of the investigator allows him to discern the bogus from the legitimate. As noted before, this presupposes a standard for comparison. Chilcutt concludes the uniqueness of the Bigfoot casts is proof of the animal. But if the Bigfoot casts have features that we do not see in any living primate, it does not follow that the casts are from an unknown type. It is as parsimonious to suppose that the longitudinal ridge patterns are an artifact of fabrication. The perspective of comparative anatomy would, in fact, lead to the sensible conclusion that, if the Bigfoot tracks have dermal patterns that correspond to no living primate, then a primate foot did not make the tracks. Nobody knows if the "unique" foot dermatoglyphics make any biological sense, but by the newspaper accounts there is something very unapelike in the details.

The case was not quite so mysterious when I phoned Chilcutt about another report that featured his Bigfoot work.[67] I had been puzzled by this story because it stated that the examined Bigfoot tracks in question did not match any known primate in their dermatoglyphic patterns along the side of the foot, with the single exception of one species of South American monkey.[68] When I asked Chilcutt to explain what he thought this meant, he told me that he had an actual mold and cast of the howler monkey's foot, whereas his other data on primate foot dermatoglyphics were in the form of prints. Chilcutt could state that Bigfoot looked like a howler monkey and didn't look like a human because he had comparative data on these two primates. He was candid in telling me that he did not know whether any other primates matched Bigfoot in this regard, because he did not have the appropriate data by which to make this judgment. When Chilcutt told me that, in his view, the media accounts of his work were by and large accurate but never developed his argument in sufficient detail, it became clear to me that the reporting of his analyses had taken a few shortcuts. It is not nearly the open-and-shut case that it is presented to be.

Chilcutt commits the same logical fallacy that bedeviled Grover Krantz and John Napier: he deduces that hoaxing is incompatible with expertise. Yet a would-be hoaxer need only contemplate the soles of their own feet to get inspiration for the subtler aspects of footprint-making. A particularly industrious one could utilize a nonhuman primate blueprint to throw the scientists off the real trail. It is a relatively simple matter to fabricate dermal ridges, even when dealing with the problem of giant feet. A human foot, latex, and kerosene permit the fabrication of fake feet with any number of dermal ridge arrangements, proportioned or distorted,[69] and, in fact, what Bigfoot advocates have identified as "sweat pores" (microscopic holes in the skin for the secretion of sweat) may be unintentional artifacts created in the process of casting such footprints.[70]

Chilcutt's insistence that the patterns he has identified can be matched to different tracks found many years and hundreds of miles apart[71] is irrelevant. Identical patterns might mean either that the same animal made them or that the same phony Sasquatch foot (or same faking technique) made them. Fake feet can travel very well, and ideas for forgery travel with even greater ease.

At the risk of belaboring the point, there is a final example that should put the Sasquatch experts on notice that the shenanigans extend to the very core of alleged Bigfoot evidence. One hallmark of "real" Bigfoot tracks is the so-called split ball or double-ball that appears as a sideways ridge along the inside part of some of the tracks behind where the big toe makes its impression. This configuration is hailed as a legitimate Sasquatch trait,[72] and it is obvious that human footprints do not bear this particular trademark. Such tracks have appeared repeatedly in print in photographs taken by René Dahinden, Ivan Sanderson, and associates of Peter Byrne.[73] The more famous published examples were found along a ridge above Bluff Creek the summer preceding Patterson's famous film in the drainage.[74] There were actually three sets of different-sized tracks found that summer on Blue Creek Mountain, and Dahinden may have considered these to be among the most convincing he had seen.[75] The tracks were, in fact, apparently instrumental in convincing Patterson to look for Bigfoot signs in the months to come. John Green describes some of the 1958 tracks as having "a sort of double ball."[76]

When Ray Wallace's family revealed that their patriarch had been involved in Bigfoot hijinks for years and years, the community of advocates rationalized that Wallace's antics were so sophomoric that he was irrelevant, since the "good" evidence would carry the day. The Blue Creek Mountain tracks made Patterson's film all the more believable because of the proximity of the events to one another. But the press photograph of Wallace's nephew holding up some of his uncle's handiwork was particularly damning: here was a fake foot that displayed, unmistakably, the split-ball feature that nobody had been able to explain up on Blue Creek Mountain as anything other than proof of the tracks' authenticity.[77] The form of the bogus foot—the split ball, the tapering forefoot, the squared-off big toe, and the curiously triangular fifth toe—is eerily reminiscent of what is featured in tracks presented as favorable evidence for Bigfoot in no less than six books![78] We do not know for certain that Ray Wallace faked tracks in 1967, but he was engaged in an operation at the appropriate times and places that indicate clearly that he was in a position to do so.[79] What his family's revelation did prove is that he had the wherewithal to manufacture Bigfoot signs of a kind that the experts would endorse over the decades. The counterargument of the advocates, that Bluff Creek has sported several different sets of Bigfoot tracks since 1958, is insipid. Wallace's family maintains he had not one, but several sets of bogus feet,[80] and Rant Mullens had more than one set to loan as well (see figs. 6.4 and 6.5).[81]

Recently, the Willow Creek–China Flat Museum has offered a $100,000 prize to anyone who can recreate the circumstances of the making of the tracks found in 1958 at Wallace's construction site.[82] It is a safe bet that no one is going to collect. The terms of demonstration are rigid. The tracks have to be made at night, without detection, with variation in toe position, track shape, and stride over sets of footprints, and, of course, they have to achieve sufficient depth to dwarf human impressions.[83] The terrain over which the tracks must be made is intimidating. In other words, to win the prize you would have to make footprints of a variety and over an area that were never properly documented in the first place. The museum's challenge is clearly a reaction to the Wallace family confession, and its terms suggest that the advocate camp has transformed the anecdotal evidence from 1958 into a body of scientifically verified facts.

Anyone can examine a mysterious footprint and read any number of details into it. Anyone can claim that the footprint cannot be explained by a human agent. With a little research, anyone can show that the print has the signature of neither human nor ape and draw the conclusion that it was made

FIGURE 6.4

Artist's reconstruction of one of the Blue Creek Mountain Sasquatch prints photographed by René Dahinden in the summer of 1967. The indentation behind the big toe marks the "double-ball" arrangement said to characterize authentic Bigfoot tracks. Drawing by Zina Deretsky.

FIGURE 6.5
Dale Lee Wallace, nephew of Ray Wallace, displays one of several sets of bogus Sasquatch feet used by his uncle in fabricating Bigfoot trackways. Compare this foot to the "authentic" footprint reproduced in Figure 6.4. The Wallace track contains a signature Sasquatch trait: the "double-ball." Wallace admitted to faking tracks as early as 1958, a statement supported by his family following his death in 2002. Photo by Dave Rubert, used with permission.

by a Sasquatch. All of these interpretations have been floated, yet the skeptics remain unmoved.

The problem with the research on the footprints is that it has been conducted with a misplaced sense of where the burden of proof ought to be. The cases of Rant Mullens and Ray Wallace should remind us that fake feet produce convincing tracks. Krantz proved that even secret knowledge of real Sasquatch traits—foolproof criteria of validation, it would seem—is no insurance against being duped. If we liken Bigfoot to an Aesop's fable, the moral of the story is that the level of your own conviction that the footprint evidence is authentic is really immaterial. When investigators rule out the possibility of a hoax without bothering to entertain seriously how such mischief might be done, it raises the question of whether the advocates are interested in finding out the hard answers or only the convenient ones.

I can come up with an idea of what a Sasquatch foot should look like and I can draw on all sorts of biological principles to defend my idea. When someone finds Bigfoot tracks, I can examine these and—based on my idea—infer whether the tracks are consistent with what I think a Sasquatch ought to look like. I can even then point to the good fit of the real tracks with my prior conception of them and announce that my idea—my anatomical model of a Sasquatch foot—has been verified. Anyone so inclined can agree with my argument, and certainly nobody is in a position to prove that I am wrong. Yet my argument in this case is entirely circular, and this is the problem with Bigfoot research. The arguments are there, but the science is not.

NOTES

1. This is Green's (1978:68) description of the area of Jerry Crew's 1958 discoveries on the Wallace road-building operation.

2. Lyle Laverty, personal communication, December 30, 2003.

3. Perez (1992:13–14).

4. Coleman (2003:122–125).

5. Dennett (1989:268–269, 1994:501); Byrne, personal correspondence, October 21, 2003.

6. Green (1971:47).

7. This interpretation is consistent with the views expressed by the Russian advocates Dmitri Bayanov and Igor Bourtsev in their initial report on the film (Hunter and Dahinden 1975:181–182).

8. McMahon, Valiant, and Frederick (1987); Schmitt (2003); Chi and Schmitt (2004).

9. The transcript of this November 1967 interview with Patterson and Gimlin can be found on the Bigfoot Encounters website: http://www.n2.net/prey/Bigfoot/.

10. This interview was recorded on videotape on March 29, 1992. John Green conducted the interview. The transcript of this can be found on the Bigfoot Encounters website: http://www.n2.net/prey/Bigfoot/.

11. Perez (1992:11).

12. Perez (1992:22); Green (1978:123).

13. Krantz (1992:20) provides a photo of one of the casts from the event with a scale grid included. I derived the area figure by calibrating and digitizing the image in Sigma Scan 5.0 (SPSS, Chicago, Illinois).

14. Krantz (1992:108–109) notes that estimates range from 280 up to 800 pounds. Krantz himself thought the form on the film weighed in the neighborhood of 500 pounds.

15. Daegling and Schmitt (1999:24–25); Fahrenbach (1998; personal correspondence, June 16, 1999).

16. The equation is $\delta = [mg + \sqrt{mg(mg + 2E\sqrt{A}h)}]/(E\sqrt{A})$. The terms refer to variables described in the text: δ is depth of the print, m is the mass of the individual, g is the acceleration due to gravity, E is elasticity (compliance) of the soil, A is the area of impact, and h is the height of the fall.

17. Perez (1992:13).

18. Cachel (1985); Krantz (1992); Fahrenbach (1998).

19. Chi and Schmitt (2004).

20. Perez (1992:11).

21. Fahrenbach (1998:67).

22. Fahrenbach (1998:68).

23. Napier (1974:93).

24. Beckjord (1982). This study is described in a December newsletter entitled *Sasquatch Search News*, a publication of Beckjord's Project Bigfoot.

25. Krantz (1992:39).

26. Baird (1989).

27. Green (1978:67).

28. Hunter and Dahinden (1975:84).

29. Green (1978:68).

30. Dennett (1994:501–502, 505), and personal correspondence from Dahinden, January 14, 1997.

31. Sanderson (1961:127).

32. Hunter and Dahinden (1975:85).

33. Daegling and Schmitt (1999:23).

34. Crew did, in fact, state that the stride was as large as 10 feet (Hunter and Dahinden, 1975:85), although it is unclear whether he observed this directly or is relating information from Ray Wallace.

35. Krantz (1992:41–42).

36. Dennett (1994:505).

37. Greenwell (1996).

38. Perez (1992:21).

39. Daniel Perez interview with Richard Henry, July 7, 2003, in personal correspondence with the author.

40. Personal communication via telephone, December 30, 2003.

41. Krantz made this assertion repeatedly in *Big Footprints* (1992) but crafted the argument in earlier contributions (1977a, 1977b) to the volume *The Scientist Looks at Sasquatch.* This volume was a collection of reprinted articles from the journal *Northwest Anthropological Research Notes*; Krantz's works appeared there in 1972. Meldrum has articulated a similar position in several television appearances. In a *USA Today* newspaper article (May 24, 1996), Meldrum said that while some footprints were obviously hoaxed, others were so anatomically consistent that it was unlikely that even a skilled hoaxer could have produced them. Perez (2000b:2) reports that Meldrum has stated that there are features of Bigfoot tracks that are impossible to fake.

42. Cachel (1985). Krantz (1992) necessarily rejected aspects of Cachel's interpretation, since her conclusion was that, given the presence of this large, flexible sole pad, inference of underlying pedal skeleton details would be tenuous.

43. Meldrum (1999, 2002, 2004).

44. Meldrum displayed these in his presentation at the 2002 meeting of the American Association of Physical Anthropologists in Buffalo, New York. Abstract of the presentation appeared in the association's journal (Meldrum 2002).

45. Meldrum (1999, 2004). The larger presentation of the 1999 abstract was given in Columbus, Ohio, in April of that year. A version of this poster presentation can be viewed at www.isu.edu/%7Emeldd/fxnlmorph.html.

46. Meldrum articulated this position in his presentation at the 2002 meeting of the American Association of Physical Anthropologists in Buffalo, New York (Meldrum 2002, 2004).

47. Gatesy et al. (1999).

48. Wasson (1994:15) suggested the use of casts for interpretive purposes was speculative and prone to misinterpretation.

49. Dahinden provided me with videotapes of his talks at the annual Sasquatch Symposium from 1995 and 1996 in which he offered blistering critiques of Krantz's work; in personal correspondence (June 28, 1996, March 6, 1997), he indicated his refusal to engage Meldrum in any discussions of Sasquatch evidence.

50. Krantz (1992:35).

51. Krantz (1992:84–85).

52. Dennett (1994:505–507).

53. J. W. Parker is a pseudonym; the individual wished not to be identified with the hoax, but there is little doubt that this person was responsible for the track (see Dennett

1994:507–508). Byrne (personal correspondence, October 21, 2003) also knows of the role that "Parker" played in the affair. I do not know the individual's identity.

54. Krantz (1999:299–300).

55. Krantz (1992:84–85).

56. Krantz (1999:299–300).

57. Dahinden provided me with a videotape of his and Meldrum's talk at this conference.

58. Dahinden had previously made this argument to skeptical investigator Michael Dennett (1989:266).

59. Dahinden (1984:131).

60. Anonymous, *Houston Chronicle*, February 21, 2000.

61. Stein (2001).

62. Sieveking (2000).

63. Chilcutt's "Dermal Ridge Examination Report: Georgia Casting" is posted online at Bobbie Short's Bigfoot Encounters website (http://www.n2.net/prey/bigfoot/).

64. Stein (2001).

65. Among his television appearances was the Discovery Channel's airing of *Sasquatch: Legend Meets Science* (2003, Whitewolf Productions). The *Houston Chronicle* featured Chilcutt in a February 2, 2000, article, and the *Denver Post* followed suit on January 14, 2001.

66. In a February 8, 2004, telephone conversation, Chilcutt indicated to me that he has no intention of publishing his results, his rationale being that he is not a professional writer and he did not see the purpose of publishing the results personally. He suggested that he hoped that other scientists would use his data in their arguments.

67. The conversation took place on February 8, 2004.

68. The article from the BBC is posted on Bobbie Short's Bigfoot Encounters website (http://www.n2.net/prey/Bigfoot/articles/jimmy.htm).

69. Baird (1989); Chilcutt (telephone conversation, February 8, 2004) says the dermal ridges in Sasquatch feet are about twice the size of humans.

70. Freeland and Rowe (1989).

71. Stein (2001).

72. Gordon (1992:24).

73. Hunter and Dahinden (1975); Sanderson (1961); Byrne (1976).

74. Green (1978:74–79).

75. Comments made at the Sasquatch Symposium, May 4, 1996, in Harrison Hot Springs, BC.

76. Green (1978:68).

77. Daegling and Radford (2003).

78. Byrne (1976:xxvii); Green (1978:77); Hunter and Dahinden (1975:inset between pp. 82–83); Wasson (1979:inset between pp. 88–89); Napier (1974:fig. 13); Halpin and Ames (1980:plate 9). Of these sources, only Napier expresses skepticism that the track might not be genuine.

79. Dale Wallace indicated (phone conversation on December 19, 2003) that his uncle was sporadically producing tracks for decades after the 1958 footprint discoveries. Ray Wallace was contributing Bigfoot stories to Ray Crowe's *The Track Record* as late as 1998 (www.internationalBigfootsociety.com).

80. Dale Wallace (phone conversation, December 19, 2003) was not certain of the number of sets of bogus feet that his uncle owned, but thought he had no more than two or three sets at any given time.

81. Mullens claimed to have had eight sets of feet made (Dennett 1982).

82. Bailey (2003).

83. Breitler (2003).

7

Three Red Herrings

On balance, the evidence for Bigfoot is inconclusive. Few advocates are so reckless to suggest otherwise. No body exists to firmly establish the creature's existence, no bones lie curated in the continent's natural history museums, and there are no agreed-on standards by which to judge the footprints, hair, and tape-recorded screeches that ostensibly serve as evidence. What we do have is a constant stream of reports of people encountering giant hairy apes deep and not-so-deep within the woods. These encounters happen all the time, throughout the lower forty-eight states, in Canada from British Columbia to Quebec, and in the Alaskan bush.

Herein lies the advocate's dilemma. The forensic evidence stinks. What purportedly good evidence does exist is tainted by surrounding circumstances—corollary evidence known to be fraudulent or associated with suspected hoaxers. The vast majority of evidence is scientifically unverifiable. It seems logically impossible to defend the position that a real animal—indeed, one standing 8 feet tall and weighing over 1,000 pounds—has somehow eluded us forever.

In crafting their arguments, however, the advocates have attempted to deal with the peculiar problem of making zoological study of an animal they can't find. If the animal is real, there must be a qualification of the argument, an explanation, an excuse for why the mundane bits of evidence that would immediately end the mystery have never been found. Rhetoric for public communication, the kind tailored for mass consumption by TV, demands simple and concise explanation—sound bytes—while the enigma of cryptic stinking half-ton apes that are thriving on the fringes of civilization would seem to require very detailed and involved argument. In practice, the advocates have opted for the simple explanation as their tactic, brushing away the skeptic's objections with glib assertions that are styled to appeal to common sense rather than to involved scientific argument.

It is an arguable point that, in the absence of definitive evidence for Sasquatch, skeptics have a responsibility to give a hearing to the apologia of the advocates. A number of advocates have sacrificed money, careers, and marriages pursuing this genuine mystery, so I don't think it is unreasonable for them to ask interested skeptics to hear the totality of their position. The mantra among career Bigfoot pursuers is that absence of evidence is not evidence of absence, which is a point well taken, but the skeptic can still reasonably ask why the evidence that should be there isn't.

The failure of Bigfoot to satisfy an evidentiary standard for qualifying as a scientifically recognized species is defended by essentially three lines of argument. The first is that Bigfoot exists because all alternative explanations are either more unlikely or more unreasonable than the simple assertion that there is a real animal out there. The second is that the absence of Bigfoot carcasses and bones is readily explicable on ecological principles. Both the first and second lines of argument have been made deliberately and repeatedly by advocates of every stripe: Ivan Sanderson, Peter Byrne, René Dahinden, and Grover Krantz have all utilized these two assertions to defend their position that the animal is real. The third argument is in some sense unintentional in its implication: the gist of it is that we have not found Bigfoot because we are, in fact, incapable of finding it. This I will call the "Bigfoot is paranormal" argument, not because the mainstream advocates really believe that Bigfoot is, in fact, paranormal (although there are plenty of UFO fans who embrace the idea), but because the essence of this argument is that Bigfoot has certain qualities that transcend what we understand to be biologically feasible. I will entertain each argument on its own merits.

If we could enumerate all the possible explanations for Bigfoot evidence and weigh the respective probabilities of these explanations, we could, hypothetically, offer a statistical assessment of how likely or unlikely the competing explanations were with respect to one another. For example, if by some means we could establish that there was a 97% probability that the Patterson film was genuine, but only a 3% probability that it was a person in a costume, we could comfortably settle on the idea that Bigfoot was filmed.

Such calculation of probabilities could presumably be made, but only by front-loading our analytical model with all manner of dubious assumptions; we could get numbers out but they wouldn't mean anything. The impossibility of the task is simply due to the fact that, where Bigfoot is concerned, we have no knowledge—none—that we can deem to be reliable. No information exists to constrain whatever statistical analysis we might choose to undertake, unless we make the dubious assumption that fake and real Bigfoot evidence can be distinguished a priori.[1]

Of course, this does not mean that we cannot enumerate the various possibilities and at least talk about their merits. This option, in fact, is all that the skeptics and advocates alike have to work with. With respect to the Patterson film, the usual discussion centers around the simple premise that either (1) the subject is a person in a fur suit or (2) the subject is an unknown animal, given that misidentification of the subject as an ambling bear is clearly out of the question. This is a simple either-or proposition that would be resolved once you established that one of the two possibilities is considerably less plausible than the other. This resolution is far from easy, but the dichotomy as presented provides a clear enough road map from which to proceed.

In a contribution to Marjorie Halpin and Michael Ames's *Manlike Monsters on Trial*, George Gill, an anthropologist at the University of Wyoming, articulated a similar choice for students of the Bigfoot phenomenon in general. In arguing for two discrete possibilities, Gill surmised that either (1) the most sophisticated hoax in history has been perpetuated unexposed for centuries or (2) Bigfoot exists despite remaining undetected by the scientific community.[2] This summation at the end of Gill's article, which was primarily concerned with examining ecogeographic variation in Sasquatch size and coloration, was the battle cry advocates had been longing for. Though not exactly original (Ivan Sanderson articulated essentially the same argument nearly twenty years before),[3] Gill provided the perfect statement for the advocate position: now the onus could be placed squarely on the skeptics. How was the conspiracy maintained for hundreds of years? The membership must have been enormous, given the level of Bigfoot activity reported since historical times all over the continent. That a collective hoax could maintain secrecy for so long, over such a wide area, is simply preposterous. Peter Byrne took to the idea and ran with it when the cameras rolled. He ridiculed the idea that a cabal could exist with such perfect organization and skill and remain completely under the radar of advocates, scientists, and the public at large.[4]

I am in complete agreement. The idea of a complex and enduring secret society dedicated to promoting Bigfoot, financially supporting its members tramping through the woods with fake feet and oversized furry costumes, is just too fantastic to be believed. At the same time, this should not be taken as a sudden conversion on my part. Gill may seem to be boiling the argument down to its very essence, but the dichotomy is bogus: the choice he presents is between the possibility of an undiscovered animal and coordinated deception on an impossibly grand scale. But the simple truth is that faking footprints, producing bogus films, and lying to newspaper writers can all be accomplished without being a card-carrying member of the Sacred Society of Sasquatch Fabrication.

What Gill promulgated, intentionally or not, was a rhetorical trick known as the false dilemma. It plays well as a sound byte but has no foundation as a reasoned argument. Why is a conspiracy required to pull off hoaxes? If both Ivan Marx and Roger Patterson made movies of Bigfoot, does it follow that they were in cahoots? Although speculative on my part, it may be that Gill's position was influenced by the consistency of the footprint evidence he was examining. But acknowledging the existence of high-quality evidence hundreds of miles apart does not in any way require belief in an underground network of confidence artists. If potential hoaxers can read a newspaper or operate a television remote, they have the ability to acquire descriptions of Bigfoot evidence and recreate that evidence in short order. Misidentification, independent hoaxing, copycat hoaxing, and the time-honored human endeavor of lying are all plausible sources of the phenomenon that Gill, and those who have cited him since, conveniently ignore.

The argument put forth is surprisingly reminiscent of arguments used to defend other odd phenomena such as crop circles.[5] The idea that consistency of evidence compels an explanation of coordinated hoaxing is irrational, because it assumes that humans are incompetent at imitation and innovation. After 1958, anybody with the wherewithal to pick up a newspaper had a template for hoaxing Sasquatch tracks. With each Bigfoot cast that made it into print, the inventory for fakery grew. There is no need to invoke some large underground network of conspirators.

The absence of physical remains—bodies or parts thereof—is, to my mind, the most devastating argument against the Sasquatch. The advocates have to account for this anomaly if they are to sustain any degree of credibility. The issue is critical enough to have burdened some veterans of the quest with a residual skepticism: René Dahinden, for one, thought the problem was so serious that he could never bring himself to fully and absolutely endorse the creature's existence, despite a lifetime devoted to its study. Others have refused to sit on the fence between belief and skepticism, convinced that, since the amount of accessory evidence was so overwhelming, the absence of a corpse, skeleton, or even a single bone or tooth must have some rational explanation.

Ivan Sanderson had a penchant for forceful, if not histrionic, argument. His rebuttal to the skeptics on the question of physical remains was uncompromising: "Ask any game warden, real woodsman or professional animal collector if he has ever found the dead body of any wild animal—except along roads of course, or if killed by man. I never have, in 40 years and 5 continents! Nature takes care of its own, and damned fast, too."[6] It is an astonishing claim: only as the result of hunting or roadkill might we expect to find the bones of not just Bigfoot, but indeed any animal at all. In a television appearance years later on the A&E network, Grover Krantz would similarly claim that, throughout his questioning of officials and hunters over his career, not one had ever reported encountering the remains of a bear that died a natural death.[7] Just how many people Krantz surveyed he doesn't say, but from his point of view, this anecdote is sufficient to posit that the reason we don't find Bigfoot bones is that we should not ever expect to. The bones are there but we can't hope to find them. The logic is extraordinary: given the virtual absence of bear remains (in print, Krantz concedes that bear remains are encountered in the wild, albeit rarely[8]) and given the greater abundance of bears relative to Sasquatches, it is a virtual certainty that Sasquatch remains would never be discovered in the wild. Thus, by this reasoning, the absence of Sasquatch bones is of no concern whatever to the advocate's position. The absence of evidence is no liability, it merely confirms the predictions that allegedly follow from consideration of the relative abundance of bears and Bigfoot.

If Krantz may be allowed to argue from anecdote, perhaps I may be allowed to do the same in making a counterpoint. I've spent a few summers prospecting for fossils in the basins surrounding the Crazy Mountains of Montana, an isolated range a few hours' drive north of Yellowstone National Park. It is ideal fossil-hunting territory, as the geological events that thrust the mountains upward also transported ancient sediments from below the surface to the flanks of the range. These sedimentary exposures aren't what we are used to seeing on *National Geographic* programs featuring Olduvai Gorge: they are not vast and continuous; instead they poke out of the hillsides and streambeds at irregular intervals, in small pockets where the grasses and pine trees haven't managed to gain a foothold. The result is that one has to spend days walking some fair distances between these exposures in search of the fossil motherlode.

One day in the summer of 1997, a colleague and I were walking between exposures through a stand of trees fairly high on the flanks of the range when we noticed something unusual on the forest floor. It was impossible to miss, a bright white dome among the beige carpet of soil and dead pine needles. Picking it up we immediately recognized it as the cranium of a black bear, beautifully preserved. What was unusual was that no other parts of the animal were visible nearby, perhaps having been carried off by scavengers. In any case, all we had was this half skull. But the point is, we found it. We had walked through the landscape over the course of perhaps ten days, but on this day we stumbled on the remains of a bear by dumb luck alone; we weren't even looking for fossils at the time. If the bear had been shot there was no indication from what we could see, and if this was roadkill, then the poor ursid had managed to amble some considerable distance from the nearest road before succumbing to the impact.

You are free to choose which anecdote you like, but perhaps you can appreciate that, based on my personal experience, I find Sanderson's and Krantz's declarations to be rather hollow. Indeed, their insistence that the only bears found are the ones that are shot is a weak caveat to get around the problem that the bones of animals of every size and shape have been culled from the wilderness to fill hundreds of cabinets in museums all over North America. Wolverines are scarce animals, but we do know what their skeletons look like for the simple reason that we have them. Where are the Bigfoot bones? Bigfoot is, by all accounts, a rather large animal. It's unlikely that every last bit of every dead Bigfoot's remains will be carried off to a raptor's nest, gnawed into dust by porcupines, or rotted into sludge by bacteria in the soil before some human observer stumbles across it, whether by luck or design. The problem is not that we infrequently find Sasquatch bones, the telling point is that we never do.

John Green attempts to get around this not-so-small problem through speculations about some behavioral quirks of the Sasquatch that might explain it. Perhaps, being a higher primate closely related to our own species, the Sasquatch has evolved some proto-cultural behaviors. Could it be that they bury their dead? Is it unreasonable to suppose, as in the legend of the elephant graveyard, that Bigfoot in the throes of death retreat to a secret locale to breathe their last?[9] Green is left troubled by these explanations because they seem inadequate to explain all conceivable cases of Bigfoot mortality. After all, some Sasquatches must die accidental deaths, and once in a blue moon we would expect someone to trip over the remains.

Green, ever optimistic, extracts himself from the problem by positing that, since it is unreasonable to suggest that the bones can't be found, perhaps the answer is that they have been found but have thus far gone unrecognized. The hope here is that there are uncatalogued or even improperly curated bones of Bigfoot in North American museums.[10] This idea is fueled by rumor: Reports are collected, rarely first hand, about bones of unusual size or shape that someone laid eyes upon at some indeterminate point in the past. Sometimes the institution where the element resides is even identified. The only problem with these rumors, and several have circulated, is that the follow-up has always been fruitless. Either the bone can't be located or it turns out to belong to some known animal.

Green's attempts to resolve the problem are admirable and constructive and they even enjoy some relative plausibility when compared to other more imaginative scenarios explaining the absence of Bigfoot remains. My personal favorite is Ivan Marx's, which he offers in his feature film *The Legend of Bigfoot.* Bigfoot, Marx explains, is migratory. Furthermore, in a touching display of concern and compassion for its fallen comrades, Bigfoot hauls the corpses of its conspecifics up north to the Alaskan glaciers and dumps the bodies into deep and impenetrable crevasses where the greedy hand of humankind cannot touch the remains.

Even Marx's narrative can appear credible compared to other accounts. One reason the Bigfoot phenomenon has gradually melded into the UFO subculture is that flying saucers give some advocates a way out of the "no bones" problem. If Bigfoot is not just a manlike ape or an apelike man but something even more fantastic, such as an extraterrestrial scout from outer space, the problem of remains is conveniently solved: Bigfoot, dead or alive, is simply beamed back to the mothership when conditions warrant.

Once talk of aliens, flying saucers, and interdimensional teleportation enters the conversation, it is clear that we have entered into the paranormal camp of Bigfoot advocacy. This could be the subject of a separate (and, I suspect more entertaining) book, so I will touch on this topic only long enough to describe the relationship of this faction to the self-proclaimed nonparanormal advocates. In terms of my own views toward paranormal explanations, suffice it to say that I agree with John Green—I see no sense in propping up one mystery on the shoulders of another improbable enigma, especially when the empirical foundation for both is lacking.

Loren Coleman deserves credit for popularizing and in some sense legitimizing the paranormal angle in Bigfoot research, despite his recent conversion to naturalistic explanations.[11] For a time, Coleman was a self-described Fortean,[12] one who dares to "believe in nonbelief."[13] In an evidentiary sense, this seems to Coleman to mean that anything goes and that it is perfectly OK to entertain opposing views simultaneously. In his books *Mysterious America* and *Creatures from the Outer Edge* (coauthored with Jerome Clark), among other contributions, Coleman has not shrunk from tying together conventional cryptozoological fare with extraterrestrial activity. His Fortean sympathies allow him to shuttle between the naturalistic and paranormal Bigfoot positions without concern for any type of paradigmatic consistency. Since Coleman has tirelessly chronicled the history and central issues of the Bigfoot phenomenon over several decades, he enjoys high status among the advocate community. His tolerance of the paranormal perspective has, by virtue of his reputation, lent it an air of credibility that it might not otherwise have, and his prolific chronicling of Bigfoot activity outside the Pacific Northwest[14] has earned him a place at the table of "biological" Sasquatch research in spite of his strange leanings.

The paranormal explanation enjoys a sort of perverse logic. Since Bigfoot is seen but never found, because it can be photographed but never captured, perhaps the solution of the mystery is very simple: Bigfoot is real and cannot be captured because it's something entirely different from our own material world. I freely admit the scientific community will have a rough time falsifying the hypotheses emerging from that particular theory.

The paranormal fringe has gradually grown in influence over the years, but they have lost their great spokesman. The first sign that Coleman was defecting to the world of the mainstream (if there can be such a thing with respect to Bigfoot) was when he published, with Patrick Huyghe, *The Field Guide to Bigfoot, Yeti and Other Mystery Primates Worldwide* in 1999. Billed as a "biologically based" work, the book succeeds in this respect only if we recognize human imagination and invention as rooted ultimately in biology. Of all the ostensibly naturalistic books on the subject, Coleman and Huyghe penned the most gullible of all.[15] Relying almost exclusively on eyewitness testimony, the authors construct a new classification system for undiscovered primates involving no less than nine classes (with numerous species nested within them) scattered about the globe. Included is a class of "merbeings": apparently amphibious primates, some of which sport the obligate fish tail. Coleman finally repudiated the utility of paranormal explanations in his 2003 book *Bigfoot! The True Story of Apes in America.* His suggestion within that UFOs have no place in the study of Bigfoot may have been born of pragmatism or of an intellectual change of heart, but whatever the reason, the paranormalists have certainly lost an articulate advocate.

At this juncture, the most infamous researcher among the paranormalists is Jon Erik Beckjord, who understands the connections between crop circles, extraterrestrials, and Bigfoot even if nobody else does. His unorthodox views have landed him on the *Tonight Show* and *Late Night with David Letterman.* He enjoys the distinction of having had well-publicized arguments with both the writers of *Skeptical Inquirer*[16] and the members of the International Society of Cryptozoology.[17] Beckjord is loathed among "mainstream" Bigfoot advocates because of his smug conclusion about the issue of physical remains. Being a student of Bigfoot history, he is familiar with how poor much of the evidence is. He insists, much as the skeptics do but for very different reasons, that the advocates must come to grips with the absence of physical remains. Often with a belligerent tone, Beckjord argues that the paranormal explanation satisfies this nagging issue: Bigfoot is an interdimensional shape-shifter that can warp in and out of physical reality. And if shape-shifting and interdimensional travel are ever verified in repeated laboratory trials, I, for one, think we should all listen to Mr. Beckjord very closely.

The paranormal fringe of the Bigfoot community creates endless headaches for the mainstream advocates who argue for nothing more than a missing species of ape. The polarization of the advocate factions over whether the phenomenon is natural or supernatural exists to the point where some Internet discussion boards ban paranormal content from their lists.[18] A large number of Bigfoot advocates publicly and privately distance themselves from the paranormal position. Grover Krantz lamented that the lunatic fringe often wasted his time,[19] and John Green displays tinges of discomfort as he reports some of the more fantastic tales of vanishing Sasquatches and associations with strange lights in the sky.[20] After all, there is no reason why Bigfoot has to be paranormal: it isn't logically impossible to have a bipedal, 8-foot-tall being living in the woods. It might be unlikely, but it is not impossible.

Science writer and *Skeptical Inquirer* editor Ken Frazier suggests that the study of Bigfoot is not a paranormal matter, or at least it does not have to be.[21] Michael Dennett, who lives in the heart of Bigfoot country in Washington State, has perhaps more first-hand experience talking to Bigfoot hunters than any other skeptical investigator. Dennett takes the view that advocacy of Bigfoot is not unlike other paranormal endeavors such as UFOology or creationism[22] and escapes the paranormal label because it has adopted the ruse of being a purely biological undertaking. The rhetoric of Bigfoot research, he argues, has paranormal undercurrents. It is important to recognize that Dennett's contention does not mean that the study of Bigfoot is intrinsically paranormal; rather, the valid assertion is that, in the arguments to legitimize Bigfoot to the public and to scientific circles, the advocates have unintentionally introduced paranormal concepts and ideas.

This is a charge to which I am confident the advocates will take exception, so some substantiation is in order. First, I submit that the conventional arguments in favor of Bigfoot, when followed to their logical consequences, require behaviors, abilities, or characteristics that transcend ordinary biology. Certainly we should discount many of the details of eyewitness accounts on this basis alone. If Bigfoot is just an ordinary animal of its described size and proportions, it cannot jump about cliffs in the manner of a mountain goat while carrying 2,000-pound rocks under its arm.[23]

Paranormal attributes inadvertently creep into the discussion, particularly when we examine the advocates' excuses for our inability to find Bigfoot. It took Dian Fossey and Jane Goodall countless hours, days, and eventually months to get close to the gorillas and chimpanzees they were tracking in the African forests. One reason they had such a difficult time was that these apes have keen senses of hearing and vision that enabled them to leave an area before the women were even aware that they were there. Bigfoot is credited with having superb sensory capabilities in all respects. Their ability to sense human proximity must be highly developed, more so than with any other living species, because despite the frequency of reports of the Sasquatch and endless speculation as to its habits and ecology, all attempts at systematically tracking the animal have failed. *The Sasquatch and Other Unknown Hominids*, for which Krantz served as coeditor, has a contribution from James Butler on "higher sensory perceptions" in Bigfoot.[24] Butler recognized the insufficiency of normal biology to explain how the giants could remain so elusive, and the higher sensory perceptions Butler attributes to the creature are indistinguishable from good old-fashioned clairvoyance.

The contention that Bigfoot consciously hides its tracks can be described as either a brilliant biological inference or as an attempt to rationalize bogus evidence as something else. As stated before, the idea of a creature hiding its tracks, given great body mass and the soft duff of the forest floor, is more than a little incongruous. If the mass of the beast obligates its prints to sink astonishingly deeply into the soil during normal locomotion, by what conceivable mechanism could the animal suspend the laws of physics and remove the variables of mass, force, and acceleration to enable it to leave no trace? Levitation would seem to do the trick, although I suspect most Bigfoot advocates would concede that this transcends biological adaptation as we know it.

John Green has always tried to base his inferences on Sasquatch biology on the facts at hand, which include at least some eyewitness accounts without accompanying physical evidence. One remarkable fact is that in all the years of hunting on the continent, during which settlers hunted the bison and grizzly to near extinction, no one has yet successfully shot, killed, and retrieved a Sasquatch. Although this would seem to compel an obvious conclusion, Green is drawn to another: it must be because Sasquatches are hard to kill.[25]

We have visited this issue already. Should we buy this argument? Polar bears are large, dangerous, and, depending on where exactly you are in circumpolar regions, infrequently encountered. I suspect they are hard to kill. But once in a while, someone with a gun succeeds in doing the job. The accounts of Bigfoot in which gunplay is involved have a particularly paranormal twinge. Shot through the head, one of the Bigfoot in Fred Beck's story merely ran away. Its eastern cousin in rural Pennsylvania, in a unique adaptive strategy, vaporized when shot.[26] Green documents a number of stories, most of them from fairly long ago, of dead Bigfoot, but needless to say the critical forensic evidence was never recovered from these incidents.

Motor vehicles are also a potential threat to the well-being of Sasquatches. Green's dictum that it is not easy to bring down a Sasquatch might apply here as well, but on balance this is a tougher call. In 1975, one unfortunate Bigfoot was struck by a motorist traveling at 50 mph in Bel Air, Maryland.[27] The animal walked away from the accident limping, but certainly not dead. The year before, a swamp ape had been able to escape a collision in the Florida Everglades in similar fashion.[28] Finally, a year before that in the Pacific Northwest a semi-truck with a load of logs plowed into a Bigfoot with sufficient force that the beast literally flew off the road. Despite some of the human-like qualities of the projectile, the driver elected not to stop until 5 miles down the road.[29] The extent of the creature's injuries was never confirmed.

These tales of Bigfoot encounters with guns and autos implicitly imbue the animal with superhuman qualities more congruent with a mythological motif than an ordinary mammal. The people who experience Bigfoot encounters often express a sense of awe; this is to be expected, perhaps, in facing the unexpected. People often leave encounters with a sense that they have witnessed something quite out of the ordinary, and not just in terms of size and stature. The epilogue to encounters is often a sense of wonder on the part of the eyewitness that is qualitatively more meaningful than a first-time encounter with a mountain lion or a grizzly bear. If Bigfoot is just an animal, why do the people who experience Bigfoot treat it as so much more?

The paranormal undercurrents of the phenomenon are disturbing to biologists who wish to soberly and systematically study Bigfoot. The existence of these undercurrents, however, is perhaps instructive as to the nature of the phenomenon. The fantastic tones that some accounts possess—the very stories that the advocates seek to play down—may be the most important clue as to why there can be the concept of Bigfoot without having an actual animal. We will return to this idea in the final chapter. At this point, however, we have at least laid the groundwork for addressing the thorny issue of whether the search for Bigfoot is truly a scientific enterprise or merely a circus without the tent.

NOTES

1. Fahrenbach (1998) published a statistical analysis of Bigfoot data in which he did not attempt to make the distinction other than to rule out obviously paranormal

events. He nevertheless concluded that the resulting distribution of footprint data was expected of a real animal, as opposed to a collection of hoaxes.

2. Gill (1980:272).

3. Sanderson (1961:432).

4. Byrne made this argument in the 1994 A&E production of *Ancient Mysteries: Bigfoot* (New York: New Video Group).

5. Schnabel (1994); also see www.circlemakers.org .

6. Quoted in Gordon (1992:29), from a 1968 piece Sanderson wrote for *Argosy*.

7. *Ancient Mysteries: Bigfoot* (1994), A&E Home Video.

8. Krantz (1992:10–11).

9. Green (1971:72).

10. Green (1971:72).

11. Coleman (2003:172).

12. The term is named after Charles Fort, an eccentric who spent a significant portion of his adult life mining periodical and newspaper reports for strange phenomena—usually meteorological in origin—with which to needle the arrogant and dogmatic scientific establishment. Although Fort's major writings were published between 1919 and 1933, his works have been reprinted numerous times, and he retains a loyal following dedicated to the idea of weirdness in nature.

13. Coleman (1983:255).

14. Coleman (1984) provides an accounting of evidence for a wide geographic range for wild North American apes.

15. See Radford (2000) for a more comprehensive critique.

16. These exchanges involve some of Beckjord's indecipherable Bigfoot photographs and a decaying bear head found in upstate New York that enjoyed brief notoriety as a Sasquatch skull. See Kurtz (1980) and Beckjord (1980).

17. Semerad and Thompson (1989).

18. For an account of the medium of cyberspace in Bigfoot research, see Zuefle (1999).

19. Krantz (1992:245–246).

20. Green (1978:263).

21. Frazier (2002).

22. Stein (1996).

23. Sanderson (1961:70–71). This Sasquatch also shook its fist at the eyewitness and stink-bombed the river below to the point where all the fish fled to an adjoining body of water. Sanderson surmises that this would be an otherwise straightforward Bigfoot encounter were it not for the teller's penchant for allowing his "precepts" to color the narrative.

24. Butler (1984:203–216).

25. Green (1971:77).
26. Green (1978:92, 262).
27. Green (1978:227).
28. Green (1978:278).
29. Green (1978:409).

8

A Science of Sasquatch?

To the chagrin of many advocates, the topic of Bigfoot frequently appears alongside the paranormal fare of extraterrestrial abductions, crop circles, disembodied spirits, and psychic phenomena. This association is not helpful to a field of inquiry that is constantly struggling to gain scientific respectability. The easiest way to dismiss the idea of Bigfoot is to simply write it off as a pseudoscientific enterprise, the domain of cranks and otherwise suggestible individuals.

The majority of advocates insist that the search for the Sasquatch resides within the legitimate field of scientific investigation. If physicists can talk about quarks and other subatomic particles that no one has ever seen, why is it that when the topic of Bigfoot arises, the scientific community turns a cold shoulder? Why doesn't Bigfoot get an aside in anthropology textbooks? The plea from the advocates isn't for unqualified acceptance of the beast's existence, only a fair hearing. When the community of advocates reads that an anthropologist living in the heart of Bigfoot country won't talk about it because "it doesn't interest me,"[1] it provides fuel for conspiracy theories about the scientific community. It seems extraordinary that scientists whose specialties include primate biology and human evolution could willingly ignore the fantastic possibility of Bigfoot. The implications to biological anthropology would seem to be huge (assuming that Bigfoot's primate status was confirmed on discovery).

This apparent enigma is seized on as a sure sign of a code of silence in the academic community. As Grover Krantz put it, scientists have squandered every opportunity to investigate Bigfoot and, having missed the boat entirely, now have to ignore the evidence to save their collective reputation.[2] If scientific methods can be applied to the problem of Bigfoot, why should there be such institutional resistance to the endeavor?

Slapping the label of "pseudoscience" on the effort allows us to wash our hands of the whole idea. The question then becomes whether this labeling is a legitimate charge or whether it is a rhetorical trick used by mainstream science to avoid engaging a mountain of embarrassing evidence. The first step in settling this issue is to arrive at an acceptable definition of what constitutes pseudoscience and to do that we have to clearly demarcate false scientific endeavors from legitimate ones.

This is easier said than done. The line separating science and pseudoscience is not sharply drawn, and the finer points of the distinction requires some involved discussion that is beyond the scope of this book. That said, I will offer here one criterion of demarcation that strikes me as reasonable and provides guidance for the problem at hand. Paul Thagard, a professor of philosophy now at the University of Waterloo, offered this definition:

> a theory which purports to be scientific is pseudoscientific if and only if 1) it has been less progressive than alternative theories over a long period of time, and faces many unsolved problems, and 2) the community of practitioners makes little attempt to develop the theory towards solutions of the problems, shows no concern for attempts to evaluate the theory in relation to others, and is selective in considering confirmations and disconfirmations.[3]

How does the search for Bigfoot square with this definition? There are several aspects of Thagard's proposed criteria that deserve additional attention. The first is that the premise of a pseudoscientific proposition is that it purports to be scientific: specifics of the theory can be subject to falsification by experiment or observation. Certainly this has been the consensus position of the advocates all along—the existence of Sasquatch is a scientifically defensible position, if only they could get scientists to bother to look into the matter.

Thagard's first criterion is two pronged: the proposed theory has to succeed in explaining things better than its competitors, with the caveat that it may take a while before it does so. In addition, to fall under the definition of pseudoscience the theory must be facing a host of unresolved issues that, because of repeated efforts to resolve them, appear to be intractable. The success of the competing explanations for the Bigfoot phenomenon is arguable, simply because very little of the vast amount of alleged data has been satisfactorily evaluated. The current status of the Patterson film is, from a purely empirical standpoint, unresolved. The advocates can crow that no one has proven that the film is fake, while the skeptics are finally at a point where they can say with a high degree of confidence that the details of the film were well within the human capacity for fabrication. In this example, the disparity of historical progress is clear. The NASI report of 1998 was really little more than high-tech window dressing for the original arguments for authenticity—the body proportions are all wrong, it walks funny, and it's not a cheap gorilla costume from the corner five-and-dime. This report, in fact, is contradicted by other data collected since the making of the film. What the advocates have left is the cheap-suit argument, which is, by any standard, a weak centerpiece. Skeptical inquiry into the film has made significant strides since 1967, even if the skeptics don't yet have the smoking gun.

In contrast, there are no data emerging since 1967 that give the film any additional credibility. The advocates will complain that this is an unfair verdict since they haven't brought in a specimen yet, but that is precisely the point—there are no supportive data of any scientific value.

This observation brings us to Thagard's next clause: a pseudoscientific endeavor has chronic unresolved problems. In fact, the Bigfoot quest suffers only from a singular problem: the beast has yet to appear. If an animal of the purported description exists and we still do not have one, then the advocates should have a theory of Bigfoot that provides a scientific explanation of why this is so. We would have an analogous problem if we were forced to posit a theory of gravitation without a means to detect mass; institutional skepticism would be expected, and that attitude would be fully justified. In the case of the Sasquatch, after thousands of sightings and footprints and not a shred of a ton-sized biped preserved, the hoax hypothesis is looking better by the day. It resolves the problem of why we still don't have a body in neat and tidy fashion.

Of course, the advocate's counterargument is that progress is made, because the prints keep showing up, strange sounds still emanate from the forest,[4] and unidentifiable hair continues to be culled from the wild. But this is progress only if the quality of the data is really becoming more and more compelling, and the collection of more hair is irrelevant if the ensuing analyses remain inconclusive. Bigfoot's hair is the perfect case in point for arguing that, in the quest for the Sasquatch, the quality of data now is as poor as it was in 1958. Mysterious hair recovered from areas of Bigfoot activity has been the subject of a number of published and Internet-posted reports.[5] The standard line of argument is that the hair cannot be attributed to a known animal, and, therefore, by virtue of its collection in Sasquatch habitat, the most parsimonious explanation is that it belongs to Bigfoot.

A closer inspection of these reports suggests this conclusion is premature. What gets lost in the secondhand accounts is that the more responsible parties engaged in the analysis will stress that they can't positively identify hair as Bigfoot in origin since there is no Sasquatch standard for objective comparison. We also have to keep in mind that the description of "unidentified" means unidentified: you cannot rationally take a sample that does not permit attribution and then attribute it to Bigfoot.

The problems faced by people in the field of Bigfoot research are encapsulated in the history of hair analysis. In 1968, some Bigfoot hair found in Idaho was sent to a police science instructor in Los Angeles. This presumably disinterested party, Ray Pinker, was reported to state that the sample did not match specimens from any known animal species, although it did have some characteristics of human and nonhuman hair.[6] This brief assessment is tantalizing, perhaps, but on closer examination, vacuous. There is not enough information here to make a judgment. By what criteria was it determined that the hair doesn't *match* anything? Did this expert have a full inventory of mammalian hair (that is, upward of 4,000 samples to cover the full spectrum of species) from which to make this sweeping claim? What is the nature of this unique combination of human and animal traits?

On examining the original source,[7] it turns out that the secondhand report, by sympathetic researchers Vaughn Bryant and Bureligh Trevor-Deutsch, is a misrepresentation. Pinker never said the hair did not match any known species, he only stated it did not correspond to anything he had access to. Moreover, Pinker's attribution of human and nonhuman characteristics is less enigmatic when one realizes that the sample contained different types of hair, and some of the "human" features could be ascribed to sheep or goat.

Bryant and Trevor-Deutsch claimed in 1980 to have samples that are "puzzling" because "they show similarities to certain known mammals yet are not identical to known hair samples from those mammals."[8] What we are to make of this analysis in unclear, because we have no clue as to what features of hair they looked at, what the comparative samples were, and what counted as a "similarity" but would not qualify as "identical." The discussion obfuscates more than it clarifies.

In the years that followed, Paul Freeman would be finding hair in his forays into the woods. Always cooperative with interested researchers, Freeman had his samples subjected to scientific scrutiny. By Freeman's account, the hair stumped the experts.[9] It would be more accurate to say that his samples proved vexing. Some samples he collected were artificial in origin,[10] although in some cases there is no question that some of the hair was real—at least it was real hair. Henner Fahrenbach commissioned some molecular geneticists at Ohio State University to extract and then amplify DNA out of some hair found by Freeman in August 1995. Fahrenbach determined ahead of time that the hair was indistinguishable from that of humans but that since the hair followed a Bigfoot sighting, further analysis was called for.[11] Apparently, the extraction of DNA was problematic (which is not unheard of with hair samples), and the decision was made not to publish results that were admittedly inconclusive. As of November 1999, Fahrenbach claims to have a dozen samples of Bigfoot hair but concedes that for analysis of DNA, the hair is not working out.[12]

Fahrenbach and his collaborators may have given up too soon. DNA amplification from hair samples is difficult, but not impossible. A sufficiently long sequence of DNA could really settle this issue. How can I be so sure? I asked my colleague Amos Deinard, a primate geneticist with a doctorate in anthropology from Yale and a veterinary degree from UC Davis. Years ago, as a favor to René Dahinden, I had a Bigfoot hair sample analyzed from a locality in rural New York State.[13] Deinard agreed to run the sample, as he has experience in extracting and amplifying DNA from the hair of nonhuman primates. He knew that using the correct extraction protocol, one could amplify DNA from shed hair. For this sample, however, there seemed to be a problem. Deinard surmised the problem was that the "hair" was not organic. He provided me with a tongue-in-cheek report that the likely origin of the sample was from the interior of a couch.

Deinard did his Ph.D. work on the genetics of chimpanzee subspecies. In the course of that research, one determination he was obviously able to make was that the subspecies could be distinguished by DNA sequences in parts of the animals' genomes. The species of Great Apes are easily identified by such sequences. Human populations may be identified by such sequences. What I am getting at here is that if Bigfoot is just another primate, perhaps a great ape in John Bindernagel's view,[14] then it follows that a suitably long sequence of Bigfoot DNA would cinch the issue. It could be identified as a higher primate, and we could definitively rule out chimpanzees, orangutans, gorillas, and humans as the source. In fairness to the Ray Pinkers who have been recruited to work on Bigfoot hair, there was a time in the past when investigators did not have the tools to make a diagnosis of "unknown species" that was credible. That time is past. When Fahrenbach says that a useful length of DNA for determining the phylogenetic status of a sample has been difficult to come by,[15] we can fairly demand to know what went wrong. These days, a mysterious result might only mean that the sample in question is useless.

In fact, DNA from hair of Bigfoot's Asian counterpart, the yeti, has been successfully analyzed. This article was published in the respected journal *Molecular Systematics and Evolution*, and the authors noted that the sample of yeti hair they were asked to examine bore startling resemblance to a subgroup of the odd-toed ungulates that included horses and zebras.[16] In the spirit of maintaining a healthy sense of humor in scientific pursuits, the authors concluded that the yeti showed a remarkable anatomical convergence on the primate body plan despite its genetic leanings.

The article was a spoof, but the analysis was properly done, and it underscores the point that such analyses ought to be decisive rather than confusing. Bigfoot's perpetually mysterious hair defines the pseudoscientific undercurrents of the search in a nutshell: the data never get any better even though there are technological and analytical advances that permit progress to be made. Bigfoot "hair" has been sequenced at Yale and Ohio State Universities. The advocates can no longer complain that nobody will examine the evidence.

Thagard's second criterion for pseudoscience is concerned with conduct. Is the proposed endeavor really committed to investigating all the alternatives? Is there a concerted effort to develop better theoretical explanations? Is there a culture of rigorous and objective scholarship? Objective practice is the issue.

Many Bigfoot hoaxes have been exposed by the very people who have been the legendary animal's most vocal proponents. Peter Byrne established that the stated circumstances of Ivan Marx's first film were contradicted once the location of filming was established.[17] Barbara Wasson was one of the first investigators to examine Paul Freeman's footprint evidence, and wrote the tracks off immediately as suspicious.[18] Daniel Perez has a reputation for challenging eyewitness accounts that are not consistent in all details.[19] Bob Titmus held Freeman's discoveries in low esteem,[20] and Dahinden was famous for his withering denouncements of bogus evidence.

This willingness to expose the human hijinks surrounding Bigfoot is, ironically, among the strongest claims that can be made that the whole affair has the status of a scientific enterprise. Why that is has to do with the fact that the investigators are prepared to consider alternative explanations for items of data, even if in deciding on a human agent as the source it undermines their core belief that Bigfoot really is out there. The ability to see past one's preconceptions and favored outcomes is a demanding but imperative prerequisite for scientific investigation. There is no question that the lay advocates—those without the adornments of titles and higher degrees—possess the intellectual tools to conduct Bigfoot research in a scientific manner. There is no reason why it cannot be a scientific endeavor. The essential problem is that, in practice, the science is often left behind, if not forgotten altogether.

Thagard's proposed demarcation of science from pseudoscience implies, in no subtle fashion, that in a scientific endeavor we should expect theory to evolve, to become better equipped to explain the data as they accumulate, and to discard speculative dead ends and replace them with more reliable tenets. When talking about Bigfoot, the idea of theory seems rather esoteric. After all, presumably the goal is finding a hairy ape in the forest, not predicting the impact of Sasquatch biomass on fern growth in the forest understory. Is a theory even necessary?

Bigfoot couldn't survive without a theory, except in the realm of myth and legend. What this theory seeks to explain is how you can have truckloads of corollary evidence without producing the vital corpus, figuratively and literally. Such evidence is essential to scientific theory: one reason physicists accept the reality of subatomic particles is that their behavior has statistically predictable outcomes that can be measured as data, even though the particles themselves aren't visible in the conventional sense. There is also a very good reason why the particles aren't visible.

If Bigfoot is real, then the animal's behavior and activity should have predictable outcomes: leaving footprints, making noise, defecating, even getting its hair stuck in shrubs with alarming frequency. These traces are data that perhaps lead us to an animal. The problem is, however, that there seems to be is no good reason why Bigfoot is not verifiable in the conventional zoological sense. At this juncture theory creeps in; it has to if the present circumstances are to support the advocate's case. Theory has to explain why we have the footprints but not the footprint maker.

In fact, we have already gone over the details of this body of theory. Bigfoot is rare. Bigfoot buries its dead. The climate of the temperate rain forest isn't conducive to preservation. The bones are there but they are never correctly identified. All of these explanations are attempts to make sense of the gaping enigma that we have never found the remains of an ape-like animal that might be four times more massive than a gorilla.

A good theory is coherent. The general proposition is consistent with observations, various planks of the theory make sense in the context of other planks, and the discrepancies that exist are trivial or suitably finite that the theory is still pretty good at explaining some phenomenon on general principles. A theory of Bigfoot—we can have a hairy giant raiding garbage dumpsters on the edge of town and miss it entirely—has to be not just persuasive but has to make sense outside of its immediate context. That is, the set of principles used to explain that Bigfoot is just another animal should be applicable to, well, just another animal. If it cannot meet this modest requirement, then it is not a very good theory.

Does Bigfoot's scarcity mean we should never find its remains? Does burial of a corpse ensure it will never be recovered? Is the Pacific Northwest climate so hostile to calcified tissues that bones and teeth are never preserved there? Are museum staff and curators so incompetent that they can't recognize a giant primate bone for what it is? A theory of Bigfoot to which the advocates adhere—we have evidence of the animal, but the absence of the animal is not problematic, but expected—is not a defensible scientific theory at all. It is special pleading, in which a set of principles is advanced to explain the absence of the creature, but the principles don't apply to any other mammal on the planet. This is not a compelling theoretical foundation. Particularly telling in the context of Thagard's proposal is that the explanations for the Bigfoot phenomenon from the advocate's point of view have not changed materially in forty years. A bad theory that is getting better might still fall within the scientific universe. But the advocate's theory of Bigfoot hasn't progressed at all.

Essential to any scientific endeavor is the ideal of scholarship. This means that when trying to sort through alternative explanations, individual scientists attempt to give a fair hearing to alternative points of view and to consider evidence that might be detrimental to their pet theory or favored explanation for something. This conduct is in the scientist's best interest, even though at first glance it seems counterproductive to spend energy undermining one's own hypothesis. In the real world, however, the social milieu of science makes this nothing less than a moral imperative.

A banal example will make this clear. You have a hypothesis that the moon is made entirely of chalk. Considering that chalk is essentially the calcified remains of microorganisms, this is a truly astounding position. Nevertheless, you note that the color of the moon on a clear night is chalky white and pictures of astronaut's footprints on the lunar surface betray a finely ground dust that is not unlike what accumulates on the lecture hall floor beneath the blackboard over the course of a semester. You note, correctly, that these twin observations are perfectly consistent with your hypothesis. But, in articulating your argument, you fail to acknowledge that anyone has ever examined the rocks brought back to earth by the Apollo missions. Whether you are ultimately proved right or wrong, you are in the meantime guilty of poor scholarship. One of your fellow scientists is going to get a cheap publication merely by pointing out that you have failed to recognize that some evidence exists that challenges your unorthodox position. Your hypothesis might be nuts, but your endorsement of it is by no means unethical. The true moral transgression is that of ignoring publicly accessible evidence that had been collected previously (if someone before you had also believed the moon was chalk and you failed to credit them, that would be equally reprehensible). Poor scholarship is one tell-tale sign of a pseudoscientific approach.

The Bigfoot literature is surprisingly voluminous, considering that the featured subject is still at large. There are examples of good scholarship and bad, and in this sense the writings that exist on the subject are not so different from other fields of study. But one can identify in the articles and books on the subject a troubling practice, one that a field on the fringe of scientific legitimacy can scarcely afford. Repeatedly, a number of investigators simply opt not to disclose the contextual information of evidence when it is crucial for deciding the legitimacy of particular data. It is what René Dahinden called lying by omission.[21]

Mark Chorvinsky, the editor of *Strange Magazine*, seems by his trade to be an unlikely debunker. He is, however, a scholar of his craft. In two 1993 columns,[22] Chorvinsky's cause was the forgotten role of Ray Wallace in the history of Bigfoot. He is clearly appalled that two of the most influential books on Bigfoot, John Green's *Sasquatch: The Apes among Us* and Grover Krantz's *Big Footprints*, fail to even acknowledge that Ray Wallace existed. We have already established that Wallace's talent for encountering Bigfoot is on par with Paul Freeman's standard of achievement. He encountered Bigfoot so often that the beast became quite used to his presence, to the point that Wallace claimed he brought it food on occasion (apples were a favorite). It is small wonder that the sober advocates wish Wallace's role in Bigfoot's history would just disappear. In these two cases the authors are trying to facilitate the disappearance, but the whitewash is not helpful to the cause. Both Green and Krantz are generally meticulous in keeping track of details of events and persons, so it seems very unlikely that the omission of Wallace is a mere oversight. If the celebrity of Ray Wallace is conveniently forgotten, what lesser-known shenanigans have been kept out of published accounts?

Chorvinsky's chronicling of events makes it fairly clear that he is not interested in destroying a legend or debunking the phenomenon. The issue is one of fair play: if the advocates are going to complain that they are not getting an unbiased public hearing, they should at least be prepared to honestly divulge what is known. Abandoning the principle of scholarship is, of course, a choice on the part of any particular investigator. Once the principle is abandoned, however, their activities amount to a campaign rather than a scientific investigation. Is the goal to be right or to discover the truth? These objectives are not one and the same. Thagard marks this distinction as the border between real and bogus science.

In the literature on Sasquatch, some errors of omission are unwitting mistakes, while others are so substantial that suspicions naturally arise. Fred Beck's 1924 account of having his cabin bombarded by an angry pair of Bigfoot is reported as a straightforward if not hair-raising encounter in its retellings by John Green,[23] Roger Patterson,[24] and others. Beck's paranormal and clairvoyant leanings are nowhere in evidence in the second-hand accounts. It is reasonable to suppose that Beck simply embellished the tale when he issued his own self-published account, but it is also possible that the advocates relaying the story decided, on editorial grounds, not to include information deemed to be irrelevant.

Other omissions are more egregious in their effects on the reader's perception of the evidence. Grover Krantz provided a thorough review of the material evidence for Bigfoot in his book *Big Footprints*. The footprint evidence alone seems, at first glance, quite impressive. Krantz also exhibited another source of evidence—Bigfoot handprints—that he considers legitimate. The first to find such handprints was none other than Ivan Marx, who Krantz properly credits. Paul Freeman began finding handprints after Krantz showed him Marx's discoveries[25] (it surprises neither skeptics nor advocates that the handprints are quite consistent in their details). Here Krantz appears to be the responsible scholar in acknowledging his sources; he offers full disclosure of the associated individuals and the readers can make an informed judgment on that basis.

Or can they? Were it not for the Bossburg incident, Krantz may well have never pursued Bigfoot as the principal focus of his career. There is no question he knew Ivan Marx from that period. But the readers of *Big Footprints* never learn of Marx's most famous contribution to the field of Bigfoot research. Krantz opined that of all motion pictures of Sasquatch, only the Patterson film was legitimate. Of the others Krantz volunteered: "I have seen eight of them and they are all fakes. A few of the most absurd of these are available on a videocassette."[26] He did not name any of the filmmakers, but it is a virtual certainty that among these eight movies was at least one contribution from Ivan Marx. These can still be found in the video Marx himself narrated entitled *The Legend of Bigfoot*.[27]

Whether deliberate or not, Krantz withholds crucial information. Marx's production of allegedly bogus films does not compel anyone to regard his handprints as phony, but the uninformed reader of Krantz's book never has the opportunity to make that judgment.[28] Marx and Freeman are both Bigfoot filmmakers, and Krantz decided that this was somehow unworthy of mention. In fact, Freeman and Marx, despite their tarnished reputations among the lay advocates, get a free ride from the professional anthropologists among the advocates across the board. Jeff Meldrum presents their evidence at face value in professional forums,[29] without disclosing their full inventory of accomplishments. Krantz was among Freeman's staunchest defenders, and John Napier declined to implicate Marx in the Bossburg affair.[30]

It is not impossible that some of the evidence an individual finds is real while some of it is not. Should we give these people the benefit of the doubt in some cases even if we don't in all? This is essentially what these professionals among the advocates are doing, especially in those cases where they are certain they cannot be fooled. This is their prerogative.

Perhaps it is my own idiosyncracy, but in cases where someone makes an unsubstantiated or fantastic claim, and I've got good cause to be dubious about similar claims that individual has made in the past, I'm loathe to embrace anything he or she subsequently peddles. This isn't subscribing to some higher principle of scientific reasoning, it's just common sense.

For example, I buy a used car from Honest Al's Preowned Vehicle Bonanza. Al gives me every assurance this car is going to run beautifully and everything has been checked out. Al strikes me as a stand-up guy and he gives me no overt reason to doubt his honesty. I buy the car. Later, I find out the V-6 engine has only four working cylinders. The "new" tires are retreads. The engine block is cracked, and the "reconditioned" water pump only had the old grime washed off of it. When it is time to buy my next car, I could go back to Al. Sure, I got taken for a ride last time, but he insists it was all a misunderstanding and the next one he has is simply the best preowned car he has ever had the pleasure of driving. On second thought, I have heard this spiel before and I, like most of us, will choose to get my next car elsewhere.

Professional scientists are, in my opinion, ill prepared to study Bigfoot. They might know all about primate biology, the fossil record, locomotor biomechanics, temperate forest ecology, and mammalian migration patterns, but they have no institutional training in confidence games. Of course, the noncredentialed advocates have had no such training either, but the veterans of the hunt have had to learn on the job—where Sasquatch was concerned, they graduated from the school of hard knocks. Scientists learn many things in graduate seminars, research laboratories, and the lecture halls, but they never experience the problem of analyzing data that are not what they are purported to be.

Science is an empirical endeavor. You observe, you replicate that observation, and then you see if your colleagues observe the same thing under the same circumstances. There is no graduate program in the country where one is encouraged to adopt an initial suspicion that the claim of a particular observation is bogus. In the institutional academic setting, there is no established pattern or culture of fabrication. This is one reason why academic fraud usually takes years to uncover: the massaging or fabrication of data is so beyond ethical norms that it is never expected. But it does happen.

The most glaring difference between the nonprofessional Bigfoot advocate and the Ph.D. types loathed by René Dahinden is not their different levels of expertise, though no doubt these are real. Instead, what sets the two apart in terms of field research is that the doctorate holders have unshakable faith in their training and powers of reasoning, while the so-called amateurs know well that nothing can be taken at face value in the universe of the Sasquatch. Anyone who has spent any time investigating Bigfoot has been fooled. The key to surviving as a legitimate player is knowing how to avoid being fooled again. In an endeavor where there are no accepted standards of authenticity, this might well be impossible. There is, however, a certain prerequisite in order to avoid being a chump twice-had. To avoid being duped repeatedly, you first have to admit to yourself that you've been fooled once.

One reason scientists have historically blundered in the Bigfoot realm is that it is terra incognita for the professional: there always exists an alternative explanation born of deception, and uncovering the lie is possible only if one is committed to finding it. Nobody classically trained in the biological sciences is psychologically prepared to deal with an area of research where the simple concept of empirical observation is nebulous. John Napier wrote apologetically that his delving into the mystery of Bigfoot was a journey into the "goblin universe."[31] It was an apt and prescient assessment of the field, although Napier may not have appreciated the disconcertingly human form of the goblins that have kept the phenomenon alive.

If Bigfoot does not count as a scientific enterprise, then scientists have no special claim to knowledge in that field. The status of Bigfoot search as science is arguable. There is no reason, in principle, that the conduct of research into the Sasquatch cannot be done scientifically. The important point is that, historically speaking, the little science that has been done has been sabotaged by special pleading, faulty premises and shoddy scholarship.

A fair question to ask at this juncture is what could have unfolded differently in the storied history of Bigfoot that would qualify it as a scientific undertaking. The short answer is that systematic study of the evidence has been chronically absent. The documentation of evidence has rarely gone beyond the anecdotal.

When René Dahinden, John Green, Peter Byrne, and Bob Titmus convened under the sponsorship of Tom Slick to participate in the Pacific Northwest Expedition, the desire to solve the mystery was there but the methods by which one could do so had not been thought out. Titmus referred to the effort in retrospect as "a half-assed operation,"[32] and Dahinden volunteered that it was "a real mess" that amounted to "one insane thing after another."[33] Years later, Dahinden was even more blunt, stating that nobody on the expedition had a clue about how to go about analyzing the evidence that was found.[34] None of the participants seemed to be particularly pleased with the expedition's accomplishments.

Part of the problem is that the seekers early on in the pursuit were bent on finding a piece of incontrovertible evidence that would render all preceding evidence and analyses thereof superfluous. They did not anticipate that the scientific community would insist that nothing less than a body would qualify as incontrovertible. Documentation of finds was incredibly lax beyond noting the length and width of the prints, the extent of trackways often went unreported, and the depth of tracks was sometimes remarked on without casts or photographs to support the claim. Those involved in the Bigfoot search from the outset may have expected that casting a few prints would settle the matter, but it would not.

In the criteria that I have invoked here for identifying pseudoscientific pursuits, Thagard sets the bar pretty low for making an endeavor scientific. Overcome some problems, make some progress, be committed to weighing all sides of the issue, and chances are you are doing some good science. Fieldwork has been an essential component of Bigfoot research. It can be conducted in a scientific manner, but the Slick expedition was by all accounts a fiasco. Much could have been learned from those mistakes. Nearly forty years after the Slick expedition, the International Society of Cryptozoology (ISC) launched another expedition into the same woods where Tom Slick's crew of investigators had tried to find Bigfoot. This 1997 "Six Rivers Expedition" (named after the national forest where it took place[35]) serves as a signature example of how the state of Bigfoot research—the rigor of investigation, the standards to which the investigators hold themselves—is as miserably deficient today as it was in 1959.

Richard Greenwell, secretary of the ISC, and Jeff Meldrum were part of this four-man expedition. They brought equipment to broadcast primate sounds into the forest in hopes of getting a reply from Bigfoot, they had night vision binoculars, cameras of every description (some with infrared thermal triggers), audio recording equipment, and a satellite phone. This operation was prepared to collect data that would further the cause for Bigfoot; their technological sophistication was beyond anything Tom Slick could have imagined. It was a tremendously successful expedition by one set of standards. By another, the proceedings were testament to the power of belief and conviction but not scientific observation and rational inference. Their report of findings was published in 1998 in the journal *Cryptozoology*.[36]

The expedition reported finding footprints attributable to Bigfoot. Incredibly, they furnished no photographs and there is no indication that the prints were cast. They heard calls from the woods beyond camp that they could not attribute to any known animal, but we do not know what the group's expertise in this matter amounts to. These were not the only sounds they heard: "thrown" rocks did not conform to conventional explanation, nor did "clicks" or "grumblings" heard around the camp. In the camp itself, at night, expedition members heard "heavy, bipedal footsteps" (how this was determined is not stated), and something had disturbed pack contents in a fashion that expedition members could not attribute to bear activity. Despite all this inexplicable activity, nobody saw a Sasquatch.

Even so, the participants ruled out the possibility of hoaxing, "since such individuals could not possibly have remained—and subsisted—in the area without detection by us."[37] Their conclusion was somber: "We are forced, by a process of elimination, to invoke the probability that a large bipedal primate—one that has been continually reported by thousands of witnesses for over a century, and is known today as Sasquatch or Bigfoot—occurs in North America at the present time quite unknown to science."[38]

The field expeditions from 1959 and 1997 reveal a pseudoscientific albatross around the necks of the Bigfoot hunters. No progress has been made. The evidence witnessed isn't available for study. Contrary explanations are dismissed without demonstration. The only difference between the two sorties into the woods is that the 1997 crew seems to know exactly what it is they didn't see. Nobody from the Slick days even pretended that they found anything definitive.

The field expeditions illustrate the larger problem: most Bigfoot evidence fails to get any supportive documentation at all. In eyewitness cases there is the occasional association of a footprint or considerately shed fur, but almost none of this is preserved and still less is evaluated. Instead, the major pillars of the advocate's evidentiary base are a remarkably limited set of footprints and images. What has been documented and analyzed as the best evidence for Bigfoot is restricted essentially to the Bluff Creek area and a few unlikely retreats in eastern Washington. Certainly there are tracks to circle the globe and a wig's worth of hair from other localities scattered throughout North America, but these are not brought forth as definitive or even compelling data. Bigfoot is a pan-continental phenomenon, but its best evidence comes from essentially three localities. Ray Wallace and Roger Patterson are connected to events surrounding Bluff Creek, and Ivan Marx and Paul Freeman have overseen Bigfoot activity in Washington State. Most of the allegedly good evidence for Bigfoot can be boiled down to three places and, as luck would have it, these four supremely talented individuals. While Sasquatches were peppering these local landscapes with scores of prints, the four men each had the presence of mind to film the Bigfoot in the course of their activities. What talents do these men possess that elude the rest of us, including professional wildlife photographers?

With Grover Krantz and John Napier joining the fray around 1970, the scientific establishment had token representation in the search for Bigfoot. Napier's involvement would be brief but very influential. He would conclude that an unknown animal might well be involved, but he was content to offer impressions and tentative endorsements and, after writing his book, apparently had little interest in devoting further energy to the mystery. Krantz was a different story. While Napier's reputation was solid enough that not even a foray into Bigfoot country could sully it, Krantz staked his career on the premise that the animal was real. He would devote himself to the cause, and in fairness, Krantz did do science in his efforts to validate the evidence. What Krantz did not do, however, is ever seriously entertain the idea that his own hypotheses about Bigfoot were provisional. He never questioned the simple proposition—the very foundation of his argument—that it was possible to infer foot bone proportions from footprints. He never supposed that his measurement estimates concerning the Patterson film could have been unreliable. He never did a thorough survey of dermal ridge patterns in primates and people; instead he peddled the casts to experts who would sign off on their authenticity. Krantz paid lip service to the idea that an alternative hypothesis existed, but he did not devote his research energies to exploring the myriad possibilities for hoaxing.

The search for Bigfoot resides beyond the fringe of science, and its status as such has more to do with what those in the search are doing rather than any principle of exclusion erected by the scientific community. If Bigfoot investigators can show that the Pacific Northwest really is inhospitable for preservation of animal remains, then the absence of bones might become more credible. A careful study of how footprints betray pedal anatomy and how pressure ridges are constrained by that anatomy would surely persuade more scientists to pay attention. One DNA sequence could settle the whole matter.[39]

Such projects don't require having Bigfoot on hand, so it is certainly feasible to undertake these studies. No technological or analytical impediments exist to undermine this type of work. This type of data collection that could easily serve as an empirical foundation for the claims of the advocates has, incredibly, never been successfully seen through.

The case for Bigfoot is not strong. The best evidence is tainted at worst and ambiguous at best. The totality of the evidence—sightings, footprints, and hair from all over the continent—looks impressive on the basis of volume only. On close examination, it reduces to anecdote, immune from verification because there is no yardstick to keep investigation on the level. Stinking like a landfill, hirsute beyond confusion, and impossible to miss at 8 feet tall, Bigfoot plods through our backyards pressing the feeble soil clear through to the earth's mantle, and yet our luck is so astonishingly, incomprehensibly bad that we just miss it, day after day, year in and year out.

NOTES

1. From "Sasquatch out there, says B.C. scientist," January 17, 1999. Published on the web by Cnews. The anthropologist quoted is primatologist Lisa Gould.
2. Krantz (1992:72).
3. Thagard (1978), quoted in Thagard (1980:19).
4. See Kirlin and Hertel (1980) for a quantitative analysis of purported Sasquatch vocalizations. While favorably disposed to the idea of Bigfoot, these authors could not rule out that the various sounds were prerecorded.
5. Hair figures in the inventory of Bigfoot evidence in most books from 1961 (Sanderson) to the present (Coleman 2003). A Google search done on December 28, 2003, yielded 161 hits for "Sasquatch hair" and 178 for "Bigfoot hair." The two searches undoubtedly overlap to some extent and I will concede that not all sites identified are relevant. The point is that hair continues to be peddled as good evidence for Bigfoot.
6. Bryant and Trevor-Deutsch (1980:296).
7. Green (1971:71).
8. Bryant and Trevor-Deutsch (1980:296).
9. Foster (1997).
10. Dennett (2003); Perez (2003b). Winn (1991) analyzed some of Freeman's hair finds.
11. Fahrenbach's account is posted on the BFRO website: http://www.bfro.net/REF/THEORIES/WHF/dnatests.htm.
12. See http://www.bfro.net/REF/THEORIES/WHF/dnatests.htm.

13. The context of the find is described by Churchill (1996).

14. Bindernagel (1998).

15. See www.bfro.net/REF/THEORIES/WHF/dnatests.htm.

16. Milinkovitch, Caccone, and Amato (2004).

17. Hunter and Dahinden (1973).

18. René Dahinden's presentation at the 1996 Sasquatch Symposium, Harrison Hot Springs, BC.

19. See Perez (1995).

20. Dennett (1989:269); Perez (2003b:4).

21. Personal communication, February 20, 1996.

22. The column, "Our Strange World," appeared in *Fate* (Chorvinsky 1993a, 1993b).

23. Green (1971:59).

24. Patterson (1966:63–70).

25. Krantz (1992:67).

26. Krantz (1992:122–123).

27. Palladium Pictures, 1982.

28. Trotti (1994).

29. Meldrum (1999, 2002). These presentations at the annual meetings of the American Association of Physical Anthropologists featured the Bossburg tracks and several of Paul Freeman's footprint finds. Meldrum did not volunteer information concerning Marx's and Freeman's success in filming Bigfoot as part of the presentations. He indicated to me, when asked, that he did not consider all these films to be genuine. Meldrum's 1999 presentation can be viewed at http://www.isu.edu/~meldd/fxnlmorph.html.

30. Napier took an agnostic position on Marx's Bossburg film, perhaps due to his opinion that it was unlikely that the footprints from that location were bogus (Napier 1974:87, 123).

31. Napier (1974:13).

32. Greenwell (1996:3).

33. Hunter and Dahinden (1975:90–92).

34. Perez (1990).

35. Greenwell et al. (1998).

36. Greenwell et al. (1998).

37. Greenwell et al. (1998:86).

38. Greenwell et al. (1998:86).

39. To establish credibility, the result would have to be duplicated from samples sent to independent laboratories.

9

The Eyewitness Problem

How to resolve all the contradictions? The answer for many people—a great many people, indeed—is that Bigfoot is real, even though there is no population of hairy bipeds lumbering through our forests. Bigfoot—or some variant of the monster—is part of human experience across the world, and has been for ages. The legend—giant, hairy human-like creatures lurking just beyond civilization—has powerful emotional and psychological meaning for many people. Bigfoot is real in the same sense that the concepts of hope and despair are shared among us, or in the sense that dragons can affect our thoughts if only because we can imagine them. Actual fire-breathing flying reptiles or malodorous Sasquatches are not required for the idea, and the consequences of that idea, to be real.

Vladimir Markotic and Robert Pyle are two students of Bigfoot who have approached the topic from different perspectives. Both have Ivy League doctorates (Markotic at Harvard and Pyle at Yale), but Pyle eschewed the dispassionate, cold-eyed scientific approach that Markotic embraced, and chose instead to cultivate an appreciation of his subject by wandering the forests where Bigfoot tread. In his account, *Where Bigfoot Walks*, Pyle casts himself in the role of the empathetic naturalist who is trying to get a feel for both the legend and the beast itself by experiencing whatever the *idea* of Bigfoot had to offer. Unlike many other books about Bigfoot, Pyle's work never descends to the verbal fist-pounding polemics of the advocate or skeptical positions. Pyle straddles the fence between skepticism and acceptance. In the end, he is left hopeful that the strange sounds he heard at twilight, the line of large footprints he found, and the pounding on the roof of his car one night were all made by a Sasquatch.[1]

Markotic, with the help of Grover Krantz, took a less stirring, more academic approach in his edited work *The Sasquatch and Other Unknown Hominoids*, assembling a group of researchers to weigh in on the possibility that the whole field of anthropology was missing something. Markotic's collection and Pyle's reflections came to the same important conclusion: the phenomenon of Bigfoot is real. It is a legitimate field of academic inquiry, but until now, that inquiry has been about finding and identifying a real animal. In recognizing the larger issue as phenomenological, Pyle and Markotic remind us that other avenues of inquiry might be more fruitful.

The skeptic who mocks Bigfoot as unworthy of academic investigation is missing the point. In fact, the skeptical position faces problems even after the poor quality of evidence for Bigfoot's biological reality is exposed. Bigfoot is not dying a discredited legend's death; instead, its reality is being championed by more and more people, and not just those living in the temperate rain forests of the Pacific Northwest. The Internet provides a home for this community of seekers where the exchange of ideas is not filtered by publishers and journal editors, and the fuel that keeps the legend burning is the steady and undiminished stream of eyewitness accounts.

These accounts are central to the phenomenon, because without them Bigfoot would not exist in the collective psyche. Without these stories, Roger Patterson would not have ventured into the woods to make his film. Bob Titmus spent his adult life tracking the animal because an encounter left him thirsting for an explanation. If we are to dismiss the possibility of a real creature, we have to explain these encounters. We have to explain why these encounters are not what they seem to be.

It is perhaps ironic that eyewitness testimony is what many advocates find to be the most compelling aspect of the case for Bigfoot, when, from the standpoint of intrinsic value as evidence, the eyewitness account is worthless. Both Henner Fahrenbach[2] and Daniel Perez[3] stressed to me that the eyewitness account was really impossible to ignore once you sat face to face with someone who was so visibly shaken and yet adamantly certain of their experience. These encounters profoundly affect the witness and, in many cases, those who chronicle the firsthand accounts. This should not surprise anyone given the vitality of Bigfoot phenomenologically: if the stories of encounters were not credible most of the time, the legend would quickly lose steam. That eyewitness credibility can prop up a phenomenon is in no way unique to Bigfoot. Investigators who champion alien abductions have to hitch their case on the perceived veracity of eyewitnesses because the aliens usually don't leave hair or giant footprints behind.

In fact, I have had the experience of interviewing an eyewitness, but it was not by design. I was surprised to find myself in that position, because it was a person I knew well, who I respected, and who I never would have guessed had an encounter with Bigfoot. She was driving with friends through the forests somewhere in the vicinity of Crater Lake in central Oregon—a suitably remote location for spotting rare wildlife. It was night. As they drove down the highway they spotted something in the headlights. It was large, she saw two legs, it was heading across the road, and then it was gone. The encounter, as it were, probably lasted all of two or three seconds. I cannot prove she was not lying, but my impression (admittedly subjective) was that she was not fabricating the account. She was positive it wasn't a bear, and none of the people she was with thought they'd seen a human, in or out of a costume.

I found the story credible, not because of the details, but because she was very certain that the encounter happened. Fahrenbach and Perez are right—the convincing eyewitness is an emotionally powerful advocate. Encounters happen; the question is whether the interpretation of events is correct. Before she began telling of her experience, my eyewitness had first stated: "I saw Bigfoot." She offered up her account, and I suggested her account was entirely plausible, but I wondered aloud how certain she was that her initial statement was true. She reflected on the encounter again for a few moments, and then with equal confidence suggested that she really wasn't entirely certain what it was she saw, but it did not correspond to anything she had seen before. For the record, I believe her. And I, too, have no idea of what she saw. I only know how she interpreted the event.

What if this is John Green's hoped-for one authentic case? If it is, we will never know. There is no way to verify the account beyond our willingness to trust the story and our confidence that what happened corresponded closely to what was seen. It may seem like I am splitting hairs, but the matter of perception is a wild card that we cannot afford to ignore if we want truly to understand what is going on.

Unraveling what is happening with the eyewitnesses may be an important key to solving the mystery, but it is at the same time hopelessly problematic. Although a committed advocate, Barbara Wasson understood better than most skeptics that there exists a psychological dimension that is always at work muddying the data. Her book *Sasquatch Apparitions* was highly critical of the work that was being done in the field of Bigfoot research. She knew that Bigfoot, even as a mere idea, was so emotionally charged for advocates that the inventory of data could not simply be taken at face value. "The reporters of all [these] data seem to have been miserably neglected."[4] It is not a trivial charge. Humans are the perceptual filter through which Bigfoot makes its way into the newspapers, the documentaries, and the occasional Sasquatch symposium. What this filter is doing is something we cannot nail down, because we don't have any Bigfoot in zoos or museums to use as a baseline for comparison. Wasson asked a simple question in 1979 that should have been broached two decades before: just who are these eyewitnesses? If the advocates are going to insist that the witnesses are credible, we can demand that they explain to us just how they know this.

Wasson's intent was to improve the way eyewitness accounts were collected and analyzed, including recommendations that the state of mind of both eyewitness and interviewer be assessed in some objective way. Wasson divides the universe of eyewitnesses into two categories, truth-tellers and liars. The liars are the ones who say they saw Bigfoot when in fact they did no such thing. Certainly these people have played a role in perpetuating Bigfoot; how much of a role is still an open question. Some liars are hapless and easily identified, but there is a subset who are convincing. No one knows how many of these are part of the Bigfoot eyewitness population.

The truth-tellers are honest—they believe that they have seen Bigfoot and they aren't actively making it all up. If Bigfoot exists, then their honesty may or may not translate into correctness, and therein lies the problem with eyewitness accounts. Truth-tellers can be honest and at the same time be wrong. The seasoned advocates know well that a dead tree, reduced to a stump some 5–10 feet off the ground, can make a suitable Sasquatch, given poor light, rotten weather, and a fleeting glimpse. Truthful eyewitnesses can make mistakes and, therefore, their honesty is not sufficient to establish that they are also right. Perceptual mistakes happen, and none of us is immune.

This line of argument sways few advocates. With Bigfoot, we are talking about not just a small mistake in judgment, but something approaching perceptual failure. How can someone be wrong about seeing 8-foot tall hairy apes in the clear light of day?

Hallucination is one explanation. That might account for one or another eyewitness account, but certainly not all accounts over so many years and across so many states. If that many people were hallucinating in the forest, we might expect the unicorn to make a comeback. Anxiety and stress can alter perception, but can a thoroughly addled person manufacture a giant hairy monster out of thin air? Can an underlying neurotic condition be powerful enough to morph a bear into a Sasquatch?

In truth, memory is astonishingly fallible. After the fact, memory is what counts, not the image that was projected onto the observer's retina. Eyewitness testimony occupies an exalted status in our society because it is an integral part of our legal system: you swear to tell the truth and your testimony is then assumed to be accurate based on that vow. Your word is golden unless forensic evidence emerges that trumps your account. If eyewitness testimony is good enough for the courts, why shouldn't it be sufficient to usher Bigfoot into the pantheon of zoological species?

In legal proceedings, eyewitness testimony gets used because it may be all the prosecution has to make its case. In science, eyewitness testimony counts for nothing if there are more objective data that can be collected. If you conduct a successful cold fusion experiment, then go out that night to celebrate, and the next morning find your lab has burned to the ground—with hard drives, notebooks, and samples gone up in smoke—you are out of luck. No scientific journal is going to publish your sworn statement (or those of your research assistants or the dean you told about it at dinner) to the effect that you have solved the energy crisis forever. It is bad luck, it is terribly unfair, and it is part of the culture of science that your word is simply not worth a damn. Is institutional science just mean-spirited, or does it know something the legal system doesn't? The answer is that law and science, partly by design and partly due to the inertia of history, have different definitions of how "truth" is established. In law, truth is established through adversarial advocacy. Eyewitness accounts are simply part of that system.

In scientific research, eyewitness testimony does serve as a source of data in some contexts (we might better rename it "informant recall" because researchers ordinarily do not take sworn oaths from their subjects). How much informant recall is going to count toward establishing the veracity of a claim really depends on what field of inquiry we are dealing with. In chemistry or physics, as the above example on cold fusion illustrates, a statement to the effect that your experiment worked but you have no data will get you laughed out of a conference. In the social sciences, however (in fields such as psychology and cultural anthropology), sometimes the information we want can only be accessed by simply asking people to remember what they did or thought at a particular time in the past. In reporting such information, researchers blithely assume that the results they obtain from their informants are accurate reflections of past events or behaviors. This assumption is simply wrong.

Russ Bernard, a colleague of mine in the Anthropology Department at the University of Florida, teamed up with anthropologists David Kronenfeld, Lee Sailer, and applied mathematician Peter Killworth to publish an article entitled "The Problem of Informant Accuracy: The Validity of Retrospective Data" in 1984.[5] This review was a damning indictment of the premise that people were accurate reporters of past events. Bernard and his colleagues called the issue a "fugitive problem"[6] for the social sciences. The poor fit between what informants said happened and what actually did happen (when it could be measured) amounted to a methodological crisis. The authors were not actually presenting information that wasn't available—the paper reviewed an existing literature of over one hundred articles—rather, they were pointing out that scientists who were relying on informant recall were burying their heads in the sand because "on average, about half of what informants report is probably incorrect in some way."[7] That means that people are unreliable reporters of facts. We cannot get around that problem very easily in psychological investigation where the variables of interest have to do with thoughts and belief systems. But if we are trying to bolster an argument in the natural sciences (where the advocates say Bigfoot research should be placed), informant recall should be the data of last resort, if it is admissible at all. In observing the poor correlation of actual behavior to reported behavior, Bernard and colleagues suggested that "this level of accuracy would be unacceptable in most fields of natural science."[8]

These findings resound in the legal arena as well, where there is a growing realization that eyewitness testimony is not nearly as reliable or accurate as we would hope. In fact, according to the work of Gary Wells, eyewitness testimony is terrible with respect to ascertaining the truth. Wells is a Distinguished Professor of Psychology at Iowa State University. He has spent years examining how well crime victims correctly identify suspects from police lineups.

What Wells has chronicled is both astonishing and chilling: eyewitnesses make mistakes in identification with alarming frequency.[9] Memory distorts, especially in contexts that are traumatic to the percipients. Several people can witness the exact same events and produce stories of the event that are wildly different. One implication this research is especially relevant to the matter of Bigfoot: *the certainty or conviction of the eyewitness has little bearing on the veracity of their claimed experience.*[10] This is bad news indeed for Bigfoot researchers, because it means that they cannot ascertain the validity of an encounter by evaluating the confidence level of the eyewitness.

A potential solution is to understand the factors that predispose eyewitnesses from misinterpreting events. Perhaps memory is better at certain times of the day. Could marital or employment status have some indirect influence on how certain events are remembered? If someone incorrectly recalls the place and time of an event, does that make the memory of that event entirely invalid? To fully understand eyewitness reports, we do need to consider such variables, but Wells maintains that—desirable as that information would be—this is knowledge we do not yet have.[11]

What we do know is that memories for events can be very unreliable. Wells and his colleague and collaborator Elizabeth Loftus, a Distinguished Professor of Psychology at UC Irvine, have demonstrated that memory can be skewed simply by assimilating misleading information after an event. The power of suggestion is very potent in this regard, and the magnitude of these effects can be astonishing. Wells and Loftus cite studies finding that, given inaccurate information after the event, people remembered seeing a barn in a bucolic setting where no buildings at all were present, and vicious animal attacks that never happened are remembered as real.[12]

Loftus has also found that imagination alone is sufficient to alter memories, whether they stem from recent events or from happenings in years past.[13] She has documented that the mere act of imagining that a past event occurred in a certain way, or had certain elements to it, is sufficient to alter memory content. Through a phenomenon called source confusion, someone can simply be told that an event happened to them (when in reality it did not), and the event becomes remembered as actually occurring. Ordinary people are susceptible to these effects. Memories are distortions of actual events.

This body of research suggests that one does not need to misperceive a bear to get a Sasquatch story; memory can conjure up Bigfoot out of thin air.

Sasquatch encounters are born of anomalous experiences, with suggestion, imagination, and expectancy contributing to many accounts. It is the nature of the human psyche to create and define categories. The forms that these categories take are going to be culturally specific in many cases. That hairy monster behavior differs between the North American Bigfoot and the Himalayan yeti may have more to do with the native culture of the reporters than the local ecology of giant primates.

This idea deserves further explanation. There is no denying that one's culture has a profound influence on perception, even to the point where contemporary social anxieties get expressed in seemingly bizarre ways. For example, in 1920 the Czech playwright Karel Capek wrote *Rossum's Universal Robots*, a science fiction piece that introduced the world to the possibilities, positive and negative, of androids in society. It was produced for the stage shortly thereafter and was immensely popular in Czechoslovakia. What happened after the play became part of public knowledge was interesting: schizophrenics began reporting that they were being stalked by robots.[14] These specific delusions weren't reported before Capek's play went public, so it seems that the form of the delusions was very much under specific cultural influence. The anthropologist Victor Barnouw offers a simple proof of the power of the social and technological environment with respect to the behavior of schizophrenics: people who are not familiar with the concept of electricity do not imagine themselves to be bombarded or monitored by malevolent electrical forces. In industrial societies, however, this is a frequent complaint of the mentally ill.[15]

Anthropologist Robert Edgerton's research into expressions of psychosis in four East African cultures makes a more subtle point about human perception.[16] Even though these separate cultures recognized the same signs of mental illness that are accepted as such in Western culture, the belief systems surrounding the underlying causes were often different from one another. That is, while people from different cultures could agree on the symptoms of mental illness, what the mental illness represented to the people who were talking about it was culturally specific. Edgerton's work shows that even a recognizable human universal—mental illness—is subjected to different interpretation based on its cultural context.

What do these examples have to do with Bigfoot? We do not need to stipulate that people who see Bigfoot are somehow deranged—this misses the point—but we have to recognize that the interpretation of an event is culture-bound. That means that consistency of reports might only tell us that the reporters share something in common in terms of attitudes, beliefs, and expectations. The apparent consistency of reports does not necessarily mean that all the eyewitnesses saw the same thing. Memory distortion is not necessarily random with respect to what is conjured; people sometimes see what they expect to see, regardless of any conscious intent to do so. Bernard and his collaborators argue that "memory is subject to systematic distortion due to cultural training. Informants respond to questions by reporting cultural norms, or 'what goes with what,' rather than dredging up actual events."[17] In the context of hairy monsters, Bigfoot goes with being scared in the woods. People can remember seeing Bigfoot if that explanation "fits" according to the circumstances of the event.

The innate need to categorize means that we do not, individually or collectively, tolerate an anomaly for long. People are remarkably inept at allowing a mystery to resolve itself in time; instead, we propose provisional solutions and try to explain the enigma in question through our current state of knowledge. Barbara Wasson referred to this as "taking refuge in the familiar."[18]

An appropriate example is the problem of things that go bump in the night. Awakened by an unfamiliar sound, your first impulse is to figure out what caused the noise. What you don't do is say to yourself, "I have no idea what that was so I will ignore it and go back to sleep." You might get out of bed to investigate, or you may merely, perhaps only semiconsciously, lie quietly in bed to run through the possibilities until you settle on a suitably plausible explanation. But you will not settle back into slumber without psychologically resolving the sound in some fashion. You may never actually find out what caused the noise, but if the event resides in your memory for long, it will be filed away in some mental folder labeled "picture falling" or "raccoon in attic." Nothing stays in the "unknown" folder for long.

It is quite plausible that a myriad of anomalous experiences gets routed into memory as Bigfoot, particularly in those cases where the context is suitable. Being alone and anxious in the woods on a foggy evening is prime time for a Bigfoot encounter, even more so if an individual is conversant with the legend or has an expectation that Bigfoot is a likely culprit in the event of unfamiliar stimuli. The wilderness can be frightening to anybody, even those with years of experience in the outdoors. A mistake of perception or a distortion of an event by fear can swiftly be transformed into an encounter with Bigfoot, even if there wasn't a bear, a tree stump or a shadow cast by a bird flying overhead. You don't have to see a hairy monster to be able to remember seeing one. This is not my opinion; it is a fact of human psychology.

Expectation is another wildcard that may be central to Bigfoot encounters. In the winter of 1978, the Rotterdam Zoo in the Netherlands lost a red panda after the animal escaped and was found dead shortly thereafter, not far from the zoo. Before the animal's body was found, officials had enlisted the press to get word out to the general populace that the animal was missing—in the hope that people seeing the animal would telephone the authorities. The calls did come in—over one hundred of them from all over the country—reporting that the panda was seen very much alive. That these calls were made after the panda's body was found suggests that all these eyewitnesses were mistaken.[19] The red panda is not native to the Netherlands, and we can be reasonably sure that the Dutch know the difference between an exotic animal and a domestic dog or cat. Thus, the reports could not be chalked up to mistaken identity alone: people expected to see a unique animal and they did. Similarly, there is no need to insist that people who see Bigfoot can't recognize a bear. The preceding example suggests instead that when people find themselves in an environment where they feel they ought to see Bigfoot, the monster is prone to make an appearance.

Ronald Binns's research at Loch Ness provides a convincing argument that monster sightings are fueled by expectation; some people favorably disposed toward the reality of the monster have managed to see a strange beast within a day or two of their arrival at Loch Ness.[20] This would not be problematic except that the loch has year-round residents, some of whom work on the water, and most of these people do not report seeing mysterious monsters.

These observations lead us to another problem: eyewitness events may not be independent. One person's Bigfoot experience might predispose another person to have an encounter retrospectively. The problem in this case is what the sociologist Ron Westrum calls "perceptual contagion."[21] Put simply, it means that the power of suggestion can take a slight anomaly and cement it into memory as a Sasquatch. This can be illustrated by considering a hypothetical series of eyewitness accounts.[22] We start with a perfectly ordinary situation that, because of the peculiarities of context, becomes something else.

It's a moonless night on a back road between two small towns; the road experiences a modest amount of nighttime traffic. Off the roadside, about 10 yards into the woods, a large owl is perched atop a tree branch some 10 feet off the ground. As it happens, the road is curving around in such a way that the headlights of the oncoming cars shine directly at the owl, but the animal is deep enough in the woods that its outline is not visible to the drivers. What does get reflected in the headlights are the creature's eyes, two of them glowing straight back at the driver. Twenty people see the set of glowing eyes high off the forest floor. Assuming none is too tired or disinterested to care about what they've seen, each person recognizes the event as something they haven't actually experienced before.

How the glowing eyes will be interpreted is bound to differ. One or a few individuals might figure out that this was an animal in a tree, even though they couldn't see the tree clearly at all and they couldn't say whether this was a possum, a raccoon, or an owl. Another individual might recognize the eyes clearly enough, but without seeing either the body or the tree's role in putting the eyes 10 feet from the ground, they figure the eyes must emanate from something just standing there. In this case, the interpretation is incorrect although it is, in some sense, consistent with the information at hand. In the amorphous shadows of the woods perhaps part of a shoulder or leg could be discerned in retrospect. The individual eventually decides this was Bigfoot staring from the woods. Nothing in the immediate experience contradicts this interpretation.

This individual might not tell anyone of the experience, but for sake of argument let us grant that he tells a sympathetic uncle one Saturday afternoon. Some weeks later, the uncle recounts the tale at the local tavern and one of the patrons was on that road the night in question and offers, "I saw it, too." This patron may have already decided what it was he saw that night, but the uncle's account provides additional information. He did not see the outline of a massive shoulder, but someone else who shared the experience did. The two accounts filter slowly through the neighboring communities, and after a month or two another witness to the event corroborates the original story.[23] After a few years, it may turn out that we seem to have seventeen witnesses to a Bigfoot lurking in the woods (three of the original witnesses may have settled on entirely different explanations, including the correct one). There is no intentional deceit involved because nobody was perpetuating a hoax. But there are seventeen people who can put themselves at a place and a time where they saw exactly the same thing.

In the sampling universe, we have twenty independent observations of two points of reflected light coming out of the woods from that night. These count as a sample of twenty. There are seventeen witnesses to Bigfoot embedded within that sample, but it is really—bowing to the imperative of independence—a sample of one that's contaminated sixteen other accounts. Reliability (all those people saw those red eyes) has been mistaken for validity.

Familiarity with landscapes or surroundings may weigh heavily in precipitating a Bigfoot encounter. My impression (and I confess I have no numbers to back this claim, but it would be a fascinating area of research) from scouring accounts over the years is that experienced hunters rarely see Bigfoot, though they would be expected to with some frequency. This suggests, circumstantially, that their familiarity with being in the woods in a variety of conditions insulates them from the type of anomalous experience that produces Bigfoot. Similarly, I have always been impressed with the ability of wildlife photographers to be able to splice together thirty- and sixty-minute segments on such rare creatures as the wolverine.[24] These people apparently don't ever see Bigfoot, even though wolverine habitat corresponds to some of Bigfoot's favorite haunts.

This situation may be analogous with astronomers rarely seeing UFOs. If flying saucers are real, it would make sense that the people who make their living stargazing would be reporting the most sightings. But this doesn't happen, and the best explanation might be that they are sufficiently familiar with things in the sky that they more easily recognize the mundane nature of what less experienced observers would classify as anomalous.[25]

A perhaps unexpected culprit in the accumulation of Bigfoot sightings over the years is the interviewer, the advocate who questions an eyewitness after an encounter. Barbara Wasson suggested that standard practice in debriefing individuals served to obscure as much as enlighten. Asking leading questions (how bad did it smell?), failing to listen to an entire account, omitting obvious questions (if you were inside the tent, how did you get a look at it?), and ignoring the greater context of the event will compromise the account in terms of the witness's actual experience and serves to interject the interviewer's personal bias. The account is immediately compromised. We can suspect that what the witness remembers at this point is susceptible to the interviewer's influence and expectations.

If an anomalous experience is interpreted as Bigfoot—or at least Bigfoot is being considered as the preferred explanation—a witness is going to seek out somebody with some familiarity or expertise with the perceived anomaly. There are two reasons for this choice: an expert (whatever that constitutes in the Bigfoot universe) is likely to be helpful and at the same time at least nominally sympathetic. The witness is seeking more than just answers; he or she is seeking validation of their experience. The interviewer is in the perfect position to provide this psychological salve. As soon as the interviewer becomes involved, the account has perhaps little chance of settling on any resolution other than Bigfoot.

Certainly no one has sufficient information from eyewitness reports to account for what anomalous stimulus caused someone to see a Sasquatch in every case. A singular explanation for sightings is neither warranted nor desirable. While it would be simpler to attribute sightings to a single source (a real Bigfoot), there is no logical reason why there cannot be multiple sources for Bigfoot encounters. Some people are lying. Some people are making mistakes. Some people are imagining things. Some people find themselves in a strange or terrifying situation, and, after the fact, Bigfoot can be molded to fit neatly into the experience. None of these human failings is unique to the Bigfoot encounter; people lie, misinterpret, invent, and rationalize in the course of innumerable endeavors in their daily lives. There is no rational reason why these real attributes of human behavior should be dismissed simply because Bigfoot is involved.

There is a rich tradition of hairy giants among Native American groups, and it is useful to inquire whether the reality of Sasquatch in two distinct cultures in North America (European versus Native) points to some independent, underlying reality of an actual creature. Anthropologist Roderick Sprague has argued that the dismissal of native Sasquatch traditions as mere myth is ethnocentric bias on the part of the anthropological and scientific community.[26] The point is well taken on one level: why should Native American accounts be whisked into the legend bin while equally fantastic accounts by European Americans be accorded greater credibility? On the other hand, if one examines the advocate position historically, it is not the case that the native accounts are marginalized by Bigfoot scholars. If anything, these stories are marshaled in support of the animal's zoological reality. The Native American tradition subverts the idea that Bigfoot was fabricated out of thin air by a handful of white pranksters in the twentieth century. The guidance that Sprague's editorial provides depends on one's initial premise. Bigfoot enjoys an oral history in both Native American and Western cultures, but this fact alone does not establish that at the tradition's foundation is a real animal.

There is no question that the idea of Bigfoot, regardless of its material status, has been borrowed and co-opted by the dominant North American culture from the native precursors. Even the finer details of Bigfoot's behavioral repertoire, such as breaking saplings in two and twisting tree branches,[27] have been usurped wholesale from native traditions[28]. Of course, the advocate position is not set back by this revelation; it is with equal ease that one can argue that the broken branches are symbolic mythological elements or a consistent behavioral sign. Yet supernatural elements infect both Native American and Western accounts. Kidnapping and gruesome murder can be found in the accounts of both Indians and descendants of European folk. Very different cultures seem to be deriving remarkably similar monster traditions from the same source, whatever that may be.

Sprague's admonition has been taken seriously by students of North American native cultures. Rather than shore up the circumstantial case for Bigfoot, however, the more detailed analyses of native traditions seem only to blur the distinction between biological and mythological entities. Wayne Suttles of Portland State University, while not hostile to the idea that a real animal underlies the myths, discovered several features of the native traditions of the Pacific Northwest that cast doubt on the notion that the source of the Bigfoot legend is a real beast.[29] Central to the problem is that the dichotomy between myth and reality is not terribly important to the Coast Salish Indians of coastal regions of Washington and British Columbia. Certainly imaginary animals exist in their cosmology (Suttles describes a two-headed beast, an adept swimmer, that transmogrifies into mallard ducks when the need arises), and ordinary animals sometimes are given to supernatural exploits. The variety of beings fitting into the category of "wild men" is large, and hairy giants are but one of these. Even within the hairy giant genre, Suttles finds that their descriptions are not consistent across Coast Salish groups, and many behaviors are very *in*consistent with what one would expect for a feral primate. There seems to be no reason ethnographically to suppose that these animals must be real.[30] This study of Suttles first appeared in 1972, and he was prescient in predicting that the mythological aspects of the Sasquatch phenomenon would soon meld with the growing American obsession with extraterrestrials.[31]

Stories of hairy wildmen are not confined to the Pacific Northwest; they are nearly universal cross-culturally. It would be a mistake to suggest that all these traditions must be attributed to a single, monolithic biological agent at their core. Yet, when the advocate position is that the myriad of tales from both indigenous and immigrant populations should be considered as legitimate evidence for Bigfoot, this begs the question. The vast wilderness areas of Canada provide fertile ground for historical and contemporary monster traditions, and people of all backgrounds see strange beings in the wild. The nature of the accounts, examined on an individual basis, makes it very clear that these people are not all seeing the same thing.[32] If one then submits that the sightings nevertheless do have a material basis, we are left accepting Loren Coleman's premise that there is not one but perhaps a dozen undetected species living in North America.[33]

Eyewitnesses may be sincere—even convincing—but as reporters of data we cannot say that they are accurate. This has no bearing on the person's moral character or sincerity; the mere act of interpretation distorts reality. If we accept that perception is flawed and that context can precipitate misperception, then what basis do we have for stating that since eyewitnesses are sincere in their belief, the case for Bigfoot is necessarily a strong one? Eyewitness accounts are a fertile and rewarding area of research—but not because they will lead us to the elusive Sasquatch. Bigfoot keeps showing up for some reason, not just in the woods through a single set of eyes, but in newspapers, TV specials, and conferences. If it isn't really there, what is it doing impressing itself on our consciousness? Why not unicorns or leprechauns? This is the remaining mystery. To make sense of Bigfoot as a phenomenon, we have to try to understand why it persists. If Bigfoot is not an animal but an invention, how do human actors keep the legend going, generation after generation?

NOTES

1. Pyle (1995), on further investigation, settled on a certain vocalization of the spotted owl as the likely source of the sounds.

2. Correspondence with the author, June 16, 1999: "The whole subject gains a different flavor when you personally interview seemingly shell-shocked eye witness (sic) right after the event."

3. Correspondence with the author, July 1, 1995: "Having interrogated many alleged eyewitnesses, I have walked away from some testimony shaken, knowing full well the witness saw what they claimed . . . they just can't prove it."

4. Wasson (1979:116).

5. *Annual Review of Anthropology* 13:495–517.

6. Bernard et al. (1984:495).

7. Bernard et al. (1984:503).
8. Bernard et al. (1984:507).
9. Gawande (2001).
10. Loftus, Miller, and Burns (1978); Wells and Murray (1984); Luus and Wells (1994); Wells and Bradfield (1999).
11. Gawande (2001:53).
12. Wells and Loftus (2002).
13. Loftus (1997:70–75); Garry, Manning, Loftus, and Sherman (1996).
14. Barnouw (1985:261).
15. Barnouw (1973).
16. Edgerton (1966).
17. Bernard et al. (1984:508).
18. Wasson (1979:126).
19. Van Kampen (1979). Ken Feder alerted me to this example.
20. Binns (1984:102, 108).
21. Westrum (1980:31–32).
22. This example is loosely based on an explanation by Joe Nickell (2000) in the case of an alleged monster sighting.
23. See Loftus and Hoffman (1989) on how easily misinformation can be incorporated into memory.
24. For example, "Wolverine: Devil of the North," produced in 2002 by the Wolverine Foundation. http://www.wolverinefoundation.org/products/cbvdo.htm.
25. See the Hamilton Amateur Astronomers' website, http://amateurastronomy.org/Events/EH387.html.
26. Sprague (1977:27).
27. See Krantz (1992:137–139).
28. Suttles (1977:49, 51).
29. Suttles (1977, 1980).
30. Suttles (1977).
31. Suttles (1977:73). The original citation is *Northwest Anthropological Research Notes* 6(1):65–90.
32. The work of Taft (1980) and Carpenter (1980) undermines the idea that Bigfoot, as traditionally conceived, is represented by all or most subhuman monstrous encounters.
33. Coleman and Huyghe (1999).

10

The Bardin Booger

The Pacific Northwest has always been the epicenter of Bigfoot activity, but a good legend will not stay geographically circumscribed for long—monster stories are just too irresistible. As Bigfoot grabbed the public imagination in the 1960s, tales of encounters with hairy bipeds started to creep eastward, and by the time John Green had published his encyclopedic *Sasquatch: The Apes among Us* in 1978, the only state in the continental United States without historical accounts attributed to Bigfoot activity was Rhode Island.[1] Interesting in this regard was that not all the stories were accounts postdating the Jerry Crew find; some came to light from decades before.

The flesh-and-blood supporters of Bigfoot are fond of these historical accounts from the eastern United States, since they further destroy the argument that the Crew find (or the Patterson film on its heels) sparked the legend. It is something of a strain to reconcile certain tales, however, with contemporary accounts of Bigfoot. There is a delightful monster tradition centered in the pine barrens of the Garden State: the "Jersey Devil" is credited with being the responsible party to a case of mass hysteria early in the twentieth century.[2] This monster is occasionally co-opted into the inventory of Bigfoot traditions[3]; the only problem is that the Jersey Devil—with its wings, claws, and tail—has a few too many adornments to qualify as a Sasquatch, although there does seem to be a more conventional Bigfoot tradition there.[4]

Florida might seem an unlikely spot to harbor Bigfoot, given its geographical and ecological remoteness with respect to the forested mountains of the

Pacific Northwest. But as aficionados of the Florida "Skunk Ape" are fond of pointing out, the swamps and forests of the Sunshine State provide a much richer potential food supply for a large primate that the temperate climate of Oregon and Washington can nurture. My present hometown, Gainesville, even had its own encounter with Bigfoot in 1974.[5] This incident took the form of a vehicular collision from which, fortunately or unfortunately depending on your point of view, the pedestrian Sasquatch was able to walk away.

A native Floridian colleague of mine, a forensic anthropologist by the name of Mike Warren, learned of my propensity to compile Bigfoot stories and informed me of a local legend emanating from a place called Bardin, a town located in the northern region of the Florida peninsula. Over lunch one day, Mike suggested that on a slow weekend we ought to make a day trip out to Putnam County to meet the Bardin Booger. Why not? Over the years, more than one Bigfoot advocate had harangued me about not doing my Bigfoot research "in the field," as it were, and here was a ready-made opportunity to investigate the history of a legend firsthand.

August in interior Florida gives new meaning to the term "oppressive." It isn't impossible to be outside, but the idea of comfort is an amusing abstraction. The usual human strategy is to hole up inside a car or dwelling with the air conditioning running, or (only if absolutely necessary) make brief forays into the sun or shade (with attendant mosquitoes) and punctuate these ill-advised ventures with long stints of recovery indoors. This particular Saturday would be perfect for our foray, since with the forecast high of 97 and the humidity at a level that makes the term "relative" laughable, we could be sure that the people we needed to talk to would be at home, indoors, with the constant hum of compressors warning them not to venture out.

You won't find Bardin on the map. It is a place insofar as someone in the know can tell you how to get there, but it is not recognizable as an incorporated entity despite having its own volunteer fire department. Bardin Road runs through it, but only the presence of Bud's Store gives the place a sense of "townness." It lies about 10 miles outside of Palatka, a typical North Florida town with plenty of churches and a downtown ruined by the arrival of several conglomerates and generic strip malls.

We arrived at Bud's store and were immediately marked as out-of-towners with our Bermuda shorts and Nikes. If you work in Bardin, chances are you're in the timber business or work in the pulp mill nearby, and that type of work doesn't mesh well with the smart casual look. Bud's store is no bigger than the convenience stores affixed to most gas stations these days, but with a rather more varied inventory. Here's where you did anything and everything commercial in Bardin. Gas, cigarettes, soft drinks, and snacks do not distinguish Bud's, but the broad inventory of chainsaws and lawnmower blades tell you that you were not just off the interstate. Off in one corner was a series of shelves with an assortment of dress and work shirts, individually loosely packed in plastic. "Over here," said Mike "is where they keep the Booger t-shirts." But we couldn't find any. "Any Booger t-shirts?" With that question, the clerk's perplexity as to what we were doing in Bardin vanished. No, she said, they've been sold out a while but there will be more coming in at some point. Anybody seen the Booger lately? No, she said, but there were always people coming by and asking about him. She said this with the nonchalance one would expect if you had inquired about which aisle to find the barbeque chips. Questions about the Booger aren't met with rolling eyes or peals of laughter here. It's good for business, and that is true whether it's out there or not. The Booger is to Bardin what Bigfoot is to Willow Creek, California. Willow Creek is home to a museum dedicated to Bigfoot. The town is situated close to the Bluff Creek footprint finds and the location of Roger Patterson's movie. The museum's president, although skeptically inclined, has said that she is a firm believer in the economic value of Bigfoot.[6]

Posted on the inside glass of the store front so one could read from the outside were two articles about the Bardin Booger, one from the Palatka newspaper from 1981 and another from some years later that appeared in the *Orlando Sentinel.* The articles carried typical monster-in-the-woods fare. Some people were parked out on a dirt road and the Booger started shaking their truck. No, they hadn't seen the Booger, but what else shakes your truck in the middle of nowhere in the middle of the night? The Bardin Booger does, apparently, match the profile of Bigfoot quite well, having the requisite attributes of bipedality, plenty of hair, and good size (8 feet is the height one usually hears). There are lots of woods around as well, and the land is sufficiently undeveloped that by nightfall the darkness can plausibly harbor a monster.

Mike knew about the Bardin Booger by means of a family connection, in that his Uncle Jody had written the only book on the subject, a tongue-in-cheek account of the legend entitled *The Enigmatic Bardin Booger.*[7] Jody Delzell was a writer and newspaperman and has written a number of columns about the Booger for the Palatka paper over the years. Mike had called ahead to alert Jody that we were on our way, and Jody assured us that he could clear up any questions about the origins of the legend.

But first we stopped for lunch in the heart of Palatka. Mike was, like his uncle, quite the local history buff, so he took me to the oldest diner in Florida—a converted railcar known as Angel's. The food was fine, the help was friendly, and by the décor you were convinced that the diner's claim to fame as Florida's oldest was at the very least close to being true. The place was nearly empty, and once we ordered Mike turned around toward the counter and asked to no one in particular "ever hear of the Bardin Booger?" Oh, sure, said the waitress, but she didn't seem to think anyone saw it these days. The next answer from one customer was not what I expected: "Hear of him?! Hell, I know him!"

I was lost for the moment, thinking I was about to be privy to one heck of an eyewitness account, but Mike knew immediately where this was headed. The woman continued, "I used to make his t-shirts." Next thing I know, Mike is asking if she knows the Booger's phone number. As the conversation progressed, I realized what she was talking about was a woman named Lena Crain, better known as the Bardin Booger who made public appearances all around Putnam County. She had a modified gorilla costume that lent flavor to all variety of local events, and was, along with Jody, perhaps the best source for the history of the legend. But no one at the diner knew how to get in touch with her.

Within a minute of meeting Jody Delzell, you realize that you are in the presence of a practiced storyteller. You get the impression from him that content without entertainment is simply a travesty. His years as a columnist, working on deadlines, had sharpened his skill for making a point with a flourish. As soon as we had shaken hands and were seated Jody launched into the history of the Bardin Booger.

In 1981, he had a young man working in his office who wanted to be a newspaper writer—in particular, a columnist—and Jody had taken the kid on with an admonition that as a columnist you had to come up with your own material. Apparently, the intern had initially risen to the task—but after two weeks and as many columns found himself creatively tapped out. He needed an idea and asked Jody if he could help him out. It was this need that spawned the Bardin Booger. Jody had spoken to a relative recently who had described her ordeal with a car breakdown in the middle of the night not far from

Bardin: "I wanted to get out of there quickly because I was afraid some booger was going to get me." Booger, Jody explained, was shorthand for bogey-man.

So Jody told the intern to write about the Bardin Booger, and the legend took hold. The boy got a better job and was soon gone, but Jody took up the Booger and adapted it to his own editorial needs. He filled in what began as a local Bigfoot and transformed it into a clothed, English-speaking, literate lost soul, quite removed from standard Sasquatch fare. His purpose in transforming the Booger, Jody said, was that it provided what he called a perfect straw man. There were comments Jody might want to make about local politics that, as a member of the community and one running the local newspaper, he really could not afford to say. In his backwoods meetings with the Booger, however, the tongue-in-cheek context provided a safe venue from which to make some unpopular suggestions—especially if it was the Booger doing the complaining.

It is Jody's opinion that the Bardin Booger did not exist per se prior to the columns written in 1981. The point is arguable, but Jody's presentation of the legend to the media certainly placed the Booger into the public consciousness of North Florida and beyond for good. After the "story" broke, Jody began to be approached by a number of Bardin residents who told him, in quite serious tones, that they had known for quite a while that "something was out there." Scaring people seemed to be the Booger's favorite pastime, and when a resident's dog turned up dead the Booger would be a prime suspect as well.

There has always been fodder for legends in the North Florida swamps. These are places where people generally don't have cause to go, so they retain mystery well. Strange lights in swamps are a common theme in the local folklore, and the mundane explanations are St. Elmo's fire, "swamp gas," or some bioluminescent phenomenon. Such legends of mysterious lights were promulgated by the local youth, Jody opined, to entice their dates into the palmetto scrub for activities other than the scientific exploration of the local ecology. Jody melded the legend of the lights with the Booger himself, noting in his columns that the light—which is often described as moving—was a lantern carried by the Booger since this poor beast was, in fact, afraid of the dark.

I asked Jody what the reaction was by the people of Bardin had been to his popularization of the legend. Had there been any complaints of any kind? He said that the reaction of the townfolk was a universally positive one of mild amusement. The legend still brings people to Bud's store, and if nothing else it's good for business. Did anyone take the Booger seriously? Jody's impression was that, by and large, the townfolk took to his light-hearted treatment of the Booger and that the popularization of the monster didn't prompt any of the locals to quit their day jobs to pursue the Booger full time.

This did not mean, however, that the humanization of the Booger didn't stop people from engaging in some time-honored pranks of the Bigfoot variety. One complaint that did make it to the newspaper office was from a local law enforcement man who asked Jody to stop writing about the Booger since it seemed to be sparking some mischief in Bardin itself. The officer explained that someone was scaring clients of Bud's store at night by hiding out in the woods and, costumed appropriately, jumping out into the parking lot and onto the beds of the parked and occupied pickup trucks. It was all in fun, the officer understood, but the problem was that an armed customer might get in on the joke just a second or two too late.

The most celebrated hijinks occurred soon after Jody had sprung the Booger on the world. Associated Press decided to run a story and soon Bardin was nationally known for its monster. Hollywood apparently took notice, and a film crew from some outfit (the popular account is "one of the networks," but nobody I talked to could remember for sure) made its way out to Bardin to do a short piece on the Booger. Some of the locals rose to the occasion in fine fashion, priming the crew the night before that they knew where the Booger was hiding out and whetting their appetites for making anthropological history the next day. By morning, the film crew was apparently quite agitated at their prospects and their local guides did not disappoint. The trademark pieces of Bigfoot evidence—footprints, hair, and broken branches—were found in sufficient quantity that the crew spent hours in pursuit. But the Booger managed to stay one step ahead of the cameras.

Jody put us in touch with Lena Crain, and Mike and I headed to the other side of town to talk to the woman who was, as far as most Floridians were concerned, *the* Bardin Booger. If Jody is responsible for hatching the Booger in its contemporary form, Lena is the force that keeps the legend alive. Her late husband, Billy, had written a song about the Booger and made a record that got a fair amount of airplay and sold close to 2,000 copies. The very idea of a feral ape inhabiting the swamps was so appealing that they had a Booger costume fashioned from a conventional gorilla getup. The Booger has since been in great local demand for parades and other events. The Crain's incarnation of

FIGURE 10.1
One version of Florida's famed skunk ape is the Bardin Booger, said to roam the woods west of the St. John's River in north-central Florida. Lena Crain has turned the Booger into a goodwill ambassador for Putnam County. Photo used with permission from Lena Crain.

the legend was much more along the conventional yeti line without the affectations or wardrobe of Delzell's creation (see fig. 10.1).

Lena sees the Booger as sort of a local goodwill ambassador; it's less a monster in public than a good-natured child of the swamp. The Booger is better known in parts of California, she told us, than in some parts of Florida, thanks to a West Coast radio talk-show host with a surname of Bardin who apparently felt a kinship with the monster. He got wind of the legend, and as anyone who looks into the matter surely will, learned of the song in its honor and arranged to have a disk sent west. Lena herself would later pen a Christmas song about the Booger that would make it onto a CD collection.[8]

What's fairly clear from our visit with Lena is that the legend has taken on a life of its own, and its popular incarnation has nothing much to do with the circumstances that spawned the legend in the first place, whatever those might be. Its popularization has made it a more well-defined entity than it would be otherwise. She seems to think that some form of the legend dates back to the early 1800s, and she concurs with Jody that among the locals, anxiety about the creature is likely confined to a minority of older residents and perhaps some rather gullible youth. And like everyone else, she said nobody seemed to have seen the Booger anytime recently.

At the end of our visit, Lena took us out to a back shed, where boxes and file drawers had Bardin Booger dolls, t-shirts, and various incarnations of the Booger that she has been wearing to events over the years. She autographed a couple of Booger publicity photos for us and assured us she would keep her ear to the ground about any inexplicable activity that might happen up the road around Bud's store, but she said this with a casualness that betrayed a confidence that no worthwhile news would emerge. Like Jody, and like the clerk at Bud's, she was much more interested in what the legend *did* than what the legend *was.* Nobody seemed much interested in Bigfoot antics among the palmetto and pines. The legend was good for a story, and it put Bardin on the map, but whether the thing was real or not did not seem to be a particularly important question, at least to the people we talked to. If the legend had utility, that was sufficient reason to keep it around. Why bother to find the thing? After all, if you settle on the question one way or another, Billy Crain figured it would take all the fun out of it.[9]

As we prepared to leave, motivated by the baking sun, Mike somehow convinced me to don the headpiece to the second-generation Booger costume, one that had been commissioned to a local art school. This head had a cartoonish expression more true to the Booger Jody had created in the newspaper accounts than the big-eared ape head that Lena preferred. As Mike snapped picture after ridiculous picture of a Booger wearing a madras shirt and Bermuda shorts, I marveled how Lena avoided heat stroke wearing this claustrophobic mask. Up the dirt road came a pickup carrying two young men, neither one much more than twenty years of age. "Don't forget to wave now Dave," Mike implored. The truck pulled up, the driver turned toward me, and proudly volunteered, "Yeah, I know the Bardin Booger!" At that moment, it occurred to me that perhaps the real reason this and other legends kept going did not revolve around cryptic animals or planted footprints. Maybe the Booger lives on for the simple reason that people want it around.

NOTES

1. Green (1978:227).
2. McCloy and Miller (1976); Lewis (1997, accessed online at www.citypaper.net/articles/102397/cover.jerseydevil.shtml).
3. According to Andrew Gable (http://www.geocities.com/Area51/Cavern/7270/jersey3.html), the wildman motif may have insinuated itself into Jersey Devil lore as early as 1927.
4. See Green (1978:264–268).
5. Green (1978:278).
6. Bailey (2003).
7. Delzell (1995).
8. "Bardin Booger's Christmas Wish" can be found on the Glad Tidings CD, Hilltop Records, Hollywood, California.
9. Kleinberg (1998:71).

11

The Phenomenon

Bigfoot is a contemporary myth. What I mean by "myth" is very important to this conclusion. Myth means different things to different people. Sometimes myth has to be about origins: of the universe, ourselves, or some important aspect of our lives. Bigfoot sort of fits this definition, if we see in its figure our primordial state in nature. The layman's idea of myth might simply be an imagined story, a fantastic tale that might have a moral to it in the end. Some Bigfoot stories certainly fall within this category. The concept of myth that I use here is that of the French literary critic Roland Barthes: myth is a means of communication, it is a message.[1] Barthes was the leading figure in developing a field known as semiology, which explores how symbols function in cultures and societies. He saw mythological elements in such diverse phenomena as big-time wrestling, the marketing of margarine and detergent, and discussions of Einstein's brain. Some of Barthes's examples of myth are more tangible than others, but his essential point is that symbols are very powerful communicators of our anxieties, hopes, and fears.

What is myth for? Barthes, like other students of mythology, understood that myth provides a connection between the mundane aspects of existence to the realm of the mystical or spiritual. This would seem to answer the obvious question of why cultures need myth as an alternative way of talking about things. Barthes believed that "myth economizes intelligence: it understands reality more cheaply."[2] The reality Barthes is talking about here is the cultural reality of values and norms, not the objective reality pursued in scientific laboratories. In other words, myth is a way of talking about things that really matter to us, through symbols that can be imbued with a variety of meanings.

Consequently, when I argue that the Sasquatch is a mythological figure, I am arguing that the search for Bigfoot means something beyond the simple question of whether there is a big hairy ape in the woods. The short answer to the question of why the legend persists is that Bigfoot symbolizes something of great concern. It is a human invention, and it is reinvented constantly. Whatever the biological status of Bigfoot might be, the beast has always been and will remain essentially a mythological figure. Part of Bigfoot's staying power is that its form can accommodate a variety of meanings; the co-opting of the legend by vastly different cultures is a testament to this fact. At the same time, Bigfoot has an essence that transcends its various manifestations; despite its survival through millennia of cultural transformation and technological innovation, it retains its basic characteristics. It is giant, wild, foul, and utterly mysterious. Marjorie Halpin notes that the enigma Bigfoot presents is the core of its appeal: "Sasquatch is pure potentiality, pure possibility."[3] It is an archetypal myth, observes Robert Pyle, a status that is independent of whether there is an undiscovered animal behind it.[4]

And then there are the footprints. Those who have encountered Bigfoot can take comfort from the fact that the being they experienced has left a tangible and unmistakable sign of its presence. The footprints are there. Only because the footprints could be seen, followed, cast, and displayed have people made the pursuit a lifelong quest. The advocates can—and should—point to these strange marks in the ground and demand an explanation. The calling card is there for everyone to see, and it makes for a monster that is impossible to ignore.

If we are to dispense with the idea of Bigfoot as just another animal, as the bulk of advocates insist it must be, then we must confront two problems. The first is figuring out what Sasquatch does for people—what need does the legend fulfill? For if it served no cultural or psychological purpose, why would it persist into our rational age with no hard evidence to back it up? The second problem has to do with the footprints. The important question is no longer who is making the footprints, because there are plenty of people who are up to the task. Instead, the interesting question is why. What possible motivation is there for fabricating tracks? Financial gain might be the initial suspect, but that explanation doesn't stand up very well. Most hoaxers are not sticking around to view the discovery of their own handiwork, and although casts of tracks have been bought and sold, no one has ever gotten rich from such commerce.

I think the principal obstacle in unraveling the mystery of Bigfoot has to do with the type of explanation that both advocates and skeptics deem satisfactory. The simple, self-contained and—most importantly—single explanation has had the most appeal for all sides. For the advocates, Bigfoot is either a real animal or an impossibly involved conspiracy. For the skeptics, it is either a real animal or a series of independent con artists having a good laugh. Each dichotomy is set up so that the conclusion is foregone: if you accept the advocate's assumptions, the animal must be real; given the skeptic's viewpoint, the work of hoaxers is the rational choice. Of course, the advocates cannot satisfactorily explain why we have no specimens, but the skeptical conclusion does not explain why Bigfoot doesn't just go away even when hoax after hoax is exposed.

Two dynamics are at work, and human agents are behind both. There is a core of believers, not necessarily identical to the population of advocates or eyewitnesses, who see the significance of Bigfoot as so profound that reducing the phenomenon to myth is unthinkable. These people see Bigfoot as, among other things, an ecological messiah. In addition, there is a less visible but no less vital assembly of individuals who, from very different motivations, keep the legend going by faking tracks, photographs, and even movies. These folks I will refer to as the "pranksters." These people do not belong to some secret society but instead work independently and unwittingly for a shared purpose. For lack of a more alliterative term, I will call my proposal the "Prankster-Ecomessiah hypothesis." The two classes of participants are at cross-purposes, but they interact to perpetuate Bigfoot in the social and cultural realm.

Bigfoot signifies wilderness and the power of nature. The Sasquatch is the ecomessiah, for if we understand this monster we might overcome our ambivalent relationship with nature. Henry Franzoni, a former NASI board member and something of a Sasquatch philosopher, has noted that his searching for Sasquatch, if nothing else, imbued in him a profound appreciation for nature.[5] Pyle surmises that Bigfoot might just be "an ambassador for truly Green spirituality."[6]

This symbolic aspect of Bigfoot is rarely talked about among advocates, but there is no denying its importance. Pyle's meditations in the heart of Bigfoot country brought him to a simple conclusion that truly sums up what the

Sasquatch evokes: if we destroy the wilderness, Bigfoot disappears as well. No real animal can compare to the Sasquatch as the embodiment of the scale, power, and ultimately the mystery of the wild. It is the perfect symbol of foreboding when our encroachment into the wild is becoming absolute and irreversible. One of the primary emotions emerging from a Sasquatch encounter is a sense of awe. It is instructive that, though people are frightened in the course of an encounter, they rarely emerge from the event determined to get rid of the creature or banish it from the forests. Instead, the event—however mundane in the details—imbues in the eyewitness the sense that, if anything, this animal is *important*.

The public pitch of the advocates is articulated most often in terms of evolutionary biology: this quest matters because we are closing in on a primate relative that is more our kin than any other. For this reason alone, the scientists should be interested. My sense is that this is more a marketing technique than true conviction. Many advocates are perfectly happy to accept the conclusions of Grover Krantz or John Bindernagel: Bigfoot is an aberrant Great Ape, nothing more. If that is the case, then Bigfoot is not our sibling so much as our distant cousin. If Bigfoot is a persistent *Gigantopithecus*, then the paleontological consensus would have to be that Bigfoot is not even our closest living relative[7]: that title would remain with the chimpanzee. So the fuss about Bigfoot potentially challenging our basic ideas of human evolution is beside the point. What really appears to matter to those who believe in Bigfoot is only that the animal is alive.

We seem incapable of fulfilling our own needs without destroying some aspect of nature; we have neither the collective will nor the wisdom to preserve the wilderness. Kenneth Wylie suggests that the Sasquatch serves to remind us that the subjugation of nature comes at a cost.[8] It is no accident that Bigfoot is perceived as existing between the realms of human and animal: How many Bigfoot encounters have ended when the hunter declared that he could not shoot the creature because it was simply too human? Bigfoot, its limitless potential maintained by its mystery, is the ideal guardian of nature. If we destroy Bigfoot, we kill part of ourselves—that core of our being that was once part of nature but then evolved out of it. Certainly one part of the appeal and persistence of Bigfoot is that it is put into the role of the ecological savior. If it survives, nature survives. We can catch a fleeting glimpse of our connection to the earth, our origins in the raw wilderness, if Bigfoot remains in our midst.

Is this just so much psychobabble, a subjective conjecture? Myth and legend, much less symbolism in general, are not empirical domains in the sense of one being able to measure their value as one can measure a footprint. Mythology breeds in the subconscious, which, by definition, is not readily accessible to objective analysis. But Bigfoot is a pliable signifier of our relationship to nature and to our primal being; it serves a very basic purpose for the human psyche. Bigfoot might persist simply because it is psychologically valuable.

The argument is made that Bigfoot really does not qualify as a mythological figure because encounters with the creature are astonishingly mundane,[9] the idea being that standard motifs of monster myths are generally absent from the accounts. On balance, I think this position is insupportable for three reasons. First, one can only argue the point by selectively eliminating the scores of reports that have paranormal or supernatural elements to them, including Fred Beck's spirit visitations and the glowing eyes of so many accounts. Many accounts of Bigfoot are obviously bogus by virtue of the fantastic narratives that accompany the encounters, yet we can dismiss these as biologically vacuous while still recognizing the psychic importance of the event.

Second, the so-called mundane encounters only qualify as such if you're judging on the basis of what Bigfoot is doing rather than on the effect that the encounter has on the eyewitness. A typical encounter in the heart of Bigfoot country is a chance occurrence, often on the edge of the wilderness but not necessarily deep within it. Bigfoot just stands there, contemplating the person, and after a time, turns and walks off. Seldom is there a violent display, no monstrous roars are brought forth, and the fear that the eyewitness feels is born of awe rather than any tangible threat behavior on the part of the Sasquatch. The lack of action in the encounter is no measure of its mythological gravity.

In fact, typical Sasquatch behavior is decidedly unnatural from a zoological perspective. Seldom does Bigfoot run off in the fashion of most wild animals; it simply walks away, unafraid, or just ignores its observer entirely. Chillingly, Bigfoot seems altogether indifferent to the human presence. It is aware that someone is there, but its curiosity is muted much of the time. Deer will run, bears may threaten, and pumas may hide when people enter their realm, but Bigfoot just goes about its business.

The same cannot be said of the human witness. Encounters often change lives. Bob Titmus, for example, lost money, friends, and family in his resolve to know what it was that just stood there on the beach in 1942.[10] Pyle is on the mark again: Native American accounts have Bigfoot stealing children, but our version steals souls.[11] The Internet is peppered with web pages detailing personal encounters where the eyewitnesses brave the certain ridicule of the public to send a clear message: Bigfoot is real, and its reality matters. It is no coincidence that this reaction also typifies UFO research, particularly with respect to alien abductions. UFOs and Bigfoot have something in common (and I don't mean that one serves as the home base for the other): both answer one of the most human of questions, "Are we alone?" with a resounding "No."[12]

There is a third reason why the supposed unremarkable nature of encounters is not an argument that we are dealing with a biological rather than a mythological entity. Our Bigfoot stories seem perfectly unremarkable to us because the stories are grounded in the familiar context of our own culture. They make sense to us even if we don't immediately recognize the mythological elements within them. Bigfoot's role as the forest guardian fulfills our expectations of the creature; this role does not contradict its history in North American culture.

This idea is illuminated by looking at Bigfoot stories from other cultures. It should not surprise us is that the narratives are culture bound, but it is enlightening to read them since it is easier for us to see the myth motifs embedded within them and it is easier still to doubt that the tales have a material basis. I'll use two sources to make the point: Panday Ramkumar's *Yeti Accounts*[13]and Dmitri Bayanov's *In the Footprints of the Russian Snowman.*[14] Both books come from areas where the bipedal hairy monster concept enjoys a long history and where, not unlike North America, there is limited scientific interest in the question of whether a real animal underlies the reports. In Nepal, the traditional yeti encounter involves decidedly less benevolence than what the North American Bigfoot brings to the table. Attacks on people and livestock are not unusual, and the preferred beverages include blood and *chang* (a Sherpa version of beer). Encounters with yetis often involve sex, consensual and otherwise. In general, the Himalayan yeti tradition has the animal much more intimately involved in human affairs, and the destructive potential of this incarnation of the wildman is more concretely realized in its penchant for wrecking crops and stealing food.

The Russian Bigfoot also differs from its American counterpart in terms of its level of human contact, but the narratives Bayanov offers (with little discernible skepticism) describe a being much closer to the human condition than the Nepali version. The Russian wildman can be found banging on dwellings and apparently begging for food; the beast is sometimes encountered sporting items of clothing that have seen better days. One account has this Asiatic Sasquatch making nocturnal visits to a stable for the purpose of braiding the manes of the horses residing therein.

Telling about these accounts is that their structure and content are decidedly un-American and un-Canadian (if the rare North American account contains a Bigfoot sporting old blue jeans, that report is generally disbelieved by the advocates). Loren Coleman might attribute this to species-specific behavioral differences among undiscovered hominids. But our understanding of mythology suggests instead that it is more parsimonious to explain the differences with the simple acknowledgment that we are dealing with separate cultural traditions. A story of a young boy having an amorous encounter with a female Bigfoot is not going to be credible in the context of the North American Bigfoot: We "know" the beast does not do such a thing. Would Albert Ostman's abduction tale be credible among Nepalis who believe in the yeti? It is hard to tell, but there can be little doubt that the meaning of the story would lose something in the translation from one culture to the other.

Panday makes clear in his discussion of the yeti that its mythological status does not significantly diminished its importance in Nepali and Sherpa cultures. The question of the creature's reality is an interesting one, he asserts, but it does not need to be resolved in order to understand the role of the monster in the native culture. Myths can have a material basis, but there is no requirement that they must.

Those of us living within the greater Western culture have evolved a rather curious relationship with our mythology. Rationalism and science hold sway as ostensible rudders of knowledge. Myth, an essential and inerasable component of human experience, has suffered a demotion in status by virtue of the fact that it is not real in a material or historical sense. Myth is as ingrained in American culture as in any other, but because a story is not "true," we fail to attribute to it the significance it deserves. That said, if Bigfoot isn't real then it cannot be important in our contemporary culture. The advocate is essentially forced, under these circumstances, to make Bigfoot a real creature to confer meaning on it. The myth is no longer good enough, since as a society we mistakenly believe we have dispensed with the need for such things.

Individuals in every culture probably entertain the notion that theirs is a rational world. Yet neither cultures nor individuals can lay claim to complete rationality: people are simply not so equipped. We are emotional beings, and rational behavior is an ideal that incompletely describes what people actually think and do. The pull of rationality is that we expect it to lead to the truth, or at the very least, to some provisional truths. Irrationality is thus stigmatized, and not always without good reason.

A peculiarity of our culture is that our popular conception of myth as inherently "false" means that myth can be stigmatized unless it is dressed up as something else. The value and meaning that myth provided historically are sublimated in the social conversation. This creates bizarre paradoxes. Belief in the literal truth of the creation account in the Bible, an unsustainable position on both logical and empirical grounds, now is manifested in the public sphere as creation science. Its proponents must make the creation story historically true to in order to validate it, which accomplishes the ultimate goal of making it meaningful. People experience missing time and are violated by extraterrestrials who kidnap them in the dead of night; they, too, see no alternative in their quest for meaning other than to mold the experience into a thing that happened.

How we deal with urban legends in public conversation is instructive. We have all heard the one about the poodle in the microwave. Its elderly owner wanted to dry the pet after a bath, and the end result of not wanting to dirty a towel was an exploded dog. There are actually several versions of the tale, and it turns out that the legend even predates microwaves (older versions have cats in clothes' dryers, for example).[15] Our concern with urban legends in contemporary society is always whether the story is true rather than what the story means. The truth of the story misses the point, though. The poodle in the microwave neatly packages our fears and concerns about technology: (1) technology is dangerous in ordinary hands; (2) there is a price to be paid for having a machine do what human labor can achieve; and (3) nature (dog) will sooner or later succumb to technology (microwave). This myth appears again and again in different guises in Western culture. Karel Capek's 1920s classic *Rossum's Universal Robots* finds the robots fashioned by men eventually rising up and overthrowing their creators. The message of the tale is unaffected by the question of its historical truth. Whether it happened or not is immaterial to what the legend does for us. For human beings, meaning has never depended on the truth of the stories conveying the message. We insist we are more enlightened now, but in practice we seem to have only confused myth and reality.

Contemporary attitudes about myth undermine its role in human experience. Bigfoot, it seems, will only get its deserved status if it joins the ranks of the real. Its meaning is cheapened if it is not made a being because the message has no value unless the messenger is known. It is indeed ironic that in adopting the imperative that only the tangible can have value, we have created a cultural milieu in which our ability to distinguish myth from reality is so hopelessly compromised. We leave ourselves no choice: Bigfoot, guardian of wild nature, our ecomessiah, has to be real.

Bigfoot encounters often happen in clusters. A sighting spurs publicity and in the following weeks, even months, a rash of encounters validates the original report. According to sociologist Robert Bartholomew, what is happening is that the encounters are fomenting a collective delusion driven by mass wish fulfillment. Bigfoot is an acceptable embodiment of mythological themes in the modern world: "an antiscientific symbol undermining secularism."[16]

It is a mistake to assume that the reality of the footprints destroys the mythological status of Bigfoot. Because Bigfoot cannot have value unless it is real, the footprints actually validate the myth by "proving" that there is a corresponding material entity behind it all. The footprints are the realm of the "pranksters," and they play an integral role in keeping Bigfoot alive. If the eyewitnesses and the true believers are the fire, the pranksters stoke that fire with fuel. These are the hoaxers, the con artists, and the liars.

As I mentioned before, it is logically unnecessary for the pranksters to all be members of a Sasquatch cabal. As individuals, they only have to know what people expect Bigfoot to be and where they expect it to be found, data which have only become easier to come by with each passing year. It helps if the pranksters are also creative and ingenious, but the truly indispensable ingredient is an audience. What demands our scrutiny is what motivates this group of people. It is likely that a number of them do not believe in Bigfoot one bit; so whatever the mythological value of Bigfoot is, it is probably inconsequential to them. Three principal factors are at work here: money, notoriety, and empowerment.

The motivational power of money is transparent. If you have acquired tangible evidence for Bigfoot, history shows that you can sell it. The evidence may be legitimate or it may be bogus, but all that is required to sell it is one buyer who believes the product is a sign of Bigfoot. If you are peddling Bigfoot merchandise, you don't even have to vouch for its legitimacy: Here are some tracks I found in the woods, take it or leave it. The seasoned advocates will tell you that going into Bigfoot for the money is a bad gamble. Certainly nobody has made their first million from Bigfoot, while it is certain that millions have been spent in the search over the decades. Of course, investing time and money in perpetual-motion machines is, in our Newtonian universe, supremely risky, but that has not stopped people from doing so. No, Bigfoot has not been a financially rewarding enterprise, but it does not follow that nobody will try to prove that it could be otherwise.

Somewhat less tangible as motivation for hoaxing is notoriety, but here again, Bigfoot's history indicates that it has been sufficient cause for hijinks. Rant Mullens and Ray Pickens were never caught in the act, but they did volunteer how they managed to fool some people. Dahinden, Krantz, and Perez have all complained about individuals bragging about encounters that were later established as bogus claims. There are few faster ways to get one's fifteen minutes of fame than to call the local paper about your Sasquatch encounter; the media will be happy to air your story. Ray Wallace was always good for a yarn, whether you were a journalist or a scientist. Bigfoot rescues from anonymity.

Finally, there is an aspect of Bigfoot hoaxing and fabrication that I think has been largely overlooked. This is the sense of empowerment that Bigfoot can bring to the individual. If hoaxing is as rampant as I suggest in this book, then it follows that the majority of hoaxers go undetected and therefore unidentified. We cannot invoke notoriety as motivation when a hoaxer chooses to remain invisible. What if most hoaxers choose to remain anonymous? If that is the case, what is the point?

Mistrust of institutional authority and perceptions of an elitist scientific community are persistent features of the American cultural landscape. It makes sense in a society that values the individualist. Orthodoxy can be seen, in the modern world, as an imposition of belief by those in power. Nobody is obliged to embrace the belief system but, at the same time, they may feel powerless to effect any substantive change in prevailing attitudes. Bigfoot is but one outlet for that kind of frustration. Author Daniel Cohen sees monster hunting in general as a means by which to challenge intellectualism:

> The buffs often celebrate the hairy-chested adventurer, the plain, straight-talking ordinary guy, the great rugged individualist, that fellow so beloved in American folklore, and so rare as to probably be mythical himself. This imaginary common-man adventurer is set up in opposition to his arch enemy, the equally mythical stuffed-shirt scientist.[17]

With Bigfoot, the pranksters cast themselves as this archetypal adventurer and do more than simply challenge the scientists: they make fools of them.

Making a statement, even anonymously, that Bigfoot exists is more than a cryptozoological opinion. Producing evidence of Bigfoot is an affront to the scientific establishment: the evidence screams that the official line, the status quo, is wrong. The Establishment is fallible, and if it is wrong about this, who knows what else might be amiss? One of the goals of the invisible hoaxer is to fool the scientists, the arrogant Ivory Tower folks who have been telling us for our whole lives what we may and may not believe. The antipathy toward the scientific community is palpable. René Dahinden's biting sarcasm in this regard speaks for hunter and hoaxer alike: "Scientists today *are* the high priests. They are all-knowing. They know the answer to every damn thing."[18] Hoaxing Bigfoot can be seen as an attempt to knock Dahinden's "priests" from their pulpits. Dahinden reviled those who perpetrated hoaxes, but the activities of the pranksters are born of the same mistrust of institutional authority that Dahinden and other Bigfoot hunters harbored. The pranksters thus validate their own suspicions: the scientists and the government that sponsors them are really fools because they can be made to believe in monsters.

This explanation might seem something of a reach, except that the search for Bigfoot is punctuated by just such episodes. What motivated the person from Indiana to mail a bogus track to Grover Krantz? The scientist's arrogance gave birth to the hoax. Similarly, confessed hoaxer Ray Pickens was clear about his motivations. His decision to fashion phony feet was provoked by derisive comments of out-of-town Bigfoot seekers that the locals were "hicks" for not even knowing there was a prize monster in the surrounding woods. Pickens responded with his feet to show the visitors who the hicks were.[19]

Of course, the full disclosure of Ray Wallace's activities reminds us that another part—perhaps the largest part—of the prankster equation is amusement. If Wallace wasn't having a good time promoting Bigfoot, no one is any the wiser today. But Wallace knew in the course of his activities that disclosing his true role with respect to tracks and photographs would invite the wrath of the serious Bigfoot investigators. Some of these earnest individuals had come a long way to have a look, and soon the law enforcement officials dealing with the fallout became very annoyed. A prank got out of hand, and the promulgator's instinct for self-preservation took over. We can be reasonably sure the same scenario has played out again and again.[20]

The last essential point of the Prankster-Ecomessiah hypothesis is that the two sets of actors reinforce one another. The hoaxers cannot have fun (or attain notoriety, or make money, or stump the experts) unless they work in conjunction or within a community that champions the cause of Bigfoot. Nor can those who sense the gravity of Bigfoot afford to have the signs of its reality disappear: What can they point to if there are no tracks? It is ironic that the activities of the folks who are into Bigfoot for the spoof value instill hope in the many others who strive to make the search a legitimate endeavor; that is, both those of the ecomessiah persuasion and the advocates who are out there actively searching.

The problem for the advocates is that they have always had a farce on their hands. The presence of a television crew is often sufficient in itself to ensure the suspension of all skepticism.[21] Bogus films, phony footprints, and fabricated stories are par for the course, but the desire to find this giant is so powerful that publicity becomes confused for truth.[22] Yet because Bigfoot is so important by virtue of what it represents, the search goes on for John Green's one bona fide case. A symbol so powerful could not be unreal.

The clumsy title of this explanation, the Prankster-Ecomessiah hypothesis, belies its usefulness. The phenomenon of Bigfoot is entirely explicable without having to argue that there is a giant undiscovered species out there. The mythological value of Bigfoot, its importance for those who seek it, has nothing at all to do with its zoological reality. If Bigfoot walks out of the woods of the Cascades into the streets of Hood River, Oregon, tomorrow evening, that has no effect whatsoever on the proposition. I do not expect that to happen, but I am not sure that I would be disappointed if it did. Bigfoot's mythological value and the willingness of people to manufacture evidence explain the phenomenon. We may need the animal, but that does not mean the animal has to be there.

The hypothesis also specifies where the focus ought to be when it comes to Bigfoot. It strikes me that the subject is a legitimate area of inquiry, even if it is not in the realm of natural history, as so many believe. René Dahinden's justification for the quest is one we can all understand: If Bigfoot is a mythological creature, "the mythology has to come from someplace, it doesn't just pop out of a Kellogg's Corn Flakes box."[23] People see Bigfoot. In terms of subjective human experience, we ought to treat this as a fact and seek an explanation for it. Unfortunately, we have been asking the wrong question through the years. "What did you see?" we ask the eyewitness. If we take the answer at face value, we miss the meaning of the phenomenon. It may be more important to ask the one question the eyewitness may be in no position to answer: "Why did you see it?" Bigfoot's persistence in our culture is testament to its value and meaning, even if we have yet to arrive at a full understanding of what it represents. It is safe to say that, as myth, Bigfoot remains useful to us; when it is obsolete, it will go the way of the unicorn. Robert Pyle sees the element of mystery as essential to Bigfoot's survival; the *possibility* of Bigfoot may be what gives this monster value.

Bigfoot is, by its suggestion of humanness, reflective of ourselves. We do not know quite what to make of the image. Figuratively and literally, its essence seems to elude us. We only know for certain that the Sasquatch is meaningful. If we can decipher why it is this particular monster stands fast in our cultural consciousness, then we will surely learn something interesting about ourselves. The search for Bigfoot is a worthwhile endeavor, but it always turns up empty because we have been asking the wrong questions and looking in the wrong places. There is a mystery here, to be sure, but it is not deep within the forests where the answer lies.

NOTES

1. Barthes (1978:109).
2. Barthes (1978:153).
3. Halpin (1980:4).
4. Pyle's comments to this effect can be seen in the 1999 video production *Sasquatch Odyssey* (Big Hairy Deal Films, West Vancouver, BC).
5. Matthew Burtch (2000). In Search of Bigfoot. *Reed Magazine* August 2000 (accessed online at http://web.reed.edu/community/newsandpub/aug2000/a_Bigfoot/index.html).
6. Pyle (1995:157).
7. Fleagle (1999) articulates the straightforward case that *Gigantopithecus* is related to modern orangutans; Krantz (1986) regards *Gigantopithecus* as more human-like than ape-like.

8. Wylie (1980:224–235).

9. Halpin (1980:21); Napier (1972:207).

10. Greenwell (1996).

11. Pyle (1995:7).

12. Denzler (2001:99–102).

13. Panday (1994).

14. Bayanov (1996).

15. The entry on the urban legends reference pages is http://www.snopes.com/horrors/techno/micropet.htm.

16. Bartholomew (1997:32). The role of Bigfoot in articulating religious themes during a perceived period of spiritual poverty is paralleled in the UFO phenomenon (see Denzler 2001).

17. Cohen (1970:8–9).

18. Wylie (1980:159).

19. Sunlin (2002). Pickens is mistakenly referred to as "Dickens" in the article.

20. Bobbie Short's Bigfoot Encounters website includes a November 2002 confession of another hoax from Citrus County, Florida, that occurred in 1975 (http://www.n2.net/prey/Bigfoot/hoaxes/sohl.htm). The incident involved some youths who manufactured a bogus encounter sufficiently well that an area teacher got the local paper to run a story. At that point, the confessor suggested that the prank was out of control and they did not see owning up to the incident was a palatable option.

21. For example, an alleged videotape of a yeti-like creature walking through a snowfield in the Himalayas was analyzed by Jeff Meldrum, who suggested that the form was between 8 and 10 feet tall on the Paranormal Borderline program in March 1996 (Perez 2003c). Meldrum's subsequent investigations determined that the footage was a hoax (http://www.bfro.net/REF/bfmedia.asp).

22. Cohen (1970:9).

23. Quoted in the 1999 video production *Sasquatch Odyssey* (Big Hairy Deal Films, West Vancouver, BC).

References

Anonymous (1967). Mrs. Bigfoot is filmed! *Eureka Times-Standard*, October 21, 1967.

Anonymous (1992). Trap designed to catch Bigfoot has outlasted its creators. Associated Press Release, November 22, 1992.

Anonymous (2000). Fingerprint expert tries to debunk Bigfoot, reaches opposite conclusion. *Houston Chronicle*, February 21, 2000.

Bailey, Eric (2003). Bigfoot's big feat: New life. *Los Angeles Times*, April 19, 2003.

Baird, Donald (1989). Sasquatch footprints: A proposed method of fabrication. *Cryptozoology* 8:43–46.

Barcott, Bruce (2002). "Sasquatch is real!" Forest love slave tells all! *Outside Magazine*, August 2002.

Barnouw, Victor (1973). *Culture and Personality*. Homewood, IL: The Dorsey Press.

Barnouw, Victor (1985). *Culture and Personality*, 4th edition. Homewood, IL: The Dorsey Press.

Barnum, Phineus (2000). *The Life of P. T. Barnum: Written by Himself*. Urbana: University of Illinois Press.

Barthes, Roland (1978). *Mythologies*. New York: Hill and Wang.

Bartholomew, Robert (1997). Collective delusions: A skeptic's guide. *Skeptical Inquirer* 21(3):29–33.

Bayanov, Dmitri (1996). *In the Footprints of the Russian Snowman*. Moscow: Crypto-Logos Books.

Bayanov, Dmitri, Igor Bourtsev, and René Dahinden (1984). Analysis of the Patterson-Gimlin film, why we find it authentic. In: Vladimir Markotic and Grover Krantz (eds.), *The Sasquatch and Other Unknown Hominoids*. Calgary: Western Publishers, pp. 219–234.

Beck, Fred (1967). *I Fought the Ape-Men of Mount St. Helens*. Private printing.

Beckjord, Jon (1980). Beckjord on Bigfoot (with commentaries from Paul Kurtz, Stuart Scott, and Charles Cazeau). *Skeptical Inquirer* 5(3):64–70.

Beckjord, Jon (1982). Bigfoot news briefs and comments. *Sasquatch Search News*, December 1982.

Bernard, H. Russell, Peter Killworth, David Kronenfeld, and Lee Sailer (1984). The problem of informant accuracy: The validity of retrospective data. *Annual Review of Anthropology* 13:495–517.

Bindernagel, John (1998). *North America's Great Ape: The Sasquatch.* Courtenay, BC: Beachcomber Books.

Binns, Ronald (1984). *The Loch Ness Mystery Solved.* Buffalo, NY: Prometheus.

Breitler, Alex (2003). Big reward offered for Bigfoot phonies. *Redding Record Searchlight,* March 9, 2003.

Bryant, Vaughn, and Burleigh Trevor-Deutsch (1980). Analysis of feces and hair suspected to be of Sasquatch origin. In: Marjorie Halpin and Michael Ames (eds.), *Manlike Monsters on Trial: Early Records and Modern Evidence.* Vancouver: University of British Columbia Press, pp. 291–300.

Buckley, Archie (1984). Report on field findings. In: Vladimir Markotic and Grover Krantz (eds.), *The Sasquatch and Other Unknown Hominoids.* Calgary: Western Publishers, pp. 187–201.

Butler, James (1984). The theoretical importance of higher sensory perceptions in the Sasquatch phenomenon. In: Vladimir Markotic and Grover Krantz (eds.), *The Sasquatch and Other Unknown Hominoids.* Calgary: Western Publishers, pp. 203–216.

Byrne, Peter (1975). *The Search for Bigfoot: Monster, Myth or Man?* Washington, DC: Acropolis.

Byrne, Peter (1976). *The Search for Bigfoot: Monster, Myth or Man?* New York: Pocket Books.

Cachel, Susan (1985). Sole pads and dermatoglyphics of the Elk Wallow footprints. *Cryptozoology* 4:45–54.

Carpenter, Carole (1980). The cultural role of monsters in Canada. In: Marjorie Halpin and Michael Ames (eds.), *Manlike Monsters on Trial: Early Records and Modern Evidence.* Vancouver: University of British Columbia Press, pp. 97–110.

Chi, Ka-Jung, and Daniel Schmitt (2004). Mechanical energy and effective foot mass during impact loading of walking and running. *Journal of Biomechanics.*

Ciochon, Russell, John Olsen, and Jamie James (1990). *Other Origins: The Search for the Giant Ape in Human Prehistory.* New York: Bantam.

Ciochon, Russell, Dolores Piperno, and Robert Thompson (1990). Opal phytoliths found on the teeth of an extinct ape, *Gigantopithecus blacki*: Implications for paleodietary studies. *Proceedings of the National Academy of Sciences* 87:8120–8124.

Chorvinsky, Mark (1993a). Our strange world: Bigfoot made in America. *Fate* July:22–28.

Chorvinsky, Mark (1993b). Our strange world: Bigfoot and the Ray Wallace connection. *Fate* November:22–29.

Chorvinsky, Mark (2003) The Patterson Bigfoot film: Questions, problems and more questions—Part I. *Fate* August:8–11.

Churchill, Ron (1996). 'Bigfoot' hairs to get DNA tests. *The Leader* (Corning, NY), January 22, 1996.

Cohen, Daniel (1970). *A Modern Look at Monsters.* New York: Dodd, Mead and Company.

Coleman, Loren (1983). *Mysterious America.* Boston: Faber and Faber.

Coleman, Loren (1984). The occurrence of wild apes in North America. In: Vladimir Markotic and Grover Krantz (eds.), *The Sasquatch and Other Unknown Hominoids.* Calgary: Western Publishers, pp. 149–173.

Coleman, Loren (1989). *Tom Slick and the Search for the Yeti.* Boston: Faber and Faber.

Coleman, Loren (2003). *Bigfoot! The True Story of Apes in America.* New York: Pocket Books.

Coleman, Loren, and Jerome Clark (1978). *Creatures of the Outer Edge.* New York: Warner.

Coleman, Loren, and Patrick Huyghe (1999). *The Field Guide to Bigfoot, Yeti, and Other Mystery Primates Worldwide.* New York: Avon Books.

Conroy, Glenn (1990). *Primate Evolution.* New York: W. W. Norton.

Cook, Janet (1998). Shedding new light on old mysteries. *NASI News* (Journal of the North American Science Institute) 1(2):10.

Crowe, Ray (2002). Early man as a model for Bigfoot. In: Craig Heinselman (ed.), *CRYPTO: Hominology Special Number* II:122-134. Private printing.

Daegling, David (2002). Cripplefoot hobbled. *Skeptical Inquirer* 26(2):35–38.

Daegling, David, and Fred Grine (1994). Bamboo feeding, dental microwear and diet of the Pleistocene ape *Gigantopithecus blacki. South African Journal of Science* 90:527–532.

Daegling, David, and Benjamin Radford (2003). Bigfoot hoaxer dies, legacy lives on. *Skeptical Inquirer* 27(2):7–8.

Daegling, David, and Daniel Schmitt (1999). Bigfoot's screen test. *Skeptical Inquirer* 23(3):20–25.

Dahinden, René (1984). Whose dermal ridges? *Cryptozoology* 3:128–131.

Delzell, Jody (1995). *The Enigmatic Bardin Booger.* Palatka, FL: JoDell Storybooks.

Dennett, Michael (1982). Bigfoot jokester reveals punchline—finally. *Skeptical Inquirer* 7(1):8–9.

Dennett, Michael (1988). An interview with René Dahinden. *The Northwest Skeptic* 16:6–8.

Dennett, Michael (1989). Evidence for Bigfoot? An investigation of the Mill Creek Sasquatch prints. *Skeptical Inquirer* 13:264–272.

Dennett, Michael (1994). Bigfoot evidence: Are these tracks real? *Skeptical Inquirer* 18:498–508.

Dennett, Michael (2003). Bigfoot proponent comes to the end of the trail. *Skeptical Briefs* 13(2):1–2.

Denzler, Brenda (2001). *The Lure of the Edge: Scientific Passions, Religious Beliefs and the Pursuit of UFOs.* Berkeley: University of California Press.

Edgerton, Robert (1966). Conceptions of psychosis in four East African societies. *American Anthropologist* 68:408–421.

Egan, Timothy (2003). Despite hoax, Big Foot believers undeterred. *Rutland Herald,* January 2, 2003.

Emery, Eugene (1981). Sasquatchsickle: The monster, the model, and the myth. *Skeptical Inquirer* 6(2):2–4.

Fahrenbach, Henner (1998). Sasquatch: Size, scaling and statistics. *Cryptozoology* 13:47–75.

Fahrenbach, Henner, and Jeff Glickman (1998). Resolution related to the Patterson/Gimlin film. *NASI News* (Journal of the North American Science Institute) 1(1):1, 3–4.

Feder, Kenneth (2002). *Frauds, Myths and Mysteries.* New York: McGraw-Hill Mayfield.

Fleagle, John G. (1999). *Primate Adaptation and Evolution.* New York: Academic Press.

Foster, David (1997). Bigfoot hunter endures ridicule to search for legend. Associated Press release, October 1, 1997.

Frazier, Kendrick (2002). Editor's note. *Skeptical Inquirer* 26(2):4.

Freeland, Deborah, and Walter Rowe (1989). Alleged pore structure in Sasquatch (Bigfoot) footprints. *Skeptical Inquirer* 13:273–276.

Gargas, Jane (2004). Bigfoot as big lie—Is someone monkeying around? *Yakima-Herald Republic,* March 9, 2004.

Garry, Maryanne, Charles Manning, Elizabeth Loftus, and Steven Sherman (1996). Imagination inflation: Imagining a childhood event inflates confidence that it occurred. *Psychonomic Bulletin & Review* 3(2):208–214.

Gatesy, Stephen, Kevein Middleton, Farish Jenkins, and Neil Shubin (1999). Three-dimensional preservation of foot movements in Triassic theropod dinosaurs. *Nature* 399:141–144.

Gawande, Atul (2001). Under suspicion: The fugitive science of criminal justice. *New Yorker* January 8:50–53.

Gill, George (1980). Population clines of the North American Sasquatch as evidenced by track length and estimated statures. In: Marjorie Halpin and Michael Ames (eds.), *Manlike Monsters on Trial: Early Records and Modern Evidence.* Vancouver: University of British Columbia Press, pp. 265–273.

Glickman, Jeff (1998). *Toward a Resolution of the Bigfoot Phenomenon.* Hood River, OR: North American Science Institute.

Goodavage, M. (1996a). In search of . . . Bigfoot. *USA Today*, May 24, 1996.

Goodavage, M. (1996b). Bigfoot merely amuses most scientists. *USA Today*, May 24, 1996.

Gordon, David George (1992). *Field Guide to the Sasquatch.* Seattle: Sasquatch Books.

Green, John (1971). *On the Track of the Sasquatch.* Agassiz, BC: Cheam Publishing.

Green, John (1978). *Sasquatch: The Apes among Us.* Saanichton, BC: Hancock House.

Green, John (1980). What is the Sasquatch? In: Marjorie Halpin and Michael Ames (eds.), *Manlike Monsters on Trial: Early Records and Modern Evidence.* Vancouver: University of British Columbia Press, pp. 237–244.

Green, John (1994). *Encounters with Bigfoot.* Surrey, BC: Hancock House.

Greenwell, Richard (1996). Bob Titmus: Bigfoot's most persistent hunter talks of his 40-year search. *ISC Newsletter* 12(2):1–6.

Greenwell, Richard, D. Jeffrey Meldrum, Mark T. Slack, and Darwin Greenwell (1998). A Sasquatch field project in Northern California: Report of the 1997 Six Rivers National Forest Expedition. *Cryptozoology* 13:76–87.

Halpin, Marjorie (1980). Investigating the goblin universe. In: Marjorie Halpin and Michael Ames (eds.), *Manlike Monsters on Trial: Early Records and Modern Evidence.* Vancouver: University of British Columbia Press, pp. 3–26.

Halpin, Marjorie, and Michael Ames (1980). *Manlike Monsters on Trial: Early Records and Modern Evidence.* Vancouver, BC: University of British Columbia Press.

Heuvelmans, Bernard (1958). *On the Track of Unknown Animals.* London: Rupert Hart-Davis.

Heuvelmans, Bernard (1969). Note préliminaire sur un spécimen conservé dans la glace, d'une forme encore inconnue d'Hominidé vivant: Homo pongoides (sp. seu subsp. nov.). *Bulletin de l'Institut Royal des Sciences Naturelles de Belgique* 45(4):1–24.

Hubbell, John (1999). Bigfoot film sets enthusiasts at odds. Associated Press Release, January 10, 1999.

Hunter, Don, and René Dahinden (1973). *Sasquatch.* Toronto: McClelland and Stewart.

Hunter, Don, and René Dahinden (1975). *Sasquatch.* New York: Signet.

Jeffrey, David (1980). Medieval monsters. In: Marjorie Halpin and Michael Ames (eds.), *Manlike Monsters on Trial: Early Records and Modern Evidence.* Vancouver: University of British Columbia Press, pp. 47–64.

Johnson, William (2002). *The Rose-tinted Menagerie.* London: Heretic.

Keith, Arthur (1929). The alleged discovery of an anthropoid ape in South America. *Man* 100:135–136.

Kirlin, R. Lynn, and Lasse Hertel (1980). Estimates of pitch and vocal tract length from recorded vocalizations of purported Bigfoot. In: Marjorie Halpin and Michael Ames (eds.), *Manlike Monsters on Trial: Early Records and Modern Evidence.* Vancouver: University of British Columbia Press, pp. 274–290.

Kleinberg, Elliot (1998). *Weird Florida.* Atlanta: Longstreet.

Kleiner, Kurt (2000). Bigfoot's buttocks. *New Scientist* 168(2270):8.

Krantz, Grover (1977a). Anatomy of the Sasquatch foot. In: Roderick Sprague and Grover Krantz (eds.), *The Scientist Looks at Sasquatch.* Moscow: University of Idaho Press, pp. 77–94.

Krantz, Grover (1977b). Additional notes on Sasquatch foot anatomy. In: Roderick Sprague and Grover Krantz (eds.), *The Scientist Looks at Sasquatch.* Moscow: University of Idaho Press, pp. 95–112.

Krantz, Grover (1977c). Sasquatch handprints. In: Roderick Sprague and Grover Krantz (eds.), *The Scientist Looks at Sasquatch.* Moscow: University of Idaho Press, pp. 113–120.

Krantz, Grover (1983). Anatomy and dermatoglyphics of three Sasquatch footprints. *Cryptozoology* 2:53–81.

Krantz, Grover (1984). Research on unknown hominoids in North America. In: Vladimir Markotic and Grover Krantz (eds.), *The Sasquatch and Other Unknown Hominoids.* Calgary: Western Publishers, pp. 128–147.

Krantz, Grover (1986). A species named from footprints. *Northwest Anthropological Research Notes* 19:93–99.

Krantz, Grover (1992). *Big Footprints.* Boulder, CO: Johnson Books.

Krantz, Grover (1999). *Bigfoot/Sasquatch Evidence.* Surrey, BC: Hancock House.

Kurtz, Paul (1980). Bigfoot on the loose: Or how to create a legend. *Skeptical Inquirer* 5(1):49–54.

Leakey, Mary D (1987). The hominid footprints: Introduction. In: Mary Leakey and J. M. Harris (eds.). *Laetoli: A Pliocene Site in Northern Tanzania.* Oxford, UK: Clarendon, pp. 490-496.

Lewis, Frank (1997). The devil went down to Jersey. *Philadelphia City Paper*, October 23, 1997.

Loftus, Elizabeth F. (1997). Creating false memories. *Scientific American* 277(3):70–75.

Loftus, Elizabeth F., and Hunter G. Hoffman (1989). Misinformation and memory, the creation of new memories. *Journal of Experimental Psychology: General* 118(1):100–104.

Loftus, Elizabeth F., D. Miller, and H. Burns (1978). Semantic integration of verbal information into a visual memory. *Journal of Experimental Psychology* 4:19–31.

Long, Greg (2004). *The Making of Bigfoot.* Amherst, NY: Prometheus.

Luus, C., and Gary Wells (1994). The malleability of eyewitness confidence: Co-witness and perseverance effects. *Journal of Applied Psychology* 79:714–724.

Markotic, Vladimir, and Grover Krantz (1984). *The Sasquatch and Other Unknown Hominoids.* Calgary: Western Publishers.

McCloy, James, and Ray Miller (1976). *The Jersey Devil.* Wallingford, PA: Middle Atlantic.

McMahon, T. A., G. Valiant, and E. C. Frederick (1987). Groucho running. *Journal of Applied Physiology* 62:2326–2337.

Meldrum, D. Jeffrey (1997). Book review: *Bigfoot of the Blues*, by Vance Orchard. *Cryptozoology* 13:109–111.

Meldrum, D. Jeffrey (1999). Evaluation of alleged Sasquatch footprints and inferred functional morphology. *American Journal of Physical Anthropology Supplement* 28:200.

Meldrum, D. Jeffrey (2002). Midfoot flexibility, footprints, and the evolution of bipedalism. *American Journal of Physical Anthropology Supplement* 34:111–112.

Meldrum, D. Jeffrey (2004). Midfoot flexibility, fossil footprints and sasquatch steps: New perspectives on the development of bipedalism. *Journal of Scientific Exploration* 18:65–79.

Milinkovitch, Michel, Algagisa Caccone, and George Amato (2004). Molecular phylogenetic analyses indicate extensive morphological convergence between the "yeti" and primates. *Molecular Phylogenetics and Evolution* 31:1–3.

Montagna, William (1976). From the director's desk. *Primate News* 14(8):7–9.

Mullens, Rant (1979). More about Big Foot. *Frontier Times* 53(6); new series 122:4–5.

Murphy, Christopher (1998a). Circumstantial evidence concerning the Patterson/Gimlin film. Part One: Coming to grips with reality. *NASI News* (Journal of the North American Science Institute) 1(2):6.

Murphy, Christopher (1998b). Circumstantial evidence concerning the Patterson/Gimlin film. Part Three: The encounter. *NASI News* (Journal of the North American Science Institute) 1(3):1, 7–12.

Murphy, Christopher (1998c). Circumstantial evidence concerning the Patterson/Gimlin film. Part Four: Crucial decisions. *NASI News* (Journal of the North American Science Institute) 1(4):1, 4–8.

Napier, John (1972). *Bigfoot.* New York: E. P. Dutton.

Napier, John (1974). *Bigfoot.* New York: Berkley Books

Nickell, Joe (2000). The Flatwoods UFO monster. *Skeptical Inquirer* 24(6):15–19.

Orchard, Vance (1993). *Bigfoot of the Blues.* Walla Walla, WA: private printing.

Osman-Hill, W. C. (1955). *Primates: Comparative Anatomy and Taxonomy.* Vol. II: *Haplorhini: Tarsioidea.* Edinburgh: Edinburgh University Press.

Osman-Hill, W. C. (1957). *Primates: Comparative Anatomy and Taxonomy.* Vol . III: *Pithecoidea: Platyrrhini.* Edinburgh: Edinburgh University Press.

Panday, Ramkumar (1994). *Yeti Accounts: Snowman's Mystery and Fantasy.* Kathmandu: Ratna Pustak Bhandar.

Patterson, Roger (1966). *Do Abominable Snowmen of America Really Exist?* Yakima, WA: Franklin Press.

Perez, Daniel (1988). *Big Footnotes: A Comprehensive Bibliography Concerning Bigfoot, the Abominable Snowmen and Related Beings.* Norwalk, CA: D. Perez Publishing.

Perez, Daniel (1990). Meet René Dahinden: "Bigfoot" hunter. *The INFO Journal* July:19–21.

Perez, Daniel (1992). *Bigfoot at Bluff Creek.* Norwalk, CA: Center for Bigfoot Studies.

Perez, Daniel (1995). The Sasquatch forum. *Fate* May:38–39.

Perez, Daniel (1999a). Abstract. *Bigfoot Times* May:1.

Perez, Daniel (1999b). Camera in question. *Bigfoot Times* November:1–2.

Perez, Daniel (2000a). As they see it. *Bigfoot Times* April:1

Perez, Daniel (2000b). Museum opens in grand style. *Bigfoot Times* May:1–3.

Perez, Daniel (2000c). Marx dead at 78. *Bigfoot Times* June:1–2.

Perez, Daniel (2003a). Television. *Bigfoot Times* February:1–3.

Perez, Daniel (2003b). St. Paul. *Bigfoot Times* April:3–4.

Perez, Daniel (2003c). They said it . . . *Bigfoot Times* April:1.

Perez, Daniel (2003d). More questions. *Bigfoot Times* July:1.

Perez, Daniel (2003e). More Skookum. *Bigfoot Times* August:2–3.

Perez, Daniel (2003f). Symposium huge success. *Bigfoot Times* September–October:1–6.

Perez, Daniel (2003g). Murphy notes. *Bigfoot Times* November:2.

Perez, Daniel (2003h). Bigfooter of the year. *Bigfoot Times* December:1–2.

Perez, Daniel (2003i). Who is this man? *Bigfoot Times* December:3.

Perez, Daniel (2003j). Strange. *Bigfoot Times* August:1.

Porshnev, Boris (1974). The Troglodytidae and the Hominidae in the taxonomy and evolution of higher primates. *Current Anthropology* 15:449–456.

Pyle, Robert Michael (1995). *Where Bigfoot Walks: Crossing the Dark Divide.* Boston: Houghton Mifflin.

Radford, Benjamin (2000). The flawed guide to Bigfoot. *Skeptical Inquirer* 24(1):55–56.

Radford, Benjamin (2002). Bigfoot at 50: A half-century of Bigfoot evidence. *Skeptical Inquirer* 26(2):29–34.

Roosevelt T. (1893). *Wilderness Hunter. An Account of the Big Game of the United States and its Chase with Horse, Hound and Rifle.* Vol. II. New York: G. P. Putnam.

Sanderson, Ivan T. (1961). *Abominable Snowmen: Legend Come to Life.* Philadelphia: Chilton Company.

Sanderson, Ivan T. (1968). First photos of "Bigfoot," California's legendary "Abominable Snowman." *Argosy* February.

Sanderson, Ivan T. (1969). Preliminary description of the external morphology of what appears to be the fresh corpse of a hitherto unknown form of living hominid. *Genus* 25:249–278.

Saxon, A. H. (1983). *Selected Letters of P. T. Barnum.* New York: Columbia University Press.

Saxon, A. H. (1989). *P. T. Barnum: The Legend and the Man.* New York: Columbia University Press.

Schmitt, Daniel (2003). Insights into the evolution of human bipedalism from experimental studies of humans and other primates. *Journal of Experimental Biology* 206:1437–1448.

Schnabel, Jim (1994). *Round in Circles.* Amherst, NY: Prometheus.

Semerad, Tony, and Steve Thompson (1989). Bigfooter jailed for allegedly threatening life of man attending conference at WSU. *Pullman Daily News,* June 24, 1989.

Shackley, Myra (1983). *Still Living? Yeti, Sasquatch and the Neanderthal Enigma.* New York: Thames and Hudson.

Short, Bobbie (1998). Reflecting on the Patterson film rumors. *NASI News* (Journal of the North American Science Institute) 1(1):5–8.

Sieveking, Paul (2000). Bigfoot helps police expert with inquiries. *London Sunday Telegraph,* May 28, 2000.

Sprague, Roderick (1977). Editorial. In: Roderick Sprague and Grover Krantz (eds.), *The Scientist Looks at Sasquatch.* Moscow: University of Idaho Press, pp. 27–29.

Stein, Gordon (1996). *Encyclopedia of the Paranormal.* Amherst, NY: Prometheus.

Stein, Theo (2001). Bigfoot legend put to the test. *Denver Post,* January 14, 2001.

Strasenburgh, Gordon (1984). The crested *Australopithecus robustus* and the Patterson-Gimlin film. In: Vladimir Markotic and Grover Krantz (eds.), *The Sasquatch and Other Unknown Hominoids.* Calgary: Western Publishers, pp. 236–248.

Sunlin, Mark (2002). The hoaxers. *Fate* August:25–27.

Suttles, Wayne (1977). On the cultural track of the Sasquatch. In: Roderick Sprague and Grover Krantz (eds.), *The Scientist Looks at Sasquatch.* Moscow: University of Idaho Press, pp. 39–76.

Suttles, Wayne (1980). Sasquatch: The testimony of tradition. In: Marjorie Halpin and Michael Ames (eds.), *Manlike Monsters on Trial: Early Records and Modern Evidence.* Vancouver: University of British Columbia Press, pp. 245–254.

Tachdjian, M (1990). *Pediatric Orthopedics,* 2nd edition, Vol. IV. Philadelphia: W. B. Saunders.

Taft, Michael (1980). Sasquatch-like creatures in Newfoundland: A study in the problems of belief, reportage and perception. In: Marjorie Halpin and Michael Ames (eds.), *Manlike Monsters on Trial: Early Records and Modern Evidence.* Vancouver: University of British Columbia Press, pp. 83–96.

Taylor, Michael (1999). Screams in the night. *San Francisco Chronicle,* January 24, 1999.

Thagard, Paul (1978). Why astrology is a pseudoscience. In: Peter D. Asquith and Ian Hacking (eds.), *PSA 1978,* Vol. I, Philosophy of Science Association, East Lansing, MI, pp. 223–234.

Thagard, Paul (1980). Resemblance, correlation and pseudoscience. In: M. P. Hanen, M. J. Osler, and R. G. Weyant (eds.), *Science, Pseudoscience and Society.* Waterloo, Ontario, Wilfrid Laurier University Press, pp.17–27.

Trotti, Hugh (1994). Did fiction give birth to Bigfoot? *Skeptical Inquirer* 18(5): 541–542.

Van Kampen, Hans (1979). The case of the lost panda. *Skeptical Inquirer* 4(1):48–50.

Wasson, Barbara (1979). *Sasquatch Apparitions.* Private printing.

Wasson, Barbara (1994). *Tracking the Sasquatch: The Elusive Northwest Hominoid.* Private printing.

Wasson, David (1999). Bigfoot believers say film no fake. *Yakima Herald Republic*, February 4, 1999.

Wells, Gary, and Amy Bradfield (1999). Distortions in eyewitnesses' recollections: Can the postidentification feedback effect be moderated? *Psychological Science* 10:138–144.

Wells, Gary, and Elizabeth F. Loftus (2002). Eyewitness memory for people and events. In: A. Goldstein (ed.), *Comprehensive Handbook of Psychology*, Vol. 11: *Forensic Psychology.* New York: John Wiley and Sons, pp. 149–160.

Wells, Gary, and Donna Murray (1984). Eyewitness confidence. In: Gary Wells and Elizabeth F. Loftus (eds.), *Eyewitness Testimony: Psychological Perspectives.* New York: Cambridge University Press pp. 155-170.

Westrum, Ron (1980). Sasquatch and scientists: Reporting Scientific Anomalies. In: Marjorie Halpin and Michael Ames (eds.), *Manlike Monsters on Trial: Early Records and Modern Evidence.* Vancouver: University of British Columbia Press, pp. 27–36.

Winn, E. (1991). Physical and morphological analysis of samples of fiber purported to be Sasquatch hair. *Cryptozoology* 10:55–65.

Woo, Ju Kang (1962). The mandibles and dentition of *Gigantopithecus. Palaeontologica Sinica.* New Series D 146(11):1–94.

Wylie, Kenneth (1980). *Bigfoot: A Personal Inquiry into a Phenomenon.* New York: Viking Press.

Zuefle, David (1997). Swift, Boone and Bigfoot: New evidence for a literary connection. *Skeptical Inquirer* 21:57–58.

Zuefle, David (1999). Tracking Bigfoot on the Internet. *Skeptical Inquirer* 23(3):26–28.

Index

Page numbers in italics represent figures.

Abominable Snowmen: Legend Come to Life (Sanderson), 28
academic fraud, 214
Academy of Applied Science, 130, 152n84–153n84
Allen, Elizabeth, 73
allometry, 49
American Association of Physical Anthropologists, 58n81, 220n29
Ames, Michael, 191
Ape Canyon encounter. *See* Beck, Fred

Bailey, George, 67
Baird, Donald, 168
Bardin, Florida, overview of, 238–38
Bardin Booger, 237; account of, 239–40, 241; birth of legend of, 239–40; pranks concerning, 242; public appearance of, 240, 242–44, *243*; public reaction to legend of, 241–42; song about, 242
Barnouw, Victor, 228
Barnum, P. T., 66–67
Barthes, Roland, 21, 247–48
Bartholomew, Robert, 255
Bauman (trapper) encounter, 30–31, 69, 70–71
Bayanov, Dmitri, 111, 252–53
Beck, Fred, 32, 69–70, 72, 212, 251
Beckjord, Jon Eric, 167, 197
Bering land bridge, 15, 16
Bernard, Russ, 226, 229
Bigfoot (Napier), 46
Bigfoot: A Personal Inquiry into a Phenomenon (Wylie), 20
Bigfoot: The Yeti and Sasquatch in Myth and Reality (Napier), 108
Bigfoot at Bluff Creek (Perez), 110, 119
Bigfoot Central, 96
Bigfoot Field Researchers Organization (BFRO), 53, 94–95, 97, 99n40, 154n98
Bigfoot Information Center Project, 36–37
Big Footnotes (Perez), 92
Big Footprints (Krantz), 101n95, 122, 212–13
The Bigfoot Research Project (TBRP), 36, 37–38, 55n2, 130
Bigfoot! The True Story of Apes in America (Coleman), 140, 197
Bindernagel, John, 250

Binns, Ronald, 26, 230
bipedal locomotion: of Bardin Booger, 239; of Bigfoot, 9, 13, 28, 51, 53, 66, 105, 198, 217; compliant gait in, 126, *127*, 129, 162, 166, 173, *174*; from fossil record, 14, 16; human, 162, 172; of Russian Bigfoot, 252; of yeti, 252
Blue Creek Mountain, tracks on, 34, 159, 177–78, 180, *181*
Bluff Creek. *See* Patterson film
body proportions, of Bigfoot, 123, 124–25
Bonebrake, George, 91
boot-on-the-fake-foot technique, 86
Bossburg Incident, 46–51, 79–87; assessment of tracks from, 82–86, 159; cast of footprint of, *48*; film of, 80–81, 86–87; reconstruction of skeletal anatomy of, *50*; size of footprint, 47
Bryant, Vaughn, 206
Bulletin of the Royal Institute of Natural Sciences of Belgium, 46
Byrne, Peter: background/character of, 35–36, 43, 57n33; on Bauman encounter, 71; as Bigfoot hunter, 18, 36–38; Bigfoot Research Project and, 130; Bossburg Incident and, 80, 81; on collective hoax, 191–92; conservation work of, 38; Freeman trackway and, 89, 91; Marx film and, 208; Patterson film and, 112, 122, 130, 131, 136–37; on scarcity of Bigfoot tracks, 95; Wallace and, 73

California Big Foot Organization (CBFO), 42
Canawest Films, Ltd., 112–13
Capek, Karel, 228, 254
Chambers, John, 116, 117
Chilcutt, Jimmy, 177–79
Chorvinsky, Mark, 73–74, 116, 117, 211–12
Clark, Jerome, 196
Coast Salish, 2, 234
Cohen, Daniel, 256
Coleman, Loren, 140; on hoaxing, 73, 75; Minnesota Iceman and, 79; paranormal Bigfoot and, 196–97; on undetected species, 235, 253
compliant gait, 126, *127*, 129, 162, 166, 173, *174*
continuity test, 10
coordinated hoaxing, 191–92
Crain, Lena. *See* Bardin Booger
Crazy Mountains, 193–94
Creatures from the Outer Edge (Coleman & Clark), 196
Crew, Gerald, 29, 33–35, 72, 99n40, 158, 168–69
crippled Bigfoot. *See* Bossburg Incident
Crook, Cliff: Patterson film and, 140–41; Skookum Cast and, 96–97, *176*
Crowe, Ray, 16
cryptozoology, 46, 216
Cryptozoology, 93, 217

Dahinden, René: on absence of Bigfoot physical remains, 193; background/character of, 38, 39, 40, 43, 55, 57n33; as Bigfoot hunter, 38, 39–40; on Bigfoot hunter/prankster, 179, 209, 257; Bluff Creek tracks and, 73; Bossburg Incident and, 50, 80, 81; Freeman trackway and, 89–*90*, 92, 93, 102n115; justification for Bigfoot quest, 258–59; on Krantz, 173, 175, 176–77; lengthy trackway and, 85–86; on nocturnal abduction, 68–69; Pacific Northwest Expedition and, 41, 215–16; Patterson film/filmmaker and, 40, 44, 106–7, 111, 113, 114, 126, 128, 141, 146, 147; as Progressive Research consultant, 130; reaction to Patterson film, 108–9, 122; split ball/double ball track and, 179
DeAtley, Al, 148, 155n121
deformed tracks. *See* Bossburg Incident
Deinard, Amos, 207
Delzell, Jody, 239–41
Dennett, Michael: Bigfoot track authentication and, 175–*76*; Bossburg Incident tracks and, 82–83; Freeman trackway and, 91, 93, 102n110; paranormal Bigfoot and, 198; on producing soft-tissue movement effect, 146
depth, of Bigfoot track: from Bossburg Incident, 86; from Crew tracks, 72, 76;

from Freeman trackway, 89; in Patterson film, 162–67
dermal ridge patterns (dermatoglyphics): Bigfoot vs. large human, 91, 177–78; of Bossburg Bigfoot, 51; at Freeman trackway, 89, 92; of Skookum Cast, 94
de Wilde, D. A. G., 91
Disney Studios, 112, 113
Do Abominable Snowmen of America Really Exist? (Patterson), 107
Donskoy, Dmitri, 111–12, 119

ecomessiah, Bigfoot as. *See* Prankster-Ecomessiah hypothesis
Edgerton, Robert, 228
eyewitness testimony: accuracy of, 226; as emotionally powerful, 222–23; hallucination and, 225; interviewer affect on, 232–33; in legal testimony, 226–27; memory and, 225, 227–28; role in perceptual contagion in, 230–32; role in scientific research, 225–26; role of culture in, 228–30; role of expectation in, 230; truth-teller/liar as eyewitness, 224–25

Fahrenbach, Henner: Bossburg Incident and, 85; on eyewitness account, 222–23; hair analysis and, 207; Skookum Cast and, 94
false dilemma, 192
The Field Guide to Bigfoot, Yeti and Other Mystery Primates Worldwide (Coleman & Huyghe), 197
Fleischmann, Martin, 62–63
fluorescent Freddie, 42
footprint. *See* track, Bigfoot
Fort, Charles, 201n12
Franzoni, Henry, 249
Frazier, Ken, 198
Freeman, Paul, 51–53, *52*; hair found by, 207; handprint discovery by, 213; multiple Bigfoot sightings by, 88–89
Freeman trackway: Bigfoot cast from, 90; evidence/investigation of, 58n81, 88–93, 101n95, 158, 167, 169, 208, 209
Genzoli, Andrew, 148
geotime pattern, 37
Gigantopithecus, 13–14, 15, 16
Gigantopithecus blacki, 13, 14
Gigantopithecus giganteus, 13
Gill, George, 191, 192
Gimlin, Bob: Dahinden investigates, 40; Patterson film and, 43–44, 105, 106, 109, 114–15, 120, 121, 146, 147–48, 162–66; on reason for not shooting Bigfoot, 115–16
Glickman, Jeff: as North American Science Institute head, 38, 130; Patterson film and, 37, 130–32, 133, 134, 135, 138, 141, 146, 153n91
great ape, 14, 16, 207–8, 250
Green, John: on absence of Bigfoot physical remains, 195; Ape Canyon encounter and, 69; Beck account and, 212; on Bigfoot behavior, 71; on Bigfoot habitat, 18; on Bigfoot research organization, 130; Blue Creek Mountain trackway and, 159; Bossburg Incident and, 80, 81; Crew tracks and, 34, 72, 74, 76, 168; Dahinden exploits published by, 39; on difficulty of killing Bigfoot, 19, 199; encyclopedia of Sasquatch of, 237; on existence of Bigfoot, 5, 10, 18, 42–43, 54; on historical Bigfoot, 65, 67; on nocturnal abduction, 68; paranormal fringe and, 198; Patterson film and, 45, 112–13, 121–22, 137, 141–42, 143; publication on Bigfoot data, 41–42; reclining Bigfoot and, 53–54; split/double ball track and, 179; trackway at road-building operation and, 44
Greenwell, Richard, 216–17
Gregory, L. H., 70
Grieve, D. W., 109, 110–11
grizzly bear, 17, 19, 66, 71, 200

habitat/ecology, of Bigfoot, 16–17, 18, 42–43
hair analysis/evidence, 51, 92, 205–8, 219n5
Halpin, Marjorie, 6–7, 191, 248
Hansen, Frank, 45–46, 77, 78, 79
Hardin, Joel, 88, 90–91, 169
Heironimus, Bob, 118

Henry, Richard, 170
Heuvelmans, Bernard, 45–46, 77, 78
hirsuteness, of Bigfoot. *See* hair analysis/evidence
historical Bigfoot (pre-1958), 65–72; Ape Canyon encounter, 32, 69–70, 72; Jacko, 33, 66–67; in Jasper, Wyoming, 65–66; nocturnal abduction, 67–69; trapper encounter with, 69, 70–71
Hitler Diaries, 177
hoax/hoaxer: Bossburg Incident and, 47, 49, 50, 81, 82, 85–86; collective, 191–92; Freeman trackway and, 88, 89, 91, 92, 93; motivation for, 255–57; Patterson film and, 44, 45, 106, 107, 108, 113, 115, 116–19, *176*; Piltdown find, 64; proposed by Bigfoot proponent, 208–9; resourcefulness/determination of, 75, 158, 169–70, 179; ruling out, 39, 159, 171–72; Six Rivers Expedition and, 217; Skookum Cast and, 96; track depth and, 160–61, 167. *See also* Wallace, Ray
Homo pongoides, 46, 78
Hoover, J. Edgar, 78
Humboldt Times, 34, 73
Hunter, Don, 39, 80, 81
Huyghe, Patrick, 197

Iceman, Minnesota, 46, 76–79
I Fought the Ape-Men of Mount Saint Helens (Beck), 70
independence, in scientific inquiry, 62–63
International Society of Cryptozoology (ISC), 216
In the Footprints of the Russian Snowman (Bayanov), 252

Jacko, 33, 66
Jersey Devil, 237
Johnson, Rodney, 88, 90–91

Katayama, Kazumichi, 91
killing Bigfoot, difficulty of, 19, 199–200
Killworth, Peter, 226
Krantz, Grover: on absence of Bigfoot physical remains, 193; on Bigfoot as great ape, 250; on Bigfoot habitat, 18; as Bigfoot track authenticator, 173, 175–77; Bossburg Incident and, 47, 48–*50*, 51–52, 79, 81, 82–84, 87, 100n82–101n82; Crew tracks and, 74; on depth of Bigfoot tracks, 167; foot skeleton analysis by, 144; Freeman trackway and, 88, 91, 92, 93, 101n95; on Jacko, 66–67; omission in publication of, 212–13; paranormal fringe and, 198; Patterson film and, 110, 122–23, 124, 125, 129, 152n74; on ruling out hoax, 171; on scarcity of Bigfoot tracks, 95; on science ignoring Bigfoot, 203–4; scientific establishment and, 218; Skookum Cast and, 97; standard of proof of Bigfoot existence for, 54; on stride of Bigfoot, 169; use of fossil record by, 14–15, 16
Kronenfeld, David, 226

La Brea tar pits, 15
Landis, John, 116, 117
Laverty, Lyle, 163, 170–71
The Legend of Bigfoot (Marx), 195
Loch Ness monster, 26, 230
The Loch Ness Mystery Solved (Binns), 26
Loftus, Elizabeth, 227
Long, Greg, 141

The Making of Bigfoot (Long), 141
Manlike Monsters on Trial (Halpin & Ames), 191
Markotic, Vladimir, 121, 222
Marx, Ivan, 43, 92, 208; on absence of Bigfoot physical remains, 195; Bossburg Incident and, 47, 80–81, 86–87, 100n79, 213; handprint discovery by, 213; Pacific Northwest Expedition and, 41
McClarin, Jim, 121–22
Meldrum, Jeff: Bossburg Incident and, 47, 53, 79, 82; cast collection of, 177; on evidence for Bigfoot, 61; foot skeleton analysis of, 144; Freeman trackway and, 88, 91–92, 93, 101n95; Patterson film and, 142, 153n93, 154n98, 173; reclining Bigfoot and, 53; on ruling out hoax, 171–72; Six

Rivers Expedition and, 216–17; Skookum Cast and, 95; standard of proof of Bigfoot existence for, 54–55; on yeti videotape, 260n21
memory, eyewitness testimony and, 225, 227–28
metatarsus adductus, 47
Metlow, Joe, 80, 81
Minnesota Iceman, 46, 76–79
Moscow Academy of Sciences, 111
Mullens, Rant, *74,* 180
Murphy, Chris, 130, 131, 134, 135, 138–39, 140–41, 153nn91&93
Mysterious America (Coleman), 196
myth, status in Western culture, 253–55
mythological figure, Bigfoot as, 20–21, 247–51; behavior as unnatural, 251; effect of reality of footprints on, 255–56; encounters with as collective delusion, 255; story from other than North American, 29, 208, 252–53; value of, 258–59

Napier, John: Bossburg Incident and, 47, 79–80, 81, 82, 220n30; Minnesota Iceman and, 78; opinion on Bigfoot evidence in Jasper, Wyoming, 66; on Patterson film, 108, 119, 166–67; scientific establishment and, 218; on search for Bigfoot, 215; Wallace and, 73
Native American, 2, 15, 35, 55n2, 233–34, 252
natural history argument: alternative explanation to, 20–21; component of, 10–12; cryptic nature of Bigfoot, 17–19; fossil record evidence, 12–16; habitat/ecology, 16–17
nocturnal, Bigfoot as, 43
nocturnal abduction, by Bigfoot. *See* Ostman, Albert
Noll, Richard, 94
North American Science Institute (NASI), 38, 130–31, 133, 137–38, 140, 141, 205

odor, of Bigfoot, 9, 30, 201n23, 219
okapi, 25, 55n1
Olsen, Robert, 91
omnivorous, Bigfoot as, 17
On the Track of Unknown Animals (Heuvelmans), 46
Ostman, Albert, 31, 67–69, 253

Pacific Northwest Expedition, 35–36, 41, 215–16
paranormal, Bigfoot as, 20, 195–99
Parker, J. W., 175–76, 185n53
parsimony, in scientific inquiry, 63
Patterson, Roger: Ape Canyon encounter and, 69; Beck account and, 212; Dahinden investigation of, 40; motivation for making film, 106–7, 114. *See also* Patterson film
Patterson film, 34, 37; Bossburg Incident and, 80; camera/film speed used in, 109–11; context of, 119–22; current status of, 205; Dahinden investigation of, 40; early verdict on, 108–13; either-or proposition of authenticity of, 191; impact of, 106; lack of institutional response to, 107–8, 109; length of, 105; making of, 43–44; misconception about making of, 106; Moscow reception of, 111; quality of, 105, 120; reconstruction of site of, 120–22; rumor of hoax concerning, 116–19; site of, 120, *124,* 158; synopsis of, 105–6; time of filming, 120, 147. *See also* Patterson film, analysis of
Patterson film, analysis of: artist reconstruction of subject of, *145*; body proportions, 123, 124–25; "fastener" around subject waist, 140–41; filming/viewing timeline, 147–49; by film technologist, 112–13; foot anatomy, 144–*45*; gait, 123, 125, 126–28, *127,* 147; limb proportions, 141–43; muscular movements, 146–47; nonacademic institution involvement in, 130–31; pressure ridges, 172, 17–174; of print depth, 162–67; sagittal crest presence, 143–44; storyline credibility, 147–49; stride length, 129; subject as primate credibility, 143–47; subject size, 131–40, *136, 137, 139,* 147, 152n74, 153n91, 163–64, 165–66, 167–68

perceptual contagion, 230–32
Perez, Daniel: annotated bibliography of Bigfoot sources by, 92; on Bossburg Incident, 100n79; on eyewitness account, 222–23; eyewitness account and, 208–9; Patterson film and, 110, 119, 121, 147–49, 166; Skookum Cast and, 97
Pickens, Ray, 87, 257
Piltdown fossils, 63–64
Pinker, Ray, 206
polar bear, 17, 167, 199
Pons, Stanley, 62–63
Porshnev, Victor, 111
Prankster-Ecomessiah hypothesis, 249–58
Progressive Research, 130, 131
pseudoscience/science, Bigfoot quest as: definition of pseudoscience, 204; objective practice issue, 208–9; scholarship principle, 211–13; systematic study/documentation of evidence, 215–18; theory evolution, 209–10; unresolved issue, 204–8, 218–19
Pyle, Robert: approach to Bigfoot research, 221–22; on Bigfoot as ecomessiah, 249–50; on Bigfoot as mythological figure, 21, 248, 252, 259; on Wallace, 99n37

Radford, Ben, 95–96
Ramkumar, Panday, 252, 253
Rapoff, Andy, 164
recognized species, defense of Bigfoot failure to qualify as: absence of physical remains, 190, 193–95; alternate explanation unlikely/unreasonable, 190–92; Bigfoot as paranormal, 190, 195–99
replication, in scientific inquiry, 62–63, 132
Roe, William, 32, 67–68, 69
Roosevelt, Theodore, 30, 56n10, 71
Rossum's Universal Robots (Capek), 228, 254
Russian Bigfoot, 252–53

Sailer, Lee, 226
Sanderson, Ivan, 35; on absence of Bigfoot physical remains, 193; on Bluff Creek tracks, 73; on eyewitness, 28; global survey of, 66; Minnesota Iceman and, 45–46, 77, 78; on nocturnal abduction, 67, 68
saola, 25, 55n1
Sasquatch. *See* Bigfoot
The Sasquatch and Other Unknown Hominoids (Markotic), 222
Sasquatch Apparitions (Wasson), 224
Sasquatch: The Apes among Us (Green), 41–42, 212, 237
Sasquatch: The Search for North America's Incredible Creature (Dahinden & Hunter), 39
Schmitt, Daniel, 125–26, 128–29, 133–34, 138, 173
scientific/anecdotal explanation, for Bigfoot, 62–63. *See also* pseudoscience/science, Bigfoot quest as
The Search for Bigfoot: Monster, Myth or Man (Byrne), 37
sensory capability, of Bigfoot, 18–19
Shipton, Eric, 29
Short, Bobbie, 117
Six Rivers Expedition, 216–17
size, of Bigfoot, 9, 16–17, 19, 49, 51, 115, 123; in Patterson film, 131–40, *136*, *137*, *139*, 147, 152n74, 153n91, 163–64, 165–66, 167–68
Skeptical Inquirer, 107, 140
Skookum Cast, 54, 94–97
Slick, Tom: Bluff Creek expedition and, 29, 34, 35–36, 73; death of, 43; Himalayan expedition of, 29, 35
Smithsonian Institution, 46, 77, 78
social history, of Bigfoot: Bigfoot hunter, 34–43; crippled Bigfoot, 46–51; debut of, 29, 33–34; discovery/fabrication of, 27–30; film of Bigfoot, 43–45; frozen Bigfoot, 45–46; origins of Bigfoot, 26–30; pre-1958 account, 30–33, 55n2; reclining Bigfoot, 53–55
source confusion, 227
Soviet Union, study of Patterson film in, 45, 111–12
Sprague, Roderick, 233–34
St. Hilaire, Roger, 80

Strange Magazine, 116, 211–12
stride length, of Bigfoot track, 34–35, 72, 75, 76, 86, 123, 129, 169
Sumerlin, Wes, 89
Suttles, Wayne, 234
Swindler, Daris, 54

Thagard, Paul, 204–5, 208, 209, 210, 212, 216
The Bigfoot Research Project (TBRP), 18–19
theory: scientific, 64. *See also* pseudoscience/science, Bigfoot quest as
Thompson, David, 33, 65–66
Titmus, Bob, 34; on Bigfoot search, 215; Bossburg Incident and, 80; Crew tracks and, 34, 168; Dahinden relationship with, 41; Freeman trackway and, 89, 90–91, 92, 209; on legitimacy of tracks, 170; Patterson film and, 121, 123, 124, 151n58, 163, 172; personal loss from Bigfoot search, 251–52; standard of proof of Bigfoot existence for, 54
trace fossil, 15
track, Bigfoot: depth of print, 159–69; ease of fabricating, 172–73; fingerprint expert on authenticity, 177–79; hoaxer determination/resourcefulness, 169–70; impossibility of recognizing real, 171–72; Krantz as authenticator of, 173, 175–77; lack of agreed-on standard for print, 170; legitimacy of, 170; location of, 157–58; number of, 159; pressure ridge, 172, *173–74*; reason to fabricate, 248–49; split ball/double ball on, 179–83, *181–82*; stride of, 34–35, 72, 75, 76, 86, 123, 129, 169
trapper encounter. *See* Bauman (trapper) encounter
Trevor-Deutsch, Bureligh, 206
type specimen, 15

UFOs, 20, 26, 42, 190, 195, 197, 232, 252
U.S. Forest Service, 51–52, 88, 167

Wallace, Dale Lee, 99n36, *182*, 187nn79&80
Wallace, Ray: character of, 35, 73, 256, 257–58; faked tracks by, 73–76, *74*, 99n36, 180, *182*; ignored in Bigfoot literature, 212; Patterson film and, 117, 118
Warren, Mike, 238
Wasson, Barbara, 40; on eyewitness, 224, 232; on Freeman trackway, 89, 208; on nocturnal abduction, 69; on toleration for anomaly, 229
Watts, David, 19
Wells, Gary, 226–27
Westrum, Ron, 230
Where Bigfoot Walks: Crossing the Dark Divide (Pyle), 21, 221–22
Willow Creek-China Flat Museum, 180
Wylie, Kenneth, 36, 43; on Bigfoot as mythological figure, 20–21; Bossburg Incident and, 87; on Green, 43; on Patterson film, 118, 121; on symbolism of Bigfoot, 250

Yeti Accounts (Ramkumar), 252
yeti tradition, 29, 208, 252, 260n21

About the Author

David J. Daegling, associate professor of anthropology at the University of Florida, is a biological anthropologist specializing in the study of primate anatomy and biomechanics.